THE BRITANNICA GUIDE TO

BASEBALL

THE WORLD OF SPORTS

THE BRITANNICA GUIDE TO
BASEBALL

EDITED BY ADAM AUGUSTYN, ASSISTANT EDITOR
AND ASSISTANT MANAGER, SPORTS

Britannica
Educational Publishing

IN ASSOCIATION WITH

ROSEN
EDUCATIONAL SERVICES

Published in 2011 by Britannica Educational Publishing
(a trademark of Encyclopædia Britannica, Inc.)
in association with Rosen Educational Services, LLC
29 East 21st Street, New York, NY 10010.

Distributed exclusively by Rosen Educational Services.
For a listing of additional Britannica Educational Publishing titles, call toll free (800) 237-9932.

First Edition

Britannica Educational Publishing
Michael I. Levy: Executive Editor
J.E. Luebering: Senior Manager
Marilyn L. Barton: Senior Coordinator, Production Control
Steven Bosco: Director, Editorial Technologies
Lisa S. Braucher: Senior Producer and Data Editor
Yvette Charboneau: Senior Copy Editor
Kathy Nakamura: Manager, Media Acquisition
Adam Augustyn, Assistant Editor and Assistant Manager, Sports

Rosen Educational Services
Hope Lourie Killcoyne: Senior Editor and Project Manager
Nelson Sá: Art Director
Cindy Reiman: Photography Manager
Karen Huang: Photo Researcher
Matthew Cauli: Designer, Cover Design
Introduction by Adam Augustyn

Library of Congress Cataloging-in-Publication Data

The Britannica guide to baseball / edited by Adam Augustyn.
    p. cm.p. cm. — (The world of sports)
"In association with Britannica Educational Publishing, Rosen Educational Services."
Includes bibliographical references and index.
ISBN 978-1-61530-521-6 (library binding)
1. Baseball. I. Augustyn, Adam. II. Encyclopaedia Britannica, inc. III. Title: Guide to baseball. IV. Title: Baseball.
GV867.B75 2012
796.357—dc22

3 4633 00248 8151   2011002630

Manufactured in the United States of America

CONTENTS

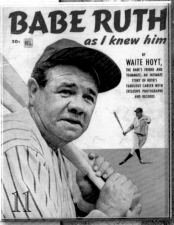

79

85

113

THE SENSATIONAL BASE BALL SON[G]

TAKE ME OUT TO THE BALL GAME

TRIXIE FRIGANZA

WORDS BY
JACK NORWORTH
MUSIC BY
ALBERT VON TILZER

THE YORK MUSIC CO
ALBERT VON TILZER, Mgr.
40 WEST 28TH ST. N.Y.

"The crack of the bat," "stealing a base," "sliding into home"—the vocabulary of baseball is well-known to all, even to people who are not fans of the sport. This familiarity speaks to the degree to which baseball has become woven into the fabric of the American experience. Baseball was the first American sport to blossom into a true countrywide sensation, played, at some point in their lives, by most every man, woman, and child in the U.S. Baseball has also had a greater influence on the larger American culture than any other sport. From "Take Me Out to the Ballgame"—the iconic song that has become inextricably linked to the ballpark experience—to the poem "Casey at the Bat" and the film *Field of Dreams*, the sport has often been used as a vehicle for Americans to express both their Americanism and themselves.

The common misconception is that the national pastime is also a national invention: New York

Front cover for the sheet music, "Take Me Out to the Ballgame," from 1908. The song is still often sung in baseball stadiums across America during the seventh-inning stretch. Diamond Images/Getty Images

state native Abner Doubleday was for years credited as the creator of the sport, a myth that was perpetuated by a self-serving 1907 commission led by American sporting-goods magnate A.G. Spalding. (Doubleday is still thought by many to be the "father of baseball," even though that story was debunked decades ago.) Baseball's true origins can be traced back to England, where rudimentary versions of the game were played as far back as the 18th century.

Modern baseball developed out of the rules established by amateur New York City baseball player Alexander Joy Cartwright in 1845. Cartwright's rules were based on the English game of rounders, but with a significant variation: base runners were put out not by being hit by a thrown ball, but by being tagged by it. This change led to the development of a harder ball that traveled farther when hit, turning a small-scale game into something much grander that would prove to be more spectator-friendly. Baseball stayed an amateur affair—played by dues-paying members of social clubs located throughout the Northeast—until the American Civil War. Around 1865 some clubs began paying select players, and in 1869 the Cincinnati Red Stockings became the first publicly announced professional baseball team. The first professional league, the National Association of Professional Base Ball Players, was formed shortly thereafter, in 1871.

In 1876 the National League of Professional Baseball Clubs—commonly known as the National League (NL)—was founded. A number of other leagues came and went in the following years, but no true rival to the National League appeared until 1893, when the Western League, which would later become the American League (AL), was organized. The AL's teams were based in the Midwest, far removed from the NL's established East Coast markets. When the AL tried to move franchises to Baltimore and Washington, D.C., the NL balked and the "baseball war" began. During the "war," the AL poached a number of star players from the NL and proved that it could compete with the established league. The two leagues agreed to a peace in 1903, and an important feature of their deal was the establishment of the World Series, which determined an annual major league champion.

The World Series was initially dominated by the Boston Red Sox (who were known as the Boston Americans when they won the inaugural Series in 1903). The Red Sox captured five of the first 15 Series played, with lineups variously featuring all-time greats such as pitcher Cy Young, centre fielder Tris Speaker, and pitcher-turned-outfielder Babe Ruth.

It was Ruth who would prove to be the key figure in the establishment of the greatest major-league dynasty of all—not with Boston, however, but with the team's greatest rival. One of the most important moments in baseball history came on Jan. 5, 1920, when Ruth was sold to the New York Yankees for $125,000. He not only led the Yankees to the franchise's first seven AL pennants and four World Series championships, but he also—over the course of his 15 seasons in New York—dominated the sport as no other player had before or has since. The gregarious "Bambino" became a cultural icon as he shattered home-run records and wowed spectators with his tape-measure blasts. What's more, his on-field success and unprecedented off-field fame catapulted the Yankees into the forefront of the country's sporting consciousness, helping the big-market team become the major's most glamorous destination in the minds of up-and-coming players for generations. The Yankees capitalized on their cachet with sound scouting and management, building a juggernaut that won 16 of the 27 World Series that followed Ruth's retirement in 1935.

Ruth's emergence in New York was perfectly timed: baseball instituted hitter-friendly rules in 1920 to usher in the "live-ball era," which made the sport much more appealing to fans than the low-scoring game dominated by pitchers such as Walter Johnson and Christy Mathewson of the previous two decades. Moreover, citizens living in booming post-World War I America had more discretionary money and entertainment options than ever before. These changes—aided by the increased prominence of newsreels and radio broadcasts, which furthered the game's reach—made the baseball stars of the era much better known than their predecessors. But Ruth and his fellow Yankees, such as Lou Gehrig and Bill Dickey, were not the only stars to make their mark during baseball's so-called "golden age." Many of the sport's all-time greats prospered in the 1920s and '30s, becoming celebrated characters in the sport's lore. These luminaries include hitting sensation Rogers Hornsby of the St. Louis Cardinals, dominant pitcher Lefty Grove, diminutive New York Giants home-run hitter Mel Ott, slugger Jimmie Foxx, and hard-nosed (which often crossed over the line into dirty) Detroit Tigers outfielder Ty Cobb.

While the sport was arguably at its pinnacle in the time between the two World Wars, there was also an ugly underside to baseball at that time. Like the broader American society, interwar baseball was beset by racial inequality. From the late 19th century until Jackie Robinson heroically broke the color barrier in 1947, the informal "gentlemen's agreement" kept black players out of the major leagues. As a result of this widespread segregation, a number of Negro leagues were formed in the 1920s and '30s in order to give standout black ballplayers an outlet for their talents. Some of the best players in the history of the sport played in the Negro leagues—notably Josh Gibson, considered by some to be the greatest home-run hitter ever, and Satchel Paige, a transcendent pitcher who was also an unparalleled showman. But the fact that white major leaguers of this era never had the opportunity to compete against any players of colour (outside of the occasional off-season exhibition game) serves as a lasting blemish on the purported golden age.

With the proliferation of television sets in the 1940s and '50s, baseball players became more visible than ever before. While maybe not as easily romanticized as the golden age icons of the diamond—whose exploits were filtered and often ameliorated by radio announcers as they were relayed to the general public—the baseball stars of this period became familiar faces in living rooms across the land. A number of these ballplayers were also hailed as real-life heroes for sacrificing prime years of their careers (as well as potentially sacrificing their lives) to serve their country in World War II. Hall of Famers such as Hank Greenberg, Warren Spahn, Joe DiMaggio, Bob Feller, and, most famously, Ted Williams forever burnished their reputations by selflessly joining the American war effort.

Major league baseball was permanently shaken up in 1958. That was the year that two New York-based teams, the Dodgers and the Giants, moved to the west coast (Los Angeles and San Francisco, respectively), kicking off a period of franchise shifts and expansions that ended with teams based in all regions of the country by the turn of the 21st century. As the major leagues expanded, the Yankee dominance slowly eroded, and a number of other teams established short dynasties. Especially noteworthy among these were the freewheeling Oakland A's squads that won three consecutive titles from 1972 to 1974, the Cincinnati Reds' "Big Red Machine" (champions in 1975 and 1976) that featured a lineup packed with future members of the Hall of Fame and is considered by many to be the greatest team of all time, and the hard-hitting A's teams of the late 1980s and early '90s.

The 1990s saw an explosion of steroid use among ballplayers, which cast a pall over nearly all of the achievements of that decade. Cheating had long been a quasi-accepted part of the game: be it the winked-at spitball of pitchers such as Gaylord Perry or the routine ingestion of amphetamines (popularly known as "greenies") that took place in baseball clubhouses for generations, these transgressions were often chalked up to simple gamesmanship or excused by the old belief that "if you ain't cheating, you ain't trying." Steroids, though, were different in that the players were not just cheating their competitors, but they were also twisting the record book, viewed as a near-sacred part of a sport that puts so much stock in its history. Baseball finally responded to the steroid problem by instituting a drug-testing program in 2006, but it was criticized by many observers for being too little, too late, and the shadow of performance-enhancing drugs continues to linger over the sport.

Steroids were not the only black mark on the sport in the last years of the 20th century. Labour strife between players and owners—which had led to a number of short work stoppages since the 1970s—reached its most acrimonious point in 1994, leading to an unprecedented strike that wiped out most of the last two months of the season, including the World Series. The strike soured many baseball fans, who did not sympathize with either side of the "millionaires versus billionaires" stand-off. It took an epic 1996 race for the single-season home run record between Mark McGwire and Sammy Sosa (which in hindsight has become clouded by accusations of steroid use against both players) to begin the slow process of bringing fans back to the game.

Eventually fans did embrace the sport again, and major league baseball in the early 21st century broke attendance records on an almost yearly basis. Part of the renewed popularity of baseball can be chalked up to the return to dominance of two of the sports' most storied franchises: the Yankees and the Red Sox. New York won four World Series in a five-year span during the mid-1990s, bringing the team back to the forefront of the major leagues after two decades of relative irrelevance. In 2004 the Red Sox famously ended 86 years of frustration and won their first title since 1918. The two teams have remained among the sport's best, and rivalry games between the two continue to draw massive media attention. Some observers have criticized baseball for the wide payroll disparities between the "haves" (such as the Red Sox and Yankees) and the "have-nots" that result from the major leagues having no salary cap. The economics of baseball have indeed left a number of teams—such as the once great Pittsburgh Pirates—with little hope to compete for a title, but supporters can point to the fact that nine different teams won championships between 2001 and 2010 and note that, despite the present massive financial inequalities, major league baseball is in one of the least dynastic periods of its history.

While the American major leagues have justifiably dominated the broader baseball culture for well over a century, the sport has made a significant impact on other countries over the years, as well. Baseball was heartily embraced by a number of Caribbean and Latin American countries, as well as Japan, which in turn produced such word-renowned stars as pitching sensation Dolf Luque and all-time home run king Oh Sadaharu. As shown by the dominance of non-American countries in the recently established World Baseball Classic, the rest of the world has in many ways caught up to the U.S.

But for all its overseas popularity, baseball will forever be first and foremost an American game. While gridiron football has recently surpassed baseball as the most popular sport in the U.S., baseball still holds a special place in the country's psyche. It may in fact never again become the nation's favorite sport, but its deep ties to the very essence of the American identity mean that it will always be the national pastime.

CHAPTER 1
A NATIONAL PASTIME

Baseball is, very basically, a game played with a bat, a ball, and gloves between two teams of nine players each on a field with four white bases laid out in a diamond (i.e., a square oriented so that its diagonal line is vertical). Teams alternate positions as batters (offense) and fielders (defense), exchanging places when three members of the batting team are "put out." As batters, players try to hit the ball out of the reach of the fielding team and make a complete circuit around the bases for a "run." The team that scores the most runs in nine innings (times at bat) wins the game.

BASEBALL'S IMPACT ON AMERICAN CULTURE

The United States is credited with developing several popular sports, including some (such as baseball, gridiron football, and basketball) that have large fan bases and, to varying degrees, have been adopted internationally. But baseball, despite the spread of the game throughout the globe and the growing influence of Asian and Latin American leagues and players, is the sport that Americans still recognize as their "national pastime." The game has long been woven into the fabric of American life and identity. "It's our game," exclaimed the poet Walt Whitman more than a century ago, "that's the chief fact in connection with it: America's game." He went on to explain that baseball

has the snap, go, fling of the American atmosphere— it belongs as much to our institutions, fits into them as

Enos Slaughter of the St. Louis Cardinals sliding home to score the winning run in game seven of the 1946 World Series; Roy Partee, catcher for the Boston Red Sox, lunges for the throw from the infield. UPI/Bettmann Newsphotos

significantly, as our constitutions, laws: is just as important in the sum total of our historic life. It is the place where memory gathers.

Perhaps Whitman exaggerated baseball's importance to and its congruency with life in the United States, but few would argue the contrary, that baseball has been merely a simple or an occasional diversion.

It was nationalistic sentiment that helped to make baseball "America's game." In the quest to obtain greater cultural autonomy, Americans yearned for a sport they could claim as exclusively their own. Just as the English had cricket and the Germans their turnvereins (gymnastic clubs), a sporting newspaper declared as early as 1857 that Americans should have a "game that could be termed a 'Native American Sport.' " A powerful confirmation of baseball as the sport to fill that need came in 1907 when a special commission appointed by A.G. Spalding, a sporting goods magnate who had formerly been a star pitcher and an executive with a baseball team, reported that baseball owed absolutely nothing to England and the children's game of rounders. Instead, the commission claimed that, to the best of its knowledge (a knowledge based on flimsy research and self-serving logic), baseball had been invented by Abner Doubleday at Cooperstown, New York, in 1839. This origin myth was perpetuated for decades.

In a country comprising a multiplicity of ethnic and religious groups, one without a monarchy, an aristocracy, or a long and mythic past, the experience of playing, watching, and talking about baseball games became one of the nation's great common denominators. It provided, in the perceptive words of British novelist Virginia Woolf, "a centre, a meeting place for the divers activities of a people whom a vast continent isolates [and] whom no tradition controls." No matter where one lived, the "hit-and-run," the "double play," and the "sacrifice bunt" were carried out the same way. The unifying power of baseball in the United States was evident in the Depression-ravaged 1930s, when a group of Cooperstown's businessmen along with officials from the major leagues established the National Baseball Hall of Fame and Museum. The Hall of Fame became a quasi-religious shrine for many Americans, and, since its founding, millions of fans have made "pilgrimages" to Cooperstown, where they have observed the "relics"—old bats, balls, and uniforms—of bygone heroes.

Baseball also reshaped the country's calendar. With the rise of industrialization, the standardized clock time of the office or factory robbed people of the earlier experience of time in its rich associations with the daylight hours, the natural rhythms of the seasons, and the traditional church calendar. Yet, for Americans, the opening of the baseball training season signaled the arrival of spring,

ABNER DOUBLEDAY

Abner Doubleday, 1862. Buyenlarge/ Archive Photos/Getty Images

(b. June 26, 1819, Ballston Spa, N.Y., U.S.—d. Jan. 26, 1893, Mendham, N.J.)

Abner Doubleday was a U.S. Army officer who was once thought to be the inventor of baseball.

Doubleday attended school in Auburn and Cooperstown, N.Y., and in 1838 he was appointed a cadet in the U.S. Military Academy (graduating in 1842). He was an artillery officer in the Mexican War and fought in the Seminole War in Florida (1856–58). At Fort Sumter, S.C., he commanded the gunners that fired the first shots by the North in the American Civil War. He fought at Bull Run (second battle), Antietam, Fredericksburg, and Gettysburg. He held the temporary rank of major general of volunteers in 1862–63, received the permanent rank of colonel in 1867, and retired from the army in 1873.

In 1907 a commission appointed by Albert G. Spalding published its conclusion that Doubleday formulated the essential rules of baseball in the summer of 1839 at Cooperstown, N.Y., where he was an instructor in a military preparatory school. Hence Cooperstown was chosen as the site of the National Baseball Hall of Fame and Museum, although it was later proved that Doubleday was not in Cooperstown in 1839.

The Spalding Commission's finding that the national game was of purely American origin was discredited by subsequent inquiries confirming baseball's evident connection with the older English game variously called rounders, feeder, or base ball.

regular-season play meant summer, and the World Series marked the arrival of fall. In the winter, baseball fans participated in "hot stove leagues," reminiscing about past games and greats and speculating about what the next season had to offer.

The World Series, inaugurated in 1903 and pitting the champions of the American and National Leagues in a postseason playoff, quickly took its place alongside the Fourth of July and Christmas as one of the most popular annual rites. The series was, said *Everybody's Magazine* in 1911, "the very quintessence and consummation of the Most Perfect Thing in America." Each fall it absorbed the entire nation.

Baseball terms and phrases, such as "He threw me a curve," "Her presentation covered all the bases," and "He's really out in left field," soon became part of the national vocabulary. So entrenched is baseball in the ordinary conversation of Americans that during the administration of President George Bush, a baseball player during his years at Yale University, the foreign press struggled to translate the president's routine use of baseball metaphors. As early as the 1850s, baseball images began to appear in periodicals, and, in the 20th century, popular illustrator Norman Rockwell often used baseball as the subject for his *The Saturday Evening Post* covers. "Casey at the Bat" and "Take Me Out to the Ballgame" remain among the best-known poems and songs, respectively, among Americans. Novelists and filmmakers frequently have turned to baseball motifs. After the mid-20th century, at the very time baseball at the grassroots level had begun a perceptible descent, baseball fiction proliferated. American colleges and universities even began to offer courses on baseball literature, and baseball films likewise proliferated. In 1994 the Public Broadcasting System released Ken Burns's nostalgic *Baseball*, arguably the most monumental historical television documentary ever made.

While baseball possessed enormous integrative powers, the game's history also has been interwoven with and reflective of major social and cultural cleavages. Until the first decades of the 20th century, middle-class Evangelical Protestants viewed the sport with profound suspicion. They associated baseball, or at least the professional version of the game, with ne'er-do-wells, immigrants, the working class, drinking, gambling, and general rowdiness. Conversely, these very qualities provided a foothold for the upward ascent of ethnic groups from the nation's ghettos. Usually encountering less discrimination in baseball (as well as in other venues of commercial entertainment) than they did in the more "respectable" occupations, in the 19th century Irish and German Americans were so conspicuous in professional baseball that some observers wondered if they had a special capacity for playing the game.

For a brief time in the 1880s, before racial segregation became the norm in the United States, black players competed with whites in professional baseball. After that period, however, blacks had to carve out a separate world of baseball. Dozens of black teams faced local semiprofessional teams while barnstorming throughout the United States, Canada, Mexico, and the Caribbean. Despite playing a high quality of baseball, the players frequently engaged in various forms of clowning that perpetuated prevailing stereotypes of blacks to appeal to spectators. From the 1920s until the '50s, separate black professional leagues—the Negro leagues—existed as well, but in 1947 Jackie Robinson crossed the long-standing colour bar in major league baseball. Because baseball was the national game, its racial integration was of enormous symbolic importance in the United States; indeed, it preceded the

U.S. Supreme Court's decision ending racial segregation in the schools (in 1954 in *Brown* v. *Board of Education of Topeka*) and helped to usher in the civil rights movement of the 1950s and '60s. Moreover, in the 1980s and '90s a huge influx of Hispanics into professional baseball reflected the country's changing ethnic composition.

Baseball likewise contributed to the shaping of American conceptions of gender roles. Although women were playing baseball as early as the 1860s, their involvement in the sport was confined for the most part to the role of spectator. To counter the game's reputation for rowdiness, baseball promoters took pains to encourage women to attend. "The presence of an assemblage of ladies purifies the moral atmosphere of a baseball gathering," reported the *Baseball Chronicle*, "repressing as it does, all the out-burst of intemperate language which the excitement of a contest so frequently induces." When women played on barnstorming teams in the 19th and the first half of the 20th century, the press routinely referred to them as "Amazons," "freaks," or "frauds." In 1943, during World War II, when it was feared that professional baseball might be forced to close down, the All-American Girls Professional Baseball League made its debut. After having provided more than 600 women an opportunity to play baseball and to entertain several million fans, the league folded in 1954.

But, even if unable to heal conflicts arising from fundamental social divisions, baseball exhibited an extraordinary capacity for fostering ties. In the 1850s, young artisans and clerks, frequently displaced in the city and finding their way of life changing rapidly in the midst of the Industrial Revolution, conceived of themselves as members of what was known as the "base ball fraternity." Like the volunteer fire departments and militia units of the day, they donned

Early baseball player in uniform. Library of Congress, Washington, D.C.

special uniforms, developed their own rituals, and, in playing baseball, shared powerful common experiences. Playing and watching baseball contests also strengthened occupational, ethnic, and racial identities. Butchers, typesetters, draymen, bricklayers, and even clergymen organized baseball clubs. So did Irish Americans, German Americans, and African Americans.

Professional baseball nourished and deepened urban identities. "If we are ahead of the big city [New York] in nothing else," crowed the *Brooklyn Eagle* as early as 1862, "we can beat her in baseball." Fans invested their emotions in their professional representative nines. "A deep gloom settled over the city," reported a Chicago newspaper in 1875 after the local White Stockings had been defeated by the St. Louis (Missouri) Brown Stockings. "Friends refused to recognize friends, lovers became estranged, and business was suspended." Even in the late 20th century, in an age more given to cynicism, the successes and failures of professional teams continued to evoke strong feelings among local residents. For example, during the 1990s, after having experienced urban decay and demoralization in the previous two decades, Cleveland experienced a great civic revival fueled in part by the success of the Indians baseball team.

The significance of specific baseball teams and individual players extended beyond the localities that they represented. The New York Yankees, who in the first half of the 20th century were the quintessential representatives of the big city, of the East, of urban America with its sophistication, and of ethnic and religious heterogeneity, became synonymous with supernal success, while the St. Louis Cardinals emerged as the quintessential champions of the Midwest, of small towns and the farms, of rural America with its simplicity, rusticity, and old-stock Protestant homogeneity.

BABE RUTH

(b. Feb. 6, 1895, Baltimore, Md., U.S.—d. Aug. 16, 1948, New York, N.Y.)

George Herman Ruth, Jr., was a professional baseball player who, largely because of his home-run hitting between 1919 and 1935, became—and perhaps remains to this day—America's most celebrated athlete.

Part of the aura surrounding Ruth arose from his modest origins. Though the legend that he was an orphan is untrue, Ruth did have a difficult childhood. Both his parents, George Herman Ruth, Sr., and Kate Shamberger Ruth, came from working-class, ethnic (German) families. Ruth, Sr., owned and operated a saloon in a tough neighbourhood on the Baltimore waterfront. Living in rooms above the saloon, the Ruths had eight children, but only George, Jr., the firstborn, and a younger sister survived to adulthood. Since neither his busy father nor his sickly mother had much time for the youngster, George roamed the streets, engaged in petty thievery, chewed tobacco, sometimes got drunk, repeatedly skipped school, and had several run-ins with the law. In 1902 his parents sent him to the St. Mary's Industrial School for Boys, a Baltimore asylum for incorrigibles and orphans run by the Xaverian Order of the Roman Catholic church. For the next 10 years Ruth was in and out of St. Mary's. When his mother died from tuberculosis in 1912, he became a permanent ward of the school.

Baseball offered Ruth an opportunity to escape both poverty and obscurity. While a teenager at St. Mary's, he achieved local renown for his baseball-playing prowess, and in 1914 Jack Dunn, owner of the local minor-league Baltimore Orioles franchise, signed him to a contract for $600. Ruth obtained the nickname "Babe" when a sportswriter referred to him as one of "Dunn's babes." For his day, Ruth was a large man; he stood more than six feet tall and weighed more than 200 pounds. Before the end of the 1914 season, his performance as a pitcher was so impressive that Dunn sold Ruth to the American League Boston Red Sox. That same year Ruth met, courted, and wed waitress Helen Woodford.

Ruth soon became the best left-handed pitcher in baseball. Between 1915 and 1919 he won 85 games, yielded a stunning earned run average (ERA) of only 2.02, won three World Series games (one in

Babe Ruth on the cover of the book Babe Ruth as I Knew Him, *written by former Yankee teammate and pitcher Waite Hoyt, 1948.* Diamond Images/ Getty Images

1916 and two in 1918), and, during a streak for scoreless World Series innings, set a record by pitching 29⅔ consecutive shutout innings.

At the same time, Ruth exhibited so much hitting clout that, on the days he did not pitch, manager Ed Barrow played him at first base or in the outfield. In an age when home runs were rare, Ruth slammed out 29 in 1919, thereby topping the single-season record of 27 set in 1884 (by Ned Williamson of the Chicago White Stockings). In 1920 Harry Frazee, the team owner and a producer of Broadway plays who was always short of money, sold Ruth to the New York Yankees for $125,000 plus a personal loan from Yankee owner Jacob Ruppert. While initially reluctant to leave Boston, Ruth signed a two-year contract with the Yankees for $10,000 a year.

As a full-time outfielder with the Yankees, Ruth quickly emerged as the greatest hitter to have ever played the game. Nicknamed by sportswriters the "Sultan of Swat," in his first season with the Yankees in 1920, he shattered his own single-season record by hitting 54 home runs, 25 more than he had hit in 1919. The next season Ruth did even better: he slammed out 59 homers and drove in 170 runs. In 1922 his salary jumped to $52,000, making him by far the highest-paid player in baseball. That summer he and Helen appeared in public with a new daughter, Dorothy, who was apparently the result of one of his many sexual escapades.

In 1922 Ruth's home run totals dropped to 35, but in 1923—with the opening of the magnificent new Yankee Stadium, dubbed by a sportswriter "The House That Ruth Built"—he hit 41 home runs, batted .393, and had a record-shattering slugging percentage (total bases divided by at bats) of .764. He continued with a strong season in 1924 when he hit a league-leading 46 home runs, but in 1925, while suffering from an intestinal disorder (thought by many to be syphilis), his offensive production declined sharply. That season, while playing in only 98 games, he hit 25 home runs.

He also struggled in his private life. Two years earlier he had met and fallen in love with actress Claire Hodgson, and in 1925 he legally separated from Helen. Helen's death from a fire in 1929 freed him to marry Hodgson the same year. The couple then formally adopted Dorothy, and Ruth adopted Hodgson's daughter, Julia.

On the field during the 1926 season, Ruth returned to his old form. Indeed, in the 1926–32 seasons, Ruth's offensive output towered over all other players in the game. For these seven seasons he averaged 49 home runs per season, batted in 152 runs, and had a batting average of .353, while taking the Yankees to four league pennants and three World Series championships. In 1927 Ruth's salary leapt to $70,000. That season he hit 60 home runs, a record that remained unbroken until Roger Maris hit 61 in 1961. That same season Ruth teamed with Lou Gehrig to form the greatest home-run hitting duo in baseball. Ruth and Gehrig were the heart of the 1927 Yankees team—nicknamed Murderer's Row—which is regarded by many baseball experts as the greatest team to ever play the game.

The 1932 World Series revealed not only Ruth's flair for exploiting the moment but produced his famous "called shot" home run. In the third game of the series against Chicago, while being heckled by the Cubs bench, Ruth, according to a story whose accuracy remains in doubt to this day, responded by pointing his finger to the centre-field bleachers. On the very next pitch, Ruth hit the ball precisely into that spot. After 1932 Ruth's playing skills rapidly diminished. Increasingly corpulent and slowed by age, his offensive numbers dropped sharply in both 1933 and 1934. He wanted to manage the Yankees, but Ruppert, the team's owner, is reported to have said that Ruth could not control his own behaviour, let alone that of the other players, and so refused to offer him the post. Hoping eventually to become a manager, in 1935 Ruth joined the Boston Braves as a player and assistant manager. But the offer to manage a big-league team never came. Ruth finished his career that season with 714 home runs, a record that remained unblemished until broken by Henry Aaron in 1974.

In 1936, sportswriters honoured Ruth by selecting him as one of five charter members to the newly established Baseball Hall of Fame in Cooperstown, New York. Ruth was a hopeless spendthrift, but, fortunately for him, in 1921 he met and employed Christy Walsh, a sports cartoonist-turned-agent. Walsh not only obtained huge contracts for Ruth's endorsement of products but also managed his finances so that Ruth lived comfortably during retirement. During his final years Ruth frequently played golf and made numerous personal appearances on behalf of products and causes but missed being actively involved in baseball. Still, he maintained his popularity with the American public; after his death from throat cancer, at least 75,000 people viewed his body in Yankee Stadium, and some

75,000 attended his funeral service (both inside and outside St. Patrick's Cathedral).

Ruth was a major figure in revolutionizing America's national game. While the frequent claim that his feats single-handedly saved the game from a massive public disillusionment that might have otherwise accompanied the Black Sox scandal of 1919 is an exaggeration, his home-run hitting did revitalize the sport. Prior to Ruth, teams had focused on what they called "scientific" or "inside" baseball—a complicated strategy of employing singles, sacrifices, hit-and-run plays, and stolen bases in order to score one run at a time. But Ruth seemed to make such tactics obsolete; with one mighty swat, he could clear the bases. While no other player in his day compared to Ruth in the ability to hit home runs, soon other players were also swinging harder and more freely. Indeed, Ruth helped to introduce an offensive revolution in baseball. In the 1920s batting averages, home runs, and runs scored soared to new heights. Ruth was also to a large extent responsible for manning the great Yankee dynasty of the 1920s and early 1930s. Between 1921 and 1932 the Yankees won seven pennants and four World Series.

In the 1920s, a decade that produced a galaxy of sports celebrities such as Red Grange in gridiron football and Jack Dempsey in prizefighting, no figure from the world of sport exceeded the public appeal of Ruth. "He has become a national curiosity," reported the *New York Times* as early as 1920, "and the sightseeing Pilgrims who daily flock into Manhattan are as anxious to rest eyes on him as they are to see the Woolworth Building." Each morning men and boys across the United States unfolded their newspapers to see if Ruth had hit yet another home run. Notorious for his enormous appetites for all things of the flesh, Ruth seemed to represent a new era in American history, a time when men and women were freer than they had been in the past to enjoy themselves. He embodied a new model of success. In an increasingly complex world of assembly lines and bureaucracies, Ruth, like other celebrities of the day, leapt to fame and fortune by his sheer natural talents and personal charisma rather than by hard work and self-control. The very words "Ruth" and "Ruthian" entered the American lexicon as benchmarks to describe outstanding performers and performances in all fields of human endeavour. As with no other sports figure in American history except perhaps Muhammad Ali, Ruth continued long after his playing career ended to occupy a towering place in America's imagination.

In the 1920s Babe Ruth became the diamond's colossal demigod. To those toiling on assembly lines or sitting at their desks in corporate bureaucracies, Ruth embodied America's continuing faith in upward social mobility. His mighty home runs furnished vivid proof that men remained masters of their own destinies and that they could still rise from mean, vulgar beginnings to fame and fortune. For African Americans, black stars such as Satchel Paige and Josh Gibson furnished equally compelling models of individual inspiration and success.

Baseball parks became important local civic monuments and repositories of collective memories. The first parks had been jerry-built, flimsy wooden structures, but between 1909 and 1923 some 15 major league clubs constructed new, more permanent parks of steel and concrete. These edifices were akin to the great public buildings, skyscrapers, and railway terminals of the day; local residents proudly pointed to them as evidence of their city's size and its achievements.

Seeing them as retreats from the noise, dirt, and squalor of the industrial city, the owners gave the first parks pastoral names—Ebbets Field, Sportsman's Park, and the Polo Grounds—but, with the construction of symmetrical, multisports facilities in the 1960s and '70s, urban and futuristic names such as Astrodome and Kingdome predominated. In a new park-building era in the 1990s, designers sought to recapture the ambience of earlier times by designing "retro parks," a term that was something of an oxymoron in that, while the new parks offered the fan the intimacy of the old-time parks, they simultaneously provided modern conveniences such as escalators, climate-controlled lounges, high-tech audiovisual systems, Disneyesque play areas for children, and space for numerous retail outlets. The increasing corporate influence on the game was reflected in park names such as Network Associates Stadium and Bank One Ballpark.

After about the mid-20th century, baseball's claim to being America's game rested on more precarious foundations than in the past. The sport faced potent competition, not only from other professional sports (especially gridiron football) but even more from a massive conversion of Americans from public to private, at-home diversions. Attendance as a percentage of population fell at all levels of baseball, the minor leagues became a shell of their former selves, and hundreds of semipro and amateur teams folded. In the 1990s, player strikes, free agency, disparities in competition, and the rising cost of attending games added to the woes of major league baseball. Yet, baseball continued to exhibit a remarkable resiliency; attendance at professional games improved, and attendance at minor league games was close to World War II records by the end of the century. As the 21st century opened, baseball still faced serious problems, but the sport was gaining in popularity around the world, and a strong case could still be made for baseball holding a special place in the hearts and minds of the American people.

HISTORY OF THE SPORT

The term *base-ball* can be dated to 1744, in John Newbery's children's book *A Little Pretty Pocket-Book*. The book has a brief poem and an illustration depicting a game called base-ball. Interestingly, the bases in the illustration are marked by posts instead of the bags and flat home plate now so familiar in the game. The book was extremely popular in England and was reprinted in North America in 1762 (New York) and 1787 (Massachusetts).

Many other early references to bat-and-ball games involving bases are known: "playing at base" at the American army camp at Valley Forge in 1778; the forbidding of students to "play with balls and sticks" on the common of Princeton College in 1787; a note in the memoirs of Thurlow Weed, an upstate New York newspaper editor and politician, of a baseball club organized about 1825; a newspaper report that the Rochester (New York) Baseball Club had about 50 members at practice in the 1820s; and a reminiscence of the elder Oliver Wendell Holmes concerning his Harvard days in the late 1820s, stating that he played a good deal of ball at college.

The Boy's Own Book (1828), a frequently reprinted book on English sports played by boys of the time, included in its second edition a chapter on the game of rounders. As described there, rounders had many resemblances to the modern game of baseball: it was played on a diamond-shaped infield with a base at each corner, the fourth being that at which the batter originally stood and to which he had to advance to score a run. When a batter hit a pitched ball through or over the infield, he could run. A ball hit elsewhere was foul, and he could not run. Three missed strikes at the ball meant the batter was out. A batted ball caught on the fly put the batter out. One notable difference from baseball was that, in rounders, when a ball hit on the ground was fielded, the fielder put the runner out by hitting him with the thrown ball; the same was true with a runner caught off base. Illustrations show flat stones used as bases and a second catcher behind the first, perhaps to catch foul balls. The descent of baseball from rounders seems indisputably clear-cut. The first American account of rounders was in *The Book of Sports* (1834) by Robin Carver, who credits *The Boy's Own Book* as his source but calls the game *base*, or *goal*, *ball*.

EARLY YEARS

In 1845, according to baseball legend, Alexander J. Cartwright, an amateur player in New York City, organized the New York Knickerbocker Base Ball Club, which formulated a set of rules for baseball, many of which still remain. The rules were much like those for rounders, but with a significant change in that the runner was put out not by being hit with the thrown ball but by being tagged with it. This change no doubt led to the substitution of a harder ball, which made possible a larger-scale game.

The adoption of these rules by the Knickerbockers and other amateur club teams in the New York City area led to an increased popularity of the game. The old game with the soft ball continued to be popular in and around Boston; a Philadelphia club that had played the old game since 1833 did not adopt the Knickerbocker or New York version of the game until 1860. Until the American Civil War (1861–65), the two versions of the game were called the Massachusetts game (using the soft ball) and the New York game (using the hard ball). During the Civil War,

An early baseball game at the Elysian Fields, Hoboken, New Jersey, 1859; engraving from Harper's magazine. Library of Congress, Washington, D.C.

soldiers from New York and New Jersey taught their game to others, and after the war the New York game became predominant.

In 1854 a revision of the rules prescribed the weight and size of the ball, along with the dimensions of the infield, specifications that have not been significantly altered since that time. The National Association of Base Ball Players was organized in 1857, comprising clubs from New York City and vicinity. In 1859 Washington, D.C., organized a club, and in the next year clubs were formed in Lowell, Massachusetts; Allegheny, Pennsylvania; and Hartford, Connecticut. The game continued to spread after the Civil War—to Maine, Kentucky, and Oregon. Baseball was on its way to becoming the national pastime. It was widely played outside the cities, but the big-city clubs were the dominant force. In 1865 a convention was called to confirm the rules and the amateur status of baseball and brought together 91 amateur teams from such cities as St. Louis; Chattanooga, Tennessee; Louisville, Kentucky; Washington, D.C.; Boston; and Philadelphia.

ORIGINS OF PROFESSIONAL BASEBALL

Two important developments in the history of baseball occurred in the post-Civil War period: the spread of the sport to Latin America and Asia (discussed later) and the professionalization of the sport in the United States. The early baseball clubs such as the New York Knickerbockers were clubs in the true sense of the word: members paid dues, the emphasis was on fraternity and socializing, and baseball games were played largely among members. But the growth of baseball's popularity soon attracted commercial interest. In 1862 William Cammeyer of Brooklyn constructed an enclosed baseball field with stands and charged admission to games. Following the Civil War, this practice quickly spread, and clubs soon learned that games with rival clubs and tournaments drew larger crowds and brought prestige to the winners. The interclub games attracted the interest and influence of gamblers. With a new emphasis on external competition, clubs felt pressure to field quality teams. Players began to specialize in playing a single position, and field time was given over to a club's top players so they could practice. Professionalism began to appear about 1865–66 as some teams hired skilled players on a per game basis. Players either were paid for playing or were compensated with jobs that required little or no actual work. Amateurs resented these practices and the gambling and bribery that often accompanied them, but the larger public was enthralled by the intense competition and the rivalries that developed. The first publicly announced all-professional team, the Cincinnati (Ohio) Red Stockings, was organized in 1869; it toured that year, playing from New York City to San Francisco and winning some 56 games and tying 1. The team's success, especially against the hallowed clubs of New York, resulted in national notoriety and proved the superior skill of professional players. The desire of many other cities and teams to win such acclaim guaranteed the professionalization of the game, though many players remained nominally in the amateur National Association of Base Ball Players until the amateurs withdrew in 1871. Thereafter professional teams largely controlled the development of the sport.

The National Association of Professional Base Ball Players was formed in 1871. The founding teams were the Philadelphia Athletics; the Chicago White Stockings (who would also play as the Chicago Colts and the Chicago Orphans before becoming the Cubs—the American

CAP ANSON

(b. April 11/17, 1851, Marshalltown, Iowa, U.S.—d. April 14, 1922, Chicago, Ill.)

The American baseball player and manager Adrian Constantine ("Cap") Anson played professionally for 27 years and was still in his team's regular lineup at the age of 46. He batted .300 or better for 23 seasons and was the most famous player of the 19th century.

Anson played in the National Association, the first professional baseball league, with the Forest City team of Rockford, Illinois, in 1871 and with the Philadelphia Athletics (1872–75). He is believed to have batted .352 during those five years. In 1876, when the Chicago National Association team—the White Stockings, later known as the Cubs—switched to the newly formed National League, Anson joined this club, and in 1879 he became its manager. Anson, who played first base for most of his career, was credited with batting championships in 1879, 1881, and 1888. His total number of hits in the National League is given as 2,995 or 3,081 (authorities differ), and thus his National League career batting average is either .329 or .339; it is certain, however, that Anson was the first player to get 3,000 lifetime hits.

Anson retired as a player and resigned as Chicago manager after the 1897 season and was nonplaying manager of the New York Gothams (later known as the Giants) in the National League in 1898. As a manager Anson led Chicago to five National League championships. He was, however, profoundly opposed to integration within professional baseball and is thought to have been one of the major forces behind the "gentlemen's agreement" that barred black players from being signed to major league teams.

He was elected to the Baseball Hall of Fame in 1939.

League Chicago White Sox were not formed until 1900); the Brooklyn (New York) Eckfords; the Cleveland (Ohio) Forest Citys; the Forest Citys of Rockford, Illinois; the Haymakers of Troy, New York; the Kekiongas of Fort Wayne, Indiana; the Olympics of Washington, D.C.; and the Mutuals of New York City. The league disbanded in 1876 with the founding of the rival National League of Professional Baseball Clubs (NL). The change from a players' association to one of clubs was particularly significant. The teams making up the new league represented Philadelphia, Hartford (Connecticut), Boston, Chicago, Cincinnati, Louisville (Kentucky), St. Louis, and New York City. When William Hulbert, president of the league (1877–82), expelled four players for dishonesty, the reputation of baseball as an institution was significantly enhanced.

LEAGUE FORMATION

In 1881 the American Association was formed with teams from cities that were not members of the National League and teams that had been expelled from the league (such as Cincinnati, which was disciplined in 1880 for playing games on Sunday and allowing liquor on the grounds). In 1890, after the National League tried to limit salaries (a $2,000 maximum for pitchers), the players formed the Players' League, but it quickly failed. The American Association unsuccessfully challenged the National League and late in 1891 merged with it in a 12-team league that constituted a monopoly, an arrangement that prevailed through 1899. By 1900 the National League had shrunk to eight teams—Boston (the team that would eventually become the Braves), Brooklyn (soon to be the Dodgers), Chicago (soon to be the Cubs), Cincinnati (the Reds, who had returned to the league in 1890), New York City (the Giants), Philadelphia (the Phillies), Pittsburgh (the Pirates), and St. Louis (the Cardinals)—and it remained so constituted until 1953, when the Boston Braves moved to Milwaukee, Wisconsin.

The Western League, organized in 1893, had Midwestern members. When in 1900 Charles Comiskey moved his St. Paul (Minnesota) team to Chicago as the White Sox and the Grand Rapids (Michigan) team was shifted to Cleveland as the Indians, the National League agreed to the moves. However, when permission was asked to put teams in Baltimore (Maryland) and Washington, D.C., the National League balked, and the "baseball war" was on. The Western League, renamed the American League (AL) and officially elevated to major league status in 1901, transferred teams from Indianapolis (Indiana), Kansas City (Missouri), Minneapolis, and Buffalo (New York) to Baltimore (the first of two American League teams to be called the Baltimore Orioles), Washington, D.C. (the Senators), Philadelphia (the Athletics), and Boston (the Red Stockings). American League teams also were established in Detroit, Michigan (the Tigers), and Milwaukee (the first of two teams to be named the Milwaukee Brewers), the latter club moving to St. Louis as the Browns in 1902. When the Baltimore club moved to New York City in 1903 to become the Highlanders (after 1912, the Yankees), the league took the form it was to keep until 1954, when the St. Louis Browns became the Baltimore Orioles.

During baseball's "war," the American League wooed away many of the National League's star players. In 1903 the leagues agreed to prohibit single ownership of two clubs in the same city and the shifting of franchises from one city to another by either league without permission of the other. They also established rules for transferring players from one league to the other and for moving minor league players into the major leagues. The peace of 1903 resulted in the first World Series, which, after a hiatus in 1904 (the New York Giants refused to play, believing the opposition unworthy), was held each year thereafter, the winner being the team to win four games out of seven (five out of nine from 1919 to 1921). In the period following the "war," the two leagues enjoyed a long period of growth. The "inside game" dominated the next two decades, until

JOHN MCGRAW

(b. April 7, 1873, Truxton, N.Y., U.S.—d. Feb. 25, 1934, New Rochelle, N.Y.)

Professional baseball player and manager John McGraw led the New York Giants to 10 National League championships.

During the 1890s McGraw was a star infielder for the Baltimore National League club. (Both the American and the National League Baltimore teams of this era were named the Orioles; neither team, however, was affiliated with the current American League Orioles, who took that name upon moving from St. Louis, Missouri, in 1954.) His .391 mark of 1899 remains the highest batting average attained by any major league third baseman.

In 1901 McGraw was appointed manager of the Baltimore club in the new American League. In that first year McGraw bought the contract of African American player Charlie Grant from the Negro league Columbia Giants. Because of the segregation that existed in baseball, McGraw tried to pass Grant off as a Cherokee Indian. The ruse was unsuccessful, and the colour bar would not be breached until Branch Rickey signed Jackie Robinson in 1947. The attempt to sign Grant was typical of McGraw, who was always on the lookout for talent and was sometimes willing to bend the rules if it enabled his team to win.

McGraw and American League president Ban Johnson had been in conflict for some time, and on July 19, 1902, McGraw returned to the National League as manager of the New York team. The enmity between McGraw and Johnson was so great that, when the Giants won the National League championship in 1904, they refused to play against the American League team in the newly organized World Series.

Until McGraw's retirement in June 1932, the Giants were generally the most feared team in the league. McGraw was a tyrant of a manger; he was abusive and difficult with umpires and put winning ahead of nearly all other considerations. His tactics succeeded, as the Giants won league championships in 1904, 1905, 1911–13, 1917, and 1921–24, taking World Series titles in 1905, 1921, and 1922. McGraw retired in 1932; in his 33 years of managing, his teams won 2,840 games, a total exceeded only by that of one other manager, Connie Mack. McGraw returned to baseball the year after his retirement to manage the National League team in the first All-Star Game. He was voted into the Baseball Hall of Fame in 1937.

hitter-friendly rules were instituted in 1920, ushering in the "live-ball era" (the period of inside-game dominance was also known as the "dead-ball era"). The inside game was a style of play that emphasized pitching, speed, and batsmanship. Bunting was very common, and doubles and triples were more heralded than home runs (which during this era were almost exclusively of the inside-the-park variety). Two managers were credited as the masters of the inside game and brought success to their respective teams: John J. McGraw, manager of the National League New York Giants (1902–32), and Connie Mack, manager of the American League Philadelphia Athletics (1901–50).

SURVIVAL AND GROWTH

Baseball suffered a major scandal—subsequently called the Black Sox scandal—when eight members of the Chicago White Sox were accused of accepting bribes from known gamblers to "throw" the 1919 World Series. Although Charles Comiskey, owner of the White Sox, suspended the players for the 1921 season, they were found not guilty because of insufficient evidence. Presuming a need to restore baseball's honour, however, Judge Kenesaw Mountain Landis banned the eight accused players from baseball for life after he was named baseball's first commissioner, supplanting the three-man National Commission that had been created in 1903.

During the 1920s, generally known as a golden age of sports in the United States, the premier hero was Babe Ruth. A New York Yankee outfielder affectionately known as the "Sultan of Swat," Ruth was a large man with an even larger personality, and his reinvention of the home run (the sort that traveled over the outfield wall) into a mythic feat enthralled the nation. His performance not only assured the success of his team but

BLACK SOX SCANDAL

The Black Sox Scandal centred on the charge that eight members of the Chicago White Sox had been bribed to lose the 1919 World Series to the Cincinnati Reds. The accused players were pitchers Eddie Cicotte and Claude ("Lefty") Williams, first baseman Arnold ("Chick") Gandil, shortstop Charles ("Swede") Risberg, third baseman George ("Buck") Weaver, outfielders Joe ("Shoeless Joe") Jackson and Oscar ("Happy") Felsch, and utility infielder Fred McMullin. Court records suggest that the eight players received $70,000 to $100,000 for losing five games to three.

Suspicions of a conspiracy were aired immediately after the World Series ended, principally by Hugh Fullerton and other sportswriters, but controversy over the allegations had died down by the beginning of the 1920 season. Then, in September, a grand jury was called to investigate various allegations of gamblers invading baseball. On Sept. 28, 1920, after Cicotte, Williams, Jackson, and Felsch admitted to the grand jury that they had thrown the 1919 series in return for a bribe, Charles Comiskey, owner of the White Sox, suspended seven of the players. (Gandil was already on suspension in a salary dispute.) The indicted players stood trial in the summer of 1921 but on August 3 were acquitted on insufficient evidence—largely because key evidence, including the original confessions of the players, had disappeared from the grand jury files. (They probably were stolen.) On August 4 the new baseball commissioner, Judge Kenesaw Mountain Landis, banned the eight players from the game for life.

Few of the alleged gamblers testified at the trial, and none were themselves ever brought to trial for the White Sox bribery, though the notorious New York racketeer Arnold Rothstein was mentioned in hearings as the probable banker of the bribery scheme.

spurred a tactical change in baseball. The inside game, with its bunts and sacrifices, gave way to the era of free swinging at the plate. The resulting explosion of offense brought fans to the ballparks in droves. Even the Great Depression of the 1930s did little to abate the rise in popularity and financial success of the game except at the minor league and Negro league levels. The commercial growth of the game was aided by several recent innovations. The first All-Star Game, an exhibition game pitting the best players in the National League against the best of the American League, was played at Comiskey Park in Chicago in 1933. During the 1920s club owners also cautiously embraced radio broadcasting of games. The first major league game broadcast took place in Pittsburgh in 1921, but during that decade only the Chicago Cubs allowed broadcasts of all their games. Many owners feared radio would dissuade fans from attending the games in person, especially during the Great Depression. However, the opposite proved to be true; radio created new fans and brought more of them to the ballpark. Night baseball, which had already been used by barnstorming and minor league teams, began in the major leagues at Cincinnati in 1935. Initially caution and tradition slowed the interest in night baseball, but the obvious commercial benefits of playing when fans were not at work eventually won out. Delayed by World War II, night baseball became almost universal by the 1960s, with all teams but the Cubs scheduling about half of their home games at night. (The Cubs acceded to night baseball at home only in 1988.) The first nighttime World Series game was played in 1971.

From 1942 until the end of World War II, baseball operated under the "green light" order of Commissioner Landis, approved by President Franklin D. Roosevelt. Soon after the Pearl Harbor attack, Landis asked Roosevelt if he felt that baseball should "close down for the duration of the war." Roosevelt, a lifelong baseball fan, replied in a letter dated Jan. 15, 1942, that he felt baseball was valuable to the nation and should continue throughout the war. Once Landis received this letter giving baseball the go-ahead, organized baseball threw itself behind the American war effort, billing itself as

KENESAW MOUNTAIN LANDIS

(b. Nov. 20, 1866, Millville, Ohio, U.S.—d. Nov. 25, 1944, Chicago, Ill.)

Kenesaw Mountain Landis was an American federal judge who, as the first commissioner of organized professional baseball, was noted for his uncompromising measures against persons guilty of dishonesty or other conduct he regarded as damaging to the sport.

He was named for a mountain near Atlanta, Ga., where his father, a Union soldier, was wounded during the Civil War. Landis attended the University of Cincinnati and in 1891 was graduated from the Union College of Law, Chicago. He practiced law in Chicago until March 1905, when President Theodore Roosevelt appointed him U.S. district judge for the northern district of Illinois. Two years later, Landis won nationwide fame by fining the Standard Oil Company more than $29,000,000 for granting unlawful freight rebates. (The decision was reversed on appeal.) During World War I he presided at sedition trials of Socialist and labour leaders.

In 1915 the Federal League, a "third major league" operating outside the structure of organized professional baseball, brought suit against the American and National leagues. The case came before Landis, who neither granted nor denied the injunction that was requested but withheld his decision until the Federal League had disbanded on terms satisfactory to all three leagues. Following the Black Sox baseball scandal (in which eight Chicago White Sox players were accused of accepting bribes to lose the 1919 World Series), Landis was proposed for the office of commissioner. Replacing the three-man National Baseball Commission, which had failed to deal adequately with the Black Sox problem, Landis took office in January 1920.

Although disliked and even feared for his autocratic methods and patriarchal sternness, the commissioner held office until his death, and none of his decisions ever was reversed. He was elected to the Baseball Hall of Fame in 1944.

"the national nerve tonic" for workers in wartime factories. Attendance at baseball games was still off slightly. Further, many players went into the armed services—most notably Ted Williams, the last man in organized baseball to have a season batting average of more than .400 (.406 in 1941)—and the quality of play suffered somewhat.

THE POSTWAR PERIOD

The years following the conclusion of World War II were marked by rising attendance, the growth of the minor leagues, and in 1947 the racial integration of the game. This period also was marked by new efforts by players to obtain better pay and conditions of employment. A portent of things to come was the formation in 1946 of the American Baseball Guild. Although the guild failed in appeals to national and state labour relations boards, its very existence led to reforms before the 1947 season: a minimum major league salary of $5,000, no salary cuts during a season for a major league player moved to the minors, weekly spring-training expense money of $25, a 25 percent limit on annual salary cuts, and establishment of a players' pension fund.

Landis's successor as commissioner, Albert B. ("Happy") Chandler (1945–51), assured the soundness of the pension fund in 1950 by signing a six-year contract for broadcasting World Series and All-Star games; the television portion alone amounted to $1 million a year, with a large proportion earmarked for the pension fund. Radio and television rights for regular-season games remained with each club. Later commissioners includeyhbd Ford C. Frick (1951–65), William D. Eckert (1965–69), Bowie Kuhn (1969–84), Peter Ueberroth (1984–89), A. Bartlett Giamatti (1989), Fay Vincent (1989–92), and Allan H. ("Bud") Selig.

MOVEMENT AND EXPANSION

The postwar boom was short-lived, however. America was going through tremendous changes. Millions were moving out of the cities and to the suburbs, and population centres in the South and West were growing. Americans had more time and money to enjoy themselves, which they did through vacationing and outdoor recreation. Moreover, the rapid growth of television preoccupied the country. Baseball was slow to adapt. Major league clubs were located only as far west as St. Louis and no farther south than Washington, D.C. Many of the ballparks had fallen into disrepair, were outdated, and were inconvenient for surburbanites driving in for a game. Despite exciting play on the field, attendance began to wane. The added revenue from radio and television broadcast rights could not offset the losses at the gate. The 1950s saw the first franchise changes since 1903. In 1953 the Braves, always overshadowed in New England by the Red Sox, moved from Boston to Milwaukee (in 1966 the franchise moved again, to Atlanta, Georgia), where they were offered a new stadium. The next year the St. Louis Browns, themselves overshadowed by the Cardinals, moved to Baltimore and became the Orioles. In 1955 the Philadelphia Athletics franchise was moved to Kansas City, Missouri (and in 1968 to Oakland, California). The impact of these moves was slight compared with the move of the Dodgers and Giants from New York City to California (the Dodgers to Los Angeles and the Giants to San Francisco) in 1958. Frustrated in his attempts to win city support for a new stadium, Dodger owner Walter O'Malley jumped at an offer to relocate the team to Los Angeles, which was then the third largest city in the country. O'Malley persuaded the Giants to move to San Francisco in order to maintain their rivalry and ease the travel burden on National League teams.

Despite the betrayal felt by fans in Brooklyn and Manhattan, the moves were a successful business decision

WALTER O'MALLEY

(b. Oct. 9, 1903, Bronx, N.Y., U.S.—d. Aug. 9, 1979, Rochester, Minn.)

American lawyer Walter O'Malley was the principal owner of the National League Brooklyn Dodgers professional baseball team (from 1958 the Los Angeles Dodgers). As owner of the Dodgers, he played a role in two of the key events in the history of both the club and the major leagues: Jackie Robinson's breaking of the colour barrier in 1947 and the expansion of the major leagues to the West Coast.

O'Malley received his law degree from Fordham University in New York City in 1930 and became a director of the Dodgers in 1932 and legal adviser in 1943. He became an owner with two other partners in 1945 and assisted general manager Branch Rickey in the signing of Robinson, which ended baseball's ban of black players. In 1950 O'Malley obtained control of 67 percent of the team's stock and was made president. He achieved sole control after the team's move to Los Angeles, becoming chairman of the board in 1970 when he passed the presidency on to his son Peter. The team won the National League pennant six times in Brooklyn and nine times in Los Angeles during the ownership of the O'Malley family (1945–98).

O'Malley was a powerful influence in baseball ownership and management; he became the National League representative to baseball's executive committee in 1951 and was reputed to have had a major role in selecting William D. Eckert and Bowie Kuhn as commissioners (in 1965 and 1969, respectively).

The Dodgers management bought the Los Angeles franchise in 1956 and moved the team there in 1958. Protests in New York were bitter, but O'Malley's business acumen was proved in 1978, when the Dodgers became the first major league team to draw more than three million fans. In 2008 he was posthumously inducted into the Baseball Hall of Fame.

O'Malley's other financial interests were in railroads, building materials, and real estate. He was also a civic leader.

for the clubs. The decade of franchise movement was followed by several rounds of expansion that lasted into the 1990s. Expansion began in 1961 when the Washington (D.C.) Senators were moved to Minneapolis–St. Paul and renamed the Twins, and a new franchise was granted to Washington (also named the Senators); however, it lasted only until 1971, when it was transferred to Dallas–Fort Worth and renamed the Texas Rangers. Another American League franchise was awarded to Los Angeles (later moved to Anaheim as the California Angels, now known as the Los Angeles Angels of Anaheim) in 1961, and in 1962 the National League also expanded to 10 teams with new franchises in New York City (the Mets) and Houston, Texas (the Colt .45s; after 1964, the Astros). The 154-game season had been expanded in the American League to 162 in 1961; the National League followed suit in 1962.

Along with this first round of expansion came an era of superb pitching that dominated the league for a generation. The earned run averages for pitchers during this era averaged 3.30, and the major league batting average fell as low as .238 in 1968. Several changes in the game were believed to account for the resurgence of pitching; the strike zone was expanded in 1963; managers explored more strategic uses of the relief pitchers; and new glove technology improved defensive play. At the same time, a new generation of large multipurpose stadiums came into use. These stadiums typically used artificial turf that was harder and faster than natural grass. As a result, new emphasis was placed on speed in the field and on the base paths. Fearing that the dominance of pitching was hurting fan interest in the game, the major league tried to improve hitting by lowering the mound and narrowing the strike zone in 1969. In hopes of further increasing offensive play, the American League introduced the designated hitter in 1973. The changes did increase offensive output, but pitching still dominated through much of the 1970s.

In 1969 new franchises were awarded to Montreal (the Expos, the first major league franchise outside the United States) and San Diego, California (the Padres), bringing the National League to 12 teams. In the American League in 1969, new franchises in Kansas City, Missouri (the Royals), and Seattle, Washington (the Pilots), brought that league to 12 teams, and both leagues were divided into Eastern and Western divisions.

Playoffs between division winners determined the league pennant winners, who then played in the World Series, which was extended into late October. California, which had had no major league baseball prior to 1958, had five teams by 1969. Of the new franchises, only Seattle failed outright and was moved to Milwaukee, where it became the Brewers (moved to the National League in a 1998 reorganization). A franchise was again granted to Seattle (the Mariners) and to Toronto (the Blue Jays), bringing the number of American League teams to 14 in 1977. In 1993 the National League also was brought to 14 with the addition of teams in Denver (the Colorado Rockies) and Miami (the Florida Marlins). In 1998 the Arizona Diamondbacks (located in Phoenix) joined the National League, and the Tampa Bay (Florida) Devil Rays (now known as the Tampa Bay Rays) began play in the American League.

In 1994 both leagues were reconfigured into East, Central, and West divisions. The playoff format was changed to include an additional round and a wild card (the team with the best record among the non-division-winning teams in each league).

An explosion of offense occurred in the mid-1980s and after. In particular, home runs increased dramatically, reaching record-breaking numbers from 1985 to 1987 and again in the late 1990s. The reasons for the change from dominant pitching to hitting were not entirely clear. Many claimed the ball had been engineered to fly farther; others claimed that continual expansion had diluted the quality of pitching. The improved off-season conditioning (that now often included weight lifting) made players stronger and quicker with their bats. The 1990s also saw another generation of new ballparks, many of which featured small dimensions that were more to the liking of power hitters.

During the later half of the 20th century, expansion was perceived by baseball executives as both a source of added revenue for clubs (large entry fees were charged to new franchises) as well as a means of generating new interest in the game. In 2001, however, concerns over economically underperforming clubs prompted owners to announce plans to eliminate two teams (widely believed to be the Minnesota Twins and the since-relocated Montreal Expos). The plan was put on hold after the players' union pursued legal action to prevent the move, and a 2002 Minnesota court order that forced the Twins to play out the lease at their home stadium effectively ended the talk of contraction for the foreseeable future.

The Minor Leagues

The minor leagues formed an association in 1901 to deal with the problems resulting from the lack of agreement on contract ownership, salaries, territoriality, and other issues. The current structure was created when the major leagues reached their agreement in 1903, and the minor leagues became a training ground for prospective major league players and a refuge for older players.

In 1919 Branch Rickey, then manager of the St. Louis Cardinals, devised what came to be known as the "farm system"; as the price of established players increased, the Cardinals began "growing" their own, signing hundreds of high-school boys. Other major league clubs followed suit, developing their own farm clubs that were tied into the minors. In 1949 the minor leagues were tremendously popular: 448 teams in the United States, Canada, Cuba, and Mexico played in 59 leagues with an aggregate attendance of some 39 million, about twice that of the 16 major league clubs. The minor leagues at that time were divided into six classifications, graded according to the level of playing skills: AAA (triple A), AA (double A), A (single A), B, C, and D.

Attendance eroded soon thereafter when the major leagues began broadcasting and televising their games into minor league attendance areas. By the early 1980s, after the American and National leagues had annexed 10 choice minor league territories, the number of minor league teams had been greatly reduced, with only 17 leagues remaining. Attendance dropped, and the minor league clubs generally looked to the major league parent clubs for heavy subsidization. The purpose of the minor leagues had evolved from mainly providing local entertainment to developing major league talent.

This situation improved in the early 1990s. As ticket prices for major league games escalated, attendance at less expensive minor league games rose apace. Further, development of new stadiums and renovation of existing facilities created more interest in minor league baseball. By 2001 attendance at minor league games reached more than 38.8 million. The minors had 15 leagues with 176 teams falling into one of five classifications—AAA, AA, A (full season), A (short season), and Rookie. The minor league franchises successfully concentrated on drawing families to their parks with both games and promotional entertainment.

LABOUR ISSUES

From the beginning of organized professional baseball, the owners controlled the game, players, managers, and umpires. Players began to organize as early as 1885, when a group of New York Giants formed the National Brotherhood of Base Ball Players, a benevolent and protective association. Under the leadership of John Montgomery Ward, who had a law degree and was a player for the Giants, the Brotherhood grew rapidly as a secret organization. It went public in 1886 to challenge the adoption of a $2,000 salary ceiling by the National League. Rebuffed in attempts to negotiate with league owners, the Brotherhood in 1890 formed the short-lived Players League.

During the National League–American League war of 1900–03, the Protective Association of Professional Baseball Players got National League players to switch to the other league, but with the peace treaty the association died. In 1912 came the Baseball Players' Fraternity, which included most professional players. It was organized after the suspension of Ty Cobb for punching a fan. Later a threatened strike was settled the day before it was to begin.

After a 1953 Supreme Court decision reaffirmed a 1922 decision stating that baseball was not a business that was subject to antitrust rules, baseball felt assured that its legal and economic foundation was firm. This foundation is primarily based on the Reserve Rule, or Reserve Clause, an agreement among major league teams, dating from 1879, whereby the rights of each team to the services of its players are observed by other teams; i.e., a team could designate a certain number of players who were not to be offered jobs by other teams. The original number of 5 such players was increased to 11 in 1883 and ultimately included a whole team roster.

The recourse the court failed to provide was in substance achieved by the Major League Baseball Players Association—founded in 1953 but largely ineffectual until 1966, when it hired as executive director Marvin Miller, a former labour-union official who also had been active in government in labour-management relations. A skillful negotiator, Miller secured players' rights and benefits contractually and established grievance procedures with recourse to impartial arbitration. In 1968 the minimum salary was doubled to $10,000, and first-class travel and meal allowances were established in 1970. A threatened players' boycott of spring training was averted in 1969 by a compromise assuring a $20,000 median salary.

In 1970 a new suit was brought in federal court contesting the Reserve Clause. The suit was supported by the players' association, which hired as counsel Arthur Goldberg, a former U.S. Supreme Court justice. The plaintiff was Curt Flood, star outfielder of the St. Louis Cardinals, and the defendants were the commissioner, the two major league presidents, and the major league clubs. Flood claimed that, in trading him to the Philadelphia Phillies without his knowledge or approval, the Cardinals had violated the antitrust laws. He refused to report to the Phillies and sat out the season. The court found against Flood, who appealed, and in 1972 the U.S. Supreme Court reaffirmed the 1922 and 1953 decisions exempting baseball from the antitrust laws, but it called on Congress to correct through legislation any inequities. Meanwhile, Flood had signed for the 1971 season with Washington on the understanding that he would not be sold or traded without his permission. He quit in midseason, however.

CURT FLOOD

Curt Flood. Focus On Sport/Getty Images

(b. Jan. 18, 1938, Houston, Texas, U.S.—d. Jan. 20, 1997, Los Angeles, Calif.)

Curtis Flood was a professional baseball player whose antitrust litigation challenging the major leagues' reserve clause was unsuccessful but led ultimately to the clause's demise.

Flood began playing baseball as a youth and was signed in 1956 by the National League Cincinnati Reds. He was traded to the St. Louis Cardinals in 1958 and played for them through the 1969 season as an outfielder. He batted over .300 in six seasons and had a career average (1956–71) of .293. When he was traded to the Philadelphia Phillies, Flood, with the backing of the Major League Baseball Players Association (MLBPA), challenged the reserve clause, which gave St. Louis the right to trade him without his permission, as violating federal antitrust laws. (Earlier attempts to overthrow the reserve clause had resulted in U.S. Supreme Court decisions in 1922 and 1953 that held the Sherman Antitrust Act law did not apply to baseball.)

Flood lost his case in 1970 but refiled it in 1971; the decision went against him. Later strike actions by the MLBPA and the consequent establishment of free agency for players with 10 years of service with the same club made the reserve clause inoperative.

After his retirement Flood became a broadcaster for the Oakland Athletics and later worked for the Oakland Department of Sports and Aquatics as commissioner of a sandlot baseball league.

Flood's autobiographical *The Way It Is*, recounting his struggle against the reserve clause, appeared in 1971.

In 1972 baseball had its first general strike, lasting 13 days and causing the cancellation of 86 regular-season games and delaying the divisional playoffs and World Series by 10 days. The players asked for and were ultimately given an addition to the pension fund. Another players' strike was averted in 1973, when an agreement was reached that provided compulsory impartial arbitration of salary negotiations and established a rule that allowed a player with 10 years of service in the major leagues and the last 5 years with the same club to refuse to be traded without his consent.

These were unprecedented victories for the players, but their greatest triumph came prior to the 1976 season. Pitchers Andy Messersmith of the Los Angeles Dodgers and Dave McNally of the Montreal Expos played the entire 1975 season without signing a contract; their contracts had expired but were automatically renewed by their clubs. Miller had been waiting for such a test case. The players' union filed a grievance on behalf of McNally and Messersmith, contending that a player's contract could not be renewed in perpetuity, a custom first established in 1879. Arbitrator Peter Seitz found for the players. This decision substantively demolished the Reserve Rule.

Stunned, the owners appealed but without success. Negotiations followed, however, and the union agreed to a modification of the Reserve Rule: players with six or more years of major league service could become free agents when their contracts expired and would be eligible to make their own deals. The ruling allowed eligible players who refused to sign their 1976 contracts to choose free agency in 1977.

Twenty-four players took immediate advantage of this new opportunity and went on the open market.

Frantic bidding by the clubs followed. Bill Campbell, a relief pitcher with the Minnesota Twins, was the first free agent to make a new connection. He signed a four-year, $1 million contract with the Boston Red Sox, which annually paid him more than 10 times his 1976 salary. The free agency procedure was the principal issue when the players struck for 50 days at the height of the 1981 season (June 12–July 31), forcing the cancellation of 714 games. Once again the players won. In the settlement it was agreed that clubs losing players to free agency would not receive direct compensation from the free agents' new teams. The union contended that such compensation would impede movement, forcing the signing club, in effect, to pay twice: a huge sum to the player and further compensation to the player's former employer. Under certain conditions relating to the quality of the player, however, the team that lost the free agent could draft a player from among those assigned to a compensation pool by their teams, and it could select an amateur draft choice from the signing team.

After another brief shutdown (August 6–7, 1985) centring on salary arbitration, the owners agreed to increase the minimum salary from $40,000 to $60,000, but the number of major league seasons a player had to serve before qualifying for arbitration was raised from two to three. Fan interest continued to rise, and major league attendance records were broken six times in the 1985–91 seasons. The major source of revenue, however, was television. The combined revenue from network television in 1984 was $90 million; one network purchased the rights to televise games in the 1990–93 seasons for $1.1 billion.

In 1994 the owners, unhappy with escalating payrolls and wary of declining television revenues and the growing financial gap between large- and small-market clubs, proposed a new collective bargaining agreement that included a salary cap (a limit on a team's payroll), elimination of salary arbitration, and a revised free agency plan. The proposal was a dramatic shift from the previous contract and was promptly rejected by the players' union. The negotiations that followed were inconclusive, and on August 12 the players went on strike, shutting down all major league play for the remainder of the season. When the owners unilaterally imposed the salary cap in December 1994, the National Labor Relations Board (NLRB) threatened legal action, and the cap was withdrawn. The owners again acted unilaterally in February 1995, eliminating salary arbitration, free agent bidding, and anticollusion provisions. Again the NLRB responded, seeking an injunction that would force ownership to operate under the old contract until a new agreement could be reached with the union. A U.S. district court granted the injunction on March 31, 1995, and the players' union quickly announced that the strike was over. The owners accepted the players' offer to return without a new agreement and to continue negotiations.

The 1994–95 strike lasted 234 days, erased 921 games (669 from the 1994 season, 252 from the 1995 season), forced the first cancellation of the World Series since 1904, disrupted the economies of cities and states, and disappointed millions of fans—all without reaching a resolution. As a result, there was an unprecedented decline in attendance during the 1995 season.

Attendance improved by 2000, but player compensation had soared; the average salary paid to a player had risen dramatically. (However, while the average player salary increased sharply, the median player salary had not, meaning that the salaries paid to superstars of the game increased at a much greater rate than those of ordinary players. The average salary was about $41,000 in 1974, $289,000 in 1983, nearly $590,000 in 1990, nearly $2,000,000 in 2000, and more than $3,300,000 in 2010. Median salaries were not compiled in the 1970s, but the 1983 median salary was $207,000, in 1990 it was $350,000, in 2000 it was $700,000, and in 2010 it was more than $1,100,000.)

Blacks in Baseball

During baseball's infancy, a colour barrier was put up by the first formal organization of baseball clubs, the National Association of Base Ball Players, which decreed in 1867 that clubs "which may be composed of one or more coloured persons" should not be permitted to compete with its teams of gentlemen amateurs. When the first professional league was formed four years later, it had no written rule barring black players, but it was tacitly understood that they were not welcome.

Segregation

The colour line was not consistently enforced, though, during the early years of professionalism. At least 60 black players performed in the minor leagues during the late 19th century—mostly in all-black clubs. In 1884 two African Americans played in a recognized major league, the American Association. They were Moses Fleetwood ("Fleet") Walker, a catcher for the Association's Toledo team, and his brother Welday, an outfielder who appeared in six games for Toledo.

The number of black players in professional leagues peaked in 1887 when Fleet Walker, second baseman Bud Fowler, pitcher George Stovey, pitcher Robert Higgins, and Frank Grant, a second baseman who was probably the best black player of the 19th century, were on rosters of clubs in the International League, one rung below the majors. At least 15 other black players were in lesser professional leagues. Although they suffered harassment and discrimination off the field, they were grudgingly accepted by most of their teammates and opponents.

A League of Colored Base Ball Clubs, organized in 1887 in cities of the Northeast and border states, was recognized as a legitimate minor league under organized baseball's National Agreement and raised hopes of sending black players to big league teams. The league's first games, however, attracted small crowds, and it collapsed after only one week. While no rule in organized baseball ever stated that black players were banned, a so-called "gentlemen's agreement" to exclude blacks eventually prevailed.

There were other disturbing signs of exclusion for black players in 1887. The Syracuse (New York) Stars of the International League suffered a mutiny when pitcher Douglas ("Dug") Crothers refused to sit for a team portrait with his black teammate Robert Higgins. In Newark, New Jersey, black pitcher Stovey was kept out of an exhibition game with the major league Chicago White Stockings at the insistence of Cap Anson, Chicago's manager and one of the most famous players of baseball's early days. And the St. Louis Browns, American Association champions, refused to play an exhibition game against the all-black Cuban Giants. The night before the scheduled game, eight members of the Browns handed a message to the team's owner that read: "[We] do not agree to play against Negroes tomorrow. We will cheerfully play against white people at any time."

In midseason that year the International League's board of directors told its secretary to approve no more contracts for black players, although it did not oust the league's five blacks. The Ohio State League also wrestled inconclusively with the colour question. It was becoming clear that the colour bar was gradually being raised. Black players were in the minor leagues for the next few years, but their numbers declined steadily. The last black players in the recognized minor leagues during 19th century were the Acme Colored Giants, who represented Celoron, New York, in the Iron and Oil Leagues in 1898.

As the 20th century dawned, separation of the races was becoming the rule, especially in the South. The U.S. Supreme Court had written segregation into national law in 1896 in *Plessy v. Ferguson*, which approved separate schools for black and white children. In the South, state laws and local ordinances placed limits on the use of public facilities by African Americans and forbade athletic competition between blacks and whites. In the North, African Americans were not usually segregated by law, but local custom dictated second-class citizenship for them.

Nevertheless, the idea of black players in the major and minor leagues was not yet unthinkable. As described earlier, in 1901 John J. McGraw, manager of the Baltimore Orioles in the new American League, tried to sign a black second baseman named Charlie Grant. McGraw tried "repackaging" Grant, saying he was a Native American named Tokohama, a member of the Cherokee tribe. The effort failed when rivals correctly identified Grant instead as a member of the Chicago Columbia Giants, a black team. Five years later there was an aborted attempt to bring African American William Clarence Matthews, Harvard University's shortstop from 1902 to 1905, into the National League.

Increasingly, black players who wanted to play professionally had to join all-black teams. (Several swarthy players in the big leagues were widely assumed to be black, although they claimed to be white Latin Americans. No admitted black men played in the white leagues at the time.) Ninety percent of the country's African American citizens lived in the South, but migration to Northern states was increasing. With the growing base of potential fans in the North, top-quality black teams appeared in the Northeast and Midwest. Among them were the Genuine Cuban Giants and Cuban X Giants of New York City (both made up of African Americans despite their names), the Cuban Stars and Havana Stars (both with real Cubans), the Lincoln Giants of New York City, the Philadelphia Giants, the Bacharach Giants of Atlantic City (New Jersey), the Homestead (Pennsylvania) Grays, the Hilldale Club of Philadelphia, and the Norfolk (Virginia) Red Stockings. In the Midwest the leaders were the Chicago American Giants, the Columbia Giants, Leland Giants, and Union Giants of Chicago, the Kansas City (Missouri) Monarchs, and the Indianapolis ABCs. Especially noteworthy was the All Nations team, composed of African Americans, whites, a Japanese, a Hawaiian, an American Indian, and several Latin Americans. On its roster at various times before World War I were two of the greatest black pitchers, John Donaldson and Jose Mendez.

These teams vied for the mythical "colored championship of the world" and also played white semipro and college teams. Salaries were modest. Journeymen players earned $40 to $75 a month, while a star might command more than $100. Some Chicago teams played in the city's semipro league on weekends, occasionally competing against big leaguers from the Cubs and White Sox who played under assumed names. During the week they played white clubs in nearby towns.

JOSH GIBSON

Josh Gibson slides safely into home base during the 1944 East-West Negro League All-Star Game at Comiskey Park in Chicago, Ill. Transcendental Graphics/Getty Images

(b. Dec. 21, 1911, Buena Vista, Ga,. U.S.—d. Jan. 20, 1947, Pittsburgh, Pa.)

Catcher Josh Gibson was one of the most prodigious home run hitters in the game's history. Known as "the black Babe Ruth," Gibson is considered to be the greatest player who never played in the major leagues—owing to the unwritten rule (enforced until the year of his death) against hiring black ballplayers.

In the 1920s Gibson moved from Georgia to Pittsburgh, where he studied to become an electrician before dropping out of trade school in 1927 to try his hand at semiprofessional baseball. He played with the Pittsburgh Crawfords through 1929, and in 1930 he joined the Homestead Grays, his first professional Negro league club. The powerful Gibson soon gained a reputation for slugging tape-measure home runs, and in 1932 he was lured back to the now-professional Crawfords by a relatively large paycheck. In 1937 he returned to the Grays, for whom he played for the remainder of his career—barring a two-year sojourn in the Mexican and Puerto Rican leagues in 1940 and 1941.

Precise records of Gibson's accomplishments do not exist. Statistics keeping was haphazard in the Negro leagues, and Gibson took part in a vast number of exhibition games and games against semiprofessional teams, but he is believed to have led the Negro National League in home runs for 10 consecutive seasons and to have had a career batting average of .347. He also reportedly hit 84 home runs in 1936 and amassed nearly 800 career homers—though those figures have been much disputed. Gibson's catching ability was praised by Walter Johnson and other major league stars against whom he played in exhibition games, and Gibson had a .426 batting average in recorded at bats against major league pitchers in those contests.

He was diagnosed with a brain tumour in 1943 but refused to let doctors operate, fearing that they might inadvertently cause more damage. His health deteriorated thereafter. Although he was frequently beset by headaches and battled a drinking problem, Gibson continued to play baseball until his death of an apparent stroke at age 36. He was elected to the Baseball Hall of Fame in 1972.

Major league teams often played black teams during spring training trips to Cuba and sometimes had post-season games against black clubs in the United States. In 1909, for example, the Chicago Cubs won three close games in a series with the Leland Giants. In 1915, eastern black teams won four of eight games against big league teams, including a five-hit shutout of the National League champion Philadelphia Phillies by Smokey Joe Williams of the Lincoln Giants. In the late 1920s Commissioner Landis forbade big league clubs from competing in toto in the off-season. Partisans of black baseball believed it was because black teams often beat the major leaguers.

In the Midwest a few teams barnstormed all season long. The Kansas City (Kansas) Giants, for example, were on the road all summer, traveling mostly by railroad. Their opponents were white semipro teams throughout the Midwestern states and southern Canada. Although a black face was a novelty in the small towns, the players remembered that by and large they had little trouble finding food and lodging in the rural areas.

Formed in 1920 and 1921, respectively, the Negro National League and the Negro Eastern League played in New York City, Chicago, St. Louis, Kansas City (Missouri), Detroit, and other cities that had absorbed a large influx of African Americans from the South during and after World War I. In the 1920s a Negro World Series was begun and was held annually until the Negro leagues failed in the 1930s. A second Negro National League was founded late in that decade, and the Negro American League, formed in 1936, ultimately had Eastern and Western divisions that in 1952 played a Negro East-West game. Among the most famous players in the various Negro leagues were Josh Gibson (who was credited with hitting 89 home runs in one season), Satchel Paige, Bill Yancey, John Henry Lloyd, Andrew ("Rube") Foster, and James Thomas ("Cool Papa") Bell. After World War II, attendance at Negro league games declined as outstanding players were lost to formerly all-white teams.

INTEGRATION

Several major league teams either discussed or attempted the racial integration of professional baseball in the 1940s. The interest in integration in the 1940s was sparked by several factors—the increasing economic and political influence of urban blacks, the success of black ballplayers in exhibition games with major leaguers, and especially the participation of African

Americans in World War II. The hypocrisy of fighting fascism abroad while tolerating segregation at home was difficult to ignore. During the war, protest signs outside Yankee Stadium read, "If we are able to stop bullets, why not balls?" A major obstacle to integration was removed in 1944 with the death of Commissioner Landis. Though he had made several public declarations that there was no colour barrier in baseball, during his tenure Landis prevented any attempts at signing black players. (He blocked, for example, Bill Veeck's purchase of the Philadelphia Phillies in 1943 after learning that Veeck planned to stock his team with Negro league All-Stars.) On the other hand, Landis's successor, Happy Chandler, was openly supportive of bringing integration to the sport.

In 1947 Jackie Robinson became the first black player in the modern major leagues. His arrival was the result of careful planning by Brooklyn Dodgers President Branch Rickey, who began researching the idea of signing a black player and scouting for the right individual when he joined the Dodgers in 1942. In a meeting with Robinson in 1945, Rickey badgered the player for several hours about the abuse and hostility he would receive from players and fans and warned him that he must not retaliate. Robinson agreed and spent the 1946 season with the Dodgers minor league franchise in Montreal in preparation for playing in the big leagues. His first season with Brooklyn was marred by all the hostility that Rickey had predicted (even from a handful of teammates), but it also was marked by Robinson's determined play, which eventually won over fans and opponents, as well as helping the Dodgers win the National League pennant. Robinson was followed into the major leagues immediately by Larry Doby and in 1948 by Paige. Both played for the American League Cleveland Indians, who won the World Series in 1948.

JACKIE ROBINSON

Jackie Robinson, c. 1945. Hulton Archive/Getty Images

(b. Jan. 31, 1919, Cairo, Ga., U.S.—d. Oct. 24, 1972, Stamford, Conn.)

Jackie Robinson was the first black baseball player to play in the American major leagues during the 20th century. On April 15, 1947, Robinson broke the decades-old colour bar of Major League Baseball (MLB) when he appeared on the field for the National League Brooklyn Dodgers. He played as an infielder and outfielder for the Dodgers from 1947 through 1956.

Reared in Pasadena, Calif., Jack Roosevelt Robinson became an outstanding all-around athlete at Pasadena Junior College and the University of California, Los Angeles (UCLA). He excelled in football, basketball, and track as well as baseball. Robinson withdrew from UCLA in his third year to help his mother care for the family. In 1942 he entered the U.S. Army and attended officer candidate school; he was commissioned a second lieutenant in 1943. Robinson faced court-martial in 1944 for refusing to follow an order that he sit at the back of a military bus. The charges against Robinson were dismissed, and he received an honourable discharge from the military. The incident, however, presaged Robinson's future activism and commitment to civil rights. Upon leaving the army, he played professional football in Hawaii and baseball with the Kansas City Monarchs of the Negro American League, where he drew the attention of the president and general manager of the Brooklyn Dodgers, Branch Rickey.

Robinson's skills on the field, his integrity, and his conservative family-oriented lifestyle all appealed greatly to Rickey, making Robinson the perfect candidate for Rickey's plans to integrate baseball. Rickey's main fear concerning Robinson was that he would be unable to withstand the racist abuse without responding in a way that would hurt integration's chances for success. During a legendary meeting Rickey shouted insults at Robinson, trying to be certain that Robinson could accept taunts without incident. On Oct. 23, 1945, Rickey signed Robinson to play on a Dodger farm team, the Montreal Royals of the International League.

Robinson led that league in batting average in 1946 and was brought up to play for Brooklyn in 1947. He was an immediate success on the field. Leading the National League in stolen bases, he was chosen Rookie of the Year. In 1949 he won the batting championship with a .342 average and was voted the league's Most Valuable Player (MVP).

His personal experiences were quite different. Fans hurled bottles and invectives at him. Some Dodger teammates openly protested against having to play with an African American, while players on opposing teams deliberately pitched balls at Robinson's head and spiked him with their shoes in deliberately rough slides into bases. Not everyone in baseball was unsupportive of Robinson, though. When players on the St. Louis Cardinals team threatened to strike if Robinson took the field, commissioner Ford Frick quashed the strike, countering that any player who did so would be suspended from baseball. Dodger captain Pee Wee Reese left his position on the field and put an arm around Robinson in a show of solidarity when fan heckling became intolerable, and the two men became lifelong friends. However, with the ugly remarks, death threats, and Jim Crow laws that forbade a black player to stay in hotels or eat in restaurants with the rest of his team, Robinson's groundbreaking experience in the major leagues was bleak. Of this period Robinson later stated,

> *Plenty of times I wanted to haul off when somebody insulted me for the color of my skin, but I had to hold to myself. I knew I was kind of an experiment. The whole thing was bigger than me.*

Robinson's career in baseball was stellar. His lifetime batting average was .311, and he led the Dodgers to six league championships and one World Series victory. As a base runner, Robinson unnerved opposing pitchers and terrorized infielders who had to try to prevent him from stealing bases.

After retiring from baseball early in 1957, Robinson engaged in business and in civil rights activism. He was a spokesperson for the National Association for the Advancement of Colored People (NAACP) and made appearances with Martin Luther King, Jr. With his induction in 1962, Robinson became the first black person in the Baseball Hall of Fame. (In the 1970s, membership in the Hall was opened to the bygone stars of the Negro leagues.) Robinson's autobiography, *I Never Had It Made*, was published in 1972. In 1984 Robinson was posthumously awarded the Presidential Medal of Freedom, the highest honour for an American civilian.

In April 1997, on the 50th anniversary of the breaking of the colour bar in baseball, baseball commissioner Bud Selig retired Robinson's jersey number, 42, from Major League Baseball. It was common for a team to retire the number of a player from that team, but for a number to be retired for all the professional teams within a sport was unprecedented. In 2004 Major League Baseball announced that it would annually honour Robinson each April 15, which would thenceforth be recognized as Jackie Robinson Day. Three years later, star slugger Ken Griffey, Jr., received permission from the commissioner of baseball to wear the number 42 on Jackie Robinson Day, and the yearly "unretiring" of Robinson's number gained more adherents until, in 2009, Major League Baseball decided that all players, coaches, and umpires would wear number 42 on April 15.

Despite the successes of Robinson, Doby, and Paige, full integration of the major leagues came about slowly and was not completed until 1959 when Elijah Green joined the Boston Red Sox.

The impact of black players on the field was significant. They brought over from the Negro leagues an aggressive style of play that combined power hitting with daring on the base paths. Black players soon established themselves as major league stars. In the 1950s and '60s players such as outfielders Willie Mays and Hank Aaron (who set the all-time career home-run record) and pitcher Bob Gibson posted statistics that ranked them among the best ever to play the game. Later Reggie Jackson, Ozzie Smith, and Barry Bonds were definitive players of their respective eras.

By the 1970s acceptance of black players was commonplace. However, inclusion of minorities in coaching and administrative positions was virtually nonexistent. In 1961 Gene Baker became the first African American to manage a minor league team, and in the mid-1960s there were only two African American coaches in the major leagues. In 1975 the Cleveland Indians made Frank Robinson the first black field manager in major league history. However, opportunities for minorities in managerial positions were rare, and their representation in leadership positions remains an issue.

Women in Baseball

Women have played organized baseball since the 1860s. Students at the all-female Vassar College formed baseball teams as early as 1866. In 1875 three men organized a women's baseball club in Springfield, Illinois, divided it into two teams, the Blondes and the Brunettes, and charged admission to see them play. In the early 20th century, barnstorming teams known as "Bloomer Girls" were formed in various parts of the United States and took on amateur and semiprofessional teams that included both men and women.

In its early stages, women's involvement in professional baseball was largely an attempt to profit from the novelty of female players. An Ohio woman, Alta Weiss, pitched for the otherwise all-male semiprofessional Vermilion Independents in 1907. Jackie Mitchell became the first female professional baseball player when she signed a contract with the minor league Chattanooga Lookouts in 1931. Mitchell pitched in an exhibition game against the New York Yankees and struck out their two star players, Babe Ruth and Lou Gehrig. Organized baseball formally banned women from signing professional contracts with men's teams in 1952, and the prohibition is still in effect.

When World War II made the suspension of major league baseball a possibility, the All-American Girls Professional Baseball League (AAGPBL) was founded with four teams—the Rockford (Illinois) Peaches, the Racine Belles and the Kenosha Comets (both of Wisconsin), and the South Bend (Indiana) Blue Sox. The AAGPBL drew large crowds because of its players' athletic abilities. The league management, however, was concerned that the players appear feminine to the fans, and rules encouraging the wearing of lipstick and long hair and banning the wearing of trousers off the field were promulgated. On the field, the women initially played fast-pitch softball (which features a larger ball and underhand pitching), but by 1948 overhand pitching was introduced, and eventually the only difference of note between men's baseball and AAGPBL baseball was the size of the diamond, which in the AAGPBL had a shorter distance between bases. During its 11-year existence (1943–54), the league received a great deal of national attention, but by the 1950s the televising of major league baseball led to dwindling interest in the women's teams, and the league folded. These female players were eventually recognized with an exhibit at the National Baseball Hall of Fame and Museum in 1988. In 1992 the feature film *A League of Their Own* dramatized the story of the AAGPBL.

Beginning in 1994, the Colorado Silver Bullets, sponsored by a brewing company and managed by Hall of Fame pitcher Phil Niekro, competed against men's teams for four years. Between 1997 and 2000 Ila Borders, a left-handed pitcher, played for two men's teams in the independent Northern League. While women have participated in professional baseball for more than a century, their impact on the game has been limited.

Amateur Baseball

After the divorce of amateur baseball in the United States from its professional counterpart in 1871, the amateur game continued to thrive on vacant lots in towns and cities and on pastures in the countryside. Becoming popular internationally, amateur baseball traveled to Latin America and Asia. Further, play by U.S. military teams helped make baseball a minor sport in the Netherlands, Italy, Belgium, England, Spain, Australia, and Tunisia. Amateur teams worldwide are represented by the International Baseball Federation (IBAF), which was formed by American Leslie Mann in 1938. The organization, headquartered in Lausanne, Switzerland, has hosted a Baseball World Cup since 1938.

As would be expected, baseball is one of the more important amateur sports in the United States. The first national amateur baseball program was the American Legion Junior League, founded in 1926 and later called the American Legion Baseball League, with an upper age limit of 19 years for players. The American Amateur Baseball Congress (founded 1935) conducts programs for youths age 8 to 19 and adults in seven divisions. By the late 1990s Little League (founded 1939), originally for boys 8 to 12 years old, had about 2,500,000 players in its baseball program and 400,000 in its softball program in 102 countries. Little League has added leagues for children as young as age 5 (Tee Ball, in which the ball is batted from a stationary pedestal) and for youths as old as age 18 (Big League). In 1974 girls were admitted into Little League play; boys and girls play together in the baseball program, but the softball program is divided by gender. Other programs for young players include the Babe Ruth League (1952) and PONY (Protect Our Nation's Youth) Baseball, Inc. (1951).

American collegiate baseball is governed by the National Collegiate Athletic Association (NCAA). By 2000 more than 850 colleges fielded baseball teams under the NCAA. From 1947 the organization has conducted the College World Series, held since 1950 in Omaha, Nebraska.

Perhaps the pinnacle of amateur baseball is the Olympics. Baseball was played at the 1904 Olympic Games and had either exhibition or demonstration status at a number of Games after that, but it was designated a full medal sport beginning with the 1992 Games in Barcelona, Spain. Professional players became eligible to participate in Olympic baseball at the 2000 Olympic Games in Sydney, Australia.

BASEBALL IN LATIN AMERICA

Baseball was first played in the United States in the 1840s but soon after became an international sport. The game was introduced in Cuba in 1864 when students returned home from the United States with a bat and ball. Baseball took hold and in fact became part of the Cuban identity in the independence struggle against Spain in the last quarter of the 19th century. Cubans helped spread the game throughout the Caribbean region. Two Cuban brothers brought baseball to the Dominican Republic in the 1880s, and Cubans, along with local nationals who had studied in the United States, introduced baseball to Venezuela in 1895 and to Puerto Rico in 1897.

Cuban refugees from the independence struggle, along with railroad workers and U.S. merchant marines, introduced baseball to various regions of Mexico between 1877 and the 1890s. Today baseball remains the most important sport in Cuba, the Dominican Republic, and Venezuela, and is among the most popular sports in Puerto Rico. Football (soccer) remains the dominant sport in Mexico but is challenged by baseball in certain regions of the country; baseball is also an important sport in Central America. In the final decades of the 20th century, players from Latin American countries and Puerto Rico became an increasingly dominant force in major league baseball in the United States.

Professional leagues currently exist in the Dominican Republic, Mexico, Puerto Rico, and Venezuela. Games are played between October and January, with the winners of the four leagues meeting in the Caribbean Series each February. In Mexico there is also a summer league affiliated with Minor League Baseball (the governing body of minor league baseball in the United States) that has been given Triple A status.

DOLF LUQUE

Dolf Luque, c. 1919. Library of Congress Prints and Photographs Division

(b. Aug. 4, 1890, Havana, Cuba—d. July 3, 1957, Havana)

Cuban Dolf Luque was the first player from Latin America to become a star in the U.S. major leagues.

Adolfo Domingo Luque Guzman, a right-handed pitcher, made his major league debut in 1914 with the Boston Braves but spent most of his career in the United States with the Cincinnati Reds from 1918 to 1929. Luque was the first player born in Latin America to play in a World Series when he pitched for Cincinnati in 1919. His 1923 season, when he recorded 27 wins and 8 losses and posted a 1.93 earned run average, is considered one of the best pitching performances of all time.

Luque is described as having an explosive temper and a caustic tongue. An incident in 1923 in Cincinnati certainly underscored those personality traits. When players on the New York Giants bench were taunting Luque, he placed his glove and ball on the pitching mound, went into the Giants dugout, and punched the player—Casey Stengel—whom he believed to be the primary instigator.

After leaving Cincinnati, Luque played two years with the Brooklyn Dodgers (1930–31) and four years with the New York Giants (1932–35). During his 20 years in the major leagues, he won 194 games and lost 179. When his major league playing career was over, Luque was a coach for the New York Giants and a title-winning manager in the Mexican League. He was elected to the Mexican Baseball Hall of Fame in Monterrey in 1985.

Although he was an outstanding player in the major leagues, Luque's most important legacy to baseball is his career in Cuba. He played more than half of his 23 Cuban seasons with Almendares, the team he debuted with in 1914. Luque had 93 wins and 62 losses in official Cuban League games, but he also barnstormed throughout the island, hiring himself out to several sugar mill teams. He managed eight Cuban League championship teams between 1919 and 1947 and was elected to the Cuban Baseball Hall of Fame in Havana in 1958.

In both the Dominican Republic and Venezuela, summer rookie leagues are affiliated with Minor League Baseball.

Professional baseball leagues existed in Cuba from 1878 until 1961, when the Cuban government abolished the professional game. With all the Cuban talent now at the amateur level, the Cubans began to dominate international amateur competition, winning the first gold medals given in baseball at the Olympic Games in Barcelona (1992) and Atlanta (1996).

BASEBALL IN ASIA AND THE PACIFIC

Baseball was introduced in Japan in the 1870s. It quickly gained popularity and by the end of the century had become a national sport. Today the annual Koshien tournament in Ōsaka, featuring the country's top high-school teams, is nationally televised and can draw more than 50,000 fans.

A professional league was organized in 1936, and the two current leagues, the Central and the Pacific, began to operate in 1950. The champions of the two leagues meet each October in the Japan Series, the equivalent of the World Series in the United States. The most famous Japanese professional player is Oh Sadaharu, who hit 868 home runs while playing for the Yomiuri Giants between 1959 and 1980.

OH SADAHARU

(b. May 20, 1940, Tokyo, Japan)

Oh Sadaharu played for the Tokyo Yomiuri Giants in the Japanese Central League for 22 seasons and holds the record for the most home runs ever hit. He is among the most revered of Japan's sporting figures. Oh led the league in hitting 5 times, led in runs batted in (RBIs) 13 times, and was selected Most Valuable Player on 9 occasions. During Oh's career with the Giants, they dominated Japanese baseball, winning the Japan Series 14 times, 9 of those times consecutively (1965–73).

In 1959 the left-handed hitter batted only .161. He then studied Zen Buddhism and several martial arts to improve his batting skills, and he adopted an unusual batting stance—known as the flamingo—in which he stood on one leg while awaiting the pitch. His batting philosophy involved an attitude far different from that found in American baseball. Oh once stated, "My opponents and I were really one. My strength and skills were only part of the equation. The other half was theirs."

Oh led the league in home runs for 15 seasons and finished with a career total of 868. By comparison, the leading home-run hitter of all time in Major League Baseball in the United States, Hank Aaron, had a career total of 755. It is difficult to compare these records. Aaron's feat was accomplished against the best pitchers in baseball at the time and in large American ballparks. Oh hit in smaller parks and against less-skilled pitching, but he forged his record while playing in a league with a 130-game season and against a large number of slow-ball, or junk-ball, pitchers. (A hitter can use the speed of the pitched ball for power; thus, it is harder to hit a home run from a ball pitched at 60 mph [97 km/hr] than from one pitched at 90 mph [145 km/hr].)

When his playing career was over, Oh managed the Tokyo Giants for the 1984–88 seasons. After several years' hiatus, he began managing again in 1995 with the Fukuoka Daiei Hawks of the Japanese Pacific League. Some of his decisions as a manager stirred controversy and called into question the notion of fair play in Japanese baseball. Randy Bass in 1985, Karl ("Tuffy") Rhodes in 2001, and Alex Cabrera in 2002, all foreign players, threatened Oh's record for most home runs (55) in a season in Japanese baseball. And in all three instances the prevailing attitude of Oh and others in Japanese baseball was that foreigners should not be allowed to break Oh's record; therefore, no hittable pitches were thrown by Oh's teams to Bass, Rhodes, or Cabrera near the end of the season. Rhodes and Cabrera did manage to tie Oh's record in 2001 and 2002, respectively, but they could not break it. In 1985 the response of the Japanese media and fans was largely supportive of Oh, but in 2001 fans at the ballpark booed the decision to pitch around Rhodes and protect Oh's record. Later the media explored the connection between Japanese baseball's diminishing fan base and its protectionist attitudes on the field. Globalism, racial attitudes, and concepts of sportsmanship were debated, and Oh's record was tarnished by the controversy. The public was quick to forgive, however, when Oh managed the Japanese team to victory in the inaugural World Baseball Classic in 2006.

In 1994 Oh was inducted into the Japanese Baseball Hall of Fame in Tokyo. His autobiography, *Sadaharu Oh: A Zen Way of Baseball* (1984), was written with David Falkner.

While the Japanese leagues have long imported players from the United States, only recently have Japanese players begun to play in the major leagues in the United States. In 1995 pitcher Hideo Nomo became the first Japanese citizen to join a U.S. major league team, after pitching professionally in the Japanese major leagues. Nomo won National League Rookie of the Year honours for his performance with the Los Angeles Dodgers in 1995, became a hero in Japan, and drew the attention of the American public to the quality of Japanese baseball. Ichiro Suzuki, as an outfielder with the Seattle Mariners at the turn of the 21st century, was another player who impressed American baseball fans.

Baseball is also an important sport in Korea, where there is a professional league, the Korea Baseball Organization, that has fielded an eight-team circuit since

1982. Taiwan, which has produced several Little League world champion teams, has two professional leagues, the Chinese Professional Baseball League, a four-team league that started in 1990, and the Taiwan Major League, a four-team league that began operations in 1997. Australia has an eight-team professional league, the International Baseball Association Australia, which started in 1989.

INTERNATIONAL COMPETITION

Baseball debuted as an Olympic sport at the 1992 Games in Barcelona, Spain, and in the late 1990s the International Baseball Federation permitted professionals to play in international competitions. But because the Olympic Summer Games take place during the Major League Baseball season, the Olympic tournament failed to attract the top players in the sport. In 2005 the International Olympic Committee voted to drop the sport from the Summer program following the 2008 Olympics. That same year the International Baseball Federation sanctioned the World Baseball Classic, a triennial international competition between national teams consisting of professional and amateur players. The inaugural World Baseball Classic was held in March 2006. It featured 16 teams from all parts of the globe and was won by Japan.

CHAPTER 2
ANALYZING BASEBALL

To a degree unequaled by any other American team sport, baseball is a game of records and statistics. No other sport provides fans with so much numerical depth and breadth. Apart from the box score (introduced in 1845) that newspapers publish to provide statistical summaries of specific games, in the 1870s annual guides began furnishing year-end tabulations of batting, fielding, and pitching exploits. Hefty encyclopaedias of baseball contain detailed records of the performances of thousands of players and team seasons, and a vast array of special statistics are offered on the Internet.

THE SCORECARD

The statistical record of a baseball game begins with the scorecard filled out by an official scorer, an employee of Major League Baseball who sits in the press box during a game and keeps track of the game's activities. The official scorer rules on each play, deciding, for example, whether a pitch that gets away from the catcher is a wild pitch (a pitch so off target that the catcher had no chance to catch it) or a passed ball (a pitch that should have been handled by the catcher). Members of the media and fans often choose to keep score of the game also. Official scorers and media professionals use detailed forms to record every pitch. Fans, who typically buy a simple scorecard at the game, record the action in a much simpler fashion. The method of keeping official score is described in detail in the game's rulebook,

A fan fills in a scorecard at a baseball game. ©www.istockphoto.com/
Lanica Klein

but for amateurs keeping score can be an idiosyncratic practice.

A basic scorecard, such as those sold at baseball parks, includes two charts, one for each team. A chart consists of the innings, marked along the top of the scorecard, and the batting order along the vertical axis. In between are boxes representing the potential at bats of each player in the lineup. Underneath each chart there is a small box used to record pitching statistics. All defensive players are assigned a number for score keeping; the methods of keeping score vary from fan to fan, but the numbers assigned to each position are the same everywhere. The pitcher is 1; the catcher is 2; first, second, and third basemen are numbered 3, 4, and 5, respectively; the shortstop is 6; and the left, centre, and right fielders are numbered 7, 8, and 9, respectively. With these numbers, plays such as a groundball to the shortstop who fields the ball and throws to first base for an out would be recorded as 6-3. There are also abbreviations, such as SB for stolen base and E for error, that are found on almost every scorecard. Software programs that allow fans to keep score on smartphones and personal digital assistants (PDAs) are now available.

The information in a scorecard is easily translated into a box score, which serves as a statistical summary of a game and is a staple of baseball news reporting.

RECORDS AND STATISTICS

Baseball records have long provided benchmarks of individual achievements. No individual accomplishment possesses more drama for fans than the tally of home runs. Babe Ruth's single-season record for home runs (60 in 1927) stood for 33 seasons until it was broken by Roger Maris (with 61 home runs in 1961). (It should be noted that, although Josh Gibson is credited with hitting 89 home runs in one season, Negro league records, which were sketchily kept, are not included in Major League Baseball statistics.) In 1998 both Mark McGwire (with 70) and Sammy Sosa (with 66) easily crashed through the 60-home-run barrier established by Ruth and Maris. In 2001 Barry Bonds broke McGwire's record with 73 home runs for the season. The record for home runs over a player's career is 762, set by Bonds, who eclipsed the mark of 755 set by Hank Aaron (though, again, it is believed that Gibson hit more). Ruth had long held that record as well, with a career home-run total of 714, until Aaron passed him in 1974.

For several decades, many of the records established by Ty Cobb, who played from 1905 through 1928, remained unbroken. While no one has successfully challenged Cobb's lifetime batting average of .367 or his 12 batting championships, Pete Rose toppled Cobb's lifetime mark of 4,189 hits in 1985 and finished his career with 4,256 hits. Cobb's single-season (20th-century) stolen-base record of 96, set in 1915, fell to Maury Wills (with 104 in 1962), then Lou Brock (with 118 in 1974), and finally Rickey Henderson (with 130 in 1982). Henderson also holds the record for career steals with 1,406. While Joe DiMaggio's consecutive hitting streak of 56 games in 1941 remained intact through the 20th century, on Sept. 6, 1995, Cal Ripken, Jr., broke Lou Gehrig's record of 2,130 consecutive games played. Ripken finished his streak in 1998 with 2,632 games.

Late in the 20th century, pitching records came under assault. While Cy Young outpaced his modern counterparts in career wins with 511, pitchers since the mid-20th century have far surpassed earlier hurlers in career strikeouts, led by Nolan Ryan, who retired in 1993 with 5,714. No one, however, has equaled the record of Grover Cleveland Alexander, who is the only four-time winner of the Triple Crown of pitching (that is, leading the league in wins, strikeouts, and the lowest earned run average). Alexander won the Triple Crown in 1915, 1916, 1917, and 1920.

In addition to individual marks, baseball fans carefully monitor record-shattering team performances. Great dynasties, teams that dominated play from year to year, have characterized much of major league baseball history. Beneficiaries of larger potential revenues because of their location, most of the dynasties have been from the country's largest metropolitan areas. Hence, New York teams appeared in 53 of 106 World Series (through the year 2010). In particular, since 1921 the New York Yankees have towered over baseball: through the 2010 season the Yankees captured 40 American League pennants, and from 1996 through 2000 they had a 46–15 postseason (divisional playoffs and World Series) record, more postseason wins than all their competitors combined.

By measuring the changes in the delicate balance between offense and defense, statistics also reveal much of baseball's history on the playing field. Lengthening the pitching distance to 60 feet 6 inches (18.4 metres) in 1893 initially touched off an offensive barrage. But increasing the size of the plate in 1900, counting the first two foul balls as strikes (adopted by the National League in 1901 and American League in 1903), the increased use of the spitball (in which moisture is applied to the surface of a ball to affect its flight), the appearance of a cadre of bigger and stronger pitchers, and conservative managerial styles (called "scientific" or "inside" baseball) all contributed to a sharp fall in total runs and hits.

PETE ROSE

(b. April 14, 1941, Cincinnati, Ohio, U.S.)

Pete Rose made an indelible impact on baseball in 1985 when he exceeded Ty Cobb's record for career hits (4,191). During his career Rose was noted for his all-around ability and enthusiasm. He was named Player of the Decade (1970–79) by *The Sporting News*. At the end of his career, he became better known for the accusations of gambling that led Major League Baseball to ban him from the sport in 1989.

Peter Edward Rose began to play in organized youth baseball at age eight. At his father's insistence, he became a switch hitter (batting either right- or left-handed). At age 18 he signed with the National League Cincinnati Reds and, after three seasons in the minor leagues, Rose joined the Reds' major league roster in 1963. Rose soon established himself at the top of the Reds' batting order and was named National League Rookie of the Year at the end of the season. He led the league in batting in 1968 and 1969, and he enjoyed his finest season in 1973, winning his third batting title while collecting a career high 230 hits; he was named the National League's Most Valuable Player that year. Rose was an integral part of the famed "Big Red Machine," the Reds teams that from 1970 to 1976 won five division titles, four National League pennants, and World Series championships in 1975 and 1976. Nicknamed "Charlie Hustle," Rose was revered for his aggressive base-running style, which included his distinctive head-first slides. During his 24 seasons in the major leagues, he played second base, left field, right field, third base, and first base (exclusively from 1980), leading the league in fielding in 1970, 1974, 1976, and 1980. In 1979 he went to the Philadelphia Phillies and helped that team win the World Series in 1980. Rose began the 1984 season with the Montreal Expos, but in mid-season he was traded back to Cincinnati, where he made his record-breaking hit in 1985 as player-manager of the Reds. By the time he retired as a player in 1986, Rose had a record career total of 4,256 hits. His other records included most games played, 3,562; most times at bat, 14,053; most runs scored, 2,165; and most seasons with 200 hits or more, 10. His lifetime batting average was .303.

Pete Rose slides into third base in a 1975 game against the Chicago Cubs.
Heinz Kluetmeier/Sports Illustrated/Getty Images

Rose retired from playing in 1986 but remained manager of the Reds until 1989 when he came under investigation by professional baseball's commissioner because of reports that he had bet repeatedly on sports teams, including his own Cincinnati Reds, in the mid-1980s. Rose denied having bet on baseball, but in August 1989 Commissioner A. Bartlett Giamatti banned him from Major League Baseball for life as a consequence of the investigation. This ruling made Rose ineligible for the Baseball Hall of Fame. In 1990 Rose was fined $50,000 and forced to serve five months in federal prison for filing false tax returns.

His autobiography, *Pete Rose: My Story* (1989), was written with Roger Kahn. In his second autobiography, *My Prison Without Bars* (2004), he admitted to gambling on baseball.

The hitting drought continued until the 1920s; then the outlawing of the spitball, the use of more balls per game, and the free swinging of Ruth produced a new offensive onslaught. Some also attributed this explosion of hitting to the introduction of what they believed to be a livelier ball, despite denials from major league authorities and the balls' manufacturers. Offense continued to dominate the game until 1963, when baseball officials sought to speed up games by increasing the size of the strike zone called by the umpires. Lowering the pitching mound and reducing the size of the strike zone in 1969, along with the advent of the designated hitter rule (replacing the pitcher in the batting order with a better-hitting player) in the American League in 1973, all served to partially reverse the decline in offensive productivity.

The 1990s witnessed a new hitting revolution, with a proliferation of home runs at its centre. Even in Ruth's heyday, homers were something of a rarity, coming at a rate of only 1 for each 91 at bats. Indeed, before 1994 a player hit 50 or more home runs in a season just 18 times;

from 1995 to 2002 there were 15 50-homer seasons. By 1999 the sluggers were averaging 1 homer for each 30 at bats. In 1998 not only did McGwire and Sosa completely alter the game's historic frame of reference for home runs in a single season, but in the very next season they again hit more than 60 homers (65 by McGwire; 63 by Sosa). Just two years later the record was shattered by Bonds.

Initially it was believed that this outburst of power was the result of lighter bats, a new style of hitting, an arguably more resilient ball, and weakened pitching in the wake of the expansion of the number of teams in the league. The slugging explosion was also attributed to the increased muscularity of hitters, though the matter of how hitters had gone about becoming stronger became increasingly controversial. In the mid-1990s, rumours circulated of the spreading use of steroids, which increase muscle mass. In 1991 it had become illegal to possess or sell anabolic steroids in the United States without a valid prescription; however, the major leagues had no formal policy on steroid use until 2002, when Ken Caminiti admitted to having used steroids while winning the 1996 Most Valuable Player award.

In 2003 it was alleged that a number of players, including Bonds, had obtained an illegal steroidal cream from the Bay Area Laboratory Co-operative (BALCO). Bonds testified before a grand jury that he had never knowingly taken steroids, but accusations of steroid use dogged his pursuit of Aaron's career home run record, and in 2007 he was indicted for perjury and obstruction of justice regarding his testimony. Bonds, however, was far from the only player whose accomplishments were called into question by the issue of performance-enhancing drugs. In March 2005 the

House of Representatives Committee on Oversight and Government Reform conducted hearings on steroid use in baseball. Among the players to testify were McGwire, Sosa, Frank Thomas, and Rafael Palmeiro (who testified, "I have never used steroids. Period"—though he later received a 10-day suspension for steroid use under the major leagues' new zero-tolerance policy). In March 2006, Major League Baseball Commissioner Bud Selig named former U.S. senator George J. Mitchell to head up an independent inquiry into steroid use in baseball. Mitchell's report was released in December 2007, and it mentioned 86 current and former players—including such stars as Bonds, Roger Clemens, Miguel Tejada, and Andy Pettitte—who were alleged to have possessed or used either steroids or human growth hormone (HGH) in the previous decade. Mitchell noted that everyone in baseball—players and management alike—shared responsibility for the "steroids era" and the effect it had on baseball's reputation with the public. In the aftermath of these developments, baseball records and statistics since the 1990s have become the topic of much debate.

AWARDS

The issuing of annual and career awards is a very serious undertaking in baseball and is done with as much fan scrutiny as any statistical analysis of the sport. Major League Baseball presents several special achievement awards each season. The Most Valuable Player (MVP) is selected in both the American League (AL) and the National League (NL). The MVP was first given in 1922; since 1931 the players have been chosen by the Baseball Writers Association of America (BBWAA). There are also MVP awards for the League Championship Series, the World Series, and the All-Star Game.

For the All-Star Game, which is played annually during baseball's midseason, the starting players from each league are selected by fan ballots. The remaining members of the squad are picked by the two All-Star managers, who are named because their teams appeared in the previous World Series.

The Cy Young Award honours the best pitcher in the National and American leagues. It was first awarded in 1956 to the outstanding pitcher in baseball, but in 1966 the baseball commissioner decided that each league would have its own Cy Young Award. Winners are selected by a vote of the BBWAA.

Begun in 1947, the Rookie of the Year award is given to the best new player in each league. A rookie is defined as a player who meets at least one of the following three criteria: fewer than 130 at bats, fewer than 50 innings pitched, or fewer than 45 days on a major league roster in the previous season. The BBWAA also select these winners.

The Gold Glove is awarded to the best defensive player at each of the nine positions (three outfielders are selected, but no consideration is given as to whether those players covered right, centre, or left field) in both the American League and the National League. The awards were first given in 1957. Players are selected by the managers and coaches of the major league teams, who are not permitted to vote for players from their own team.

The highest honour for a major league baseball player is induction into the Baseball Hall of Fame at Cooperstown, New York. The first selections were made in 1936 (the Hall actually opened in 1939), and inductees to the hall now include players, Negro league players, managers, baseball executives, and umpires.

CY YOUNG

Cy Young. Library of Congress, Washington, D.C.

(b. March 29, 1867, Gilmore, Ohio, U.S.—d. Nov. 4, 1955, Newcomerstown, Ohio)

Cy Young was the winner of more major league games (511) than any other pitcher.

Denton True Young grew up on a farm, and his formal education ended in sixth grade so he could help his family with their daily farming duties. He began playing baseball at this time and became so proficient at the sport that he joined two local semi-professional teams in the summer of 1884. In 1890 Young signed his first professional contract: with a Canton, Ohio, minor league team, with whom he acquired the nickname "Cyclone," which was soon shortened to "Cy." A big right-hander, standing 6 feet 2 inches (1.88 metres) tall and weighing 210 pounds (95 kg), he drew the attention of major league clubs, and his contract was purchased by the Cleveland Spiders of the National League after Young had played just half of a season in Canton.

Young made his debut with the Spiders late in the 1890 season. Quickly acclimating to pitching to big-league hitters, he led the NL in wins (36), earned run average (1.93), and shutouts (nine) in his third season. In 1899 he was shifted to the St. Louis Perfectos by the Spiders' ownership, who controlled both teams and wanted to create a powerhouse team in St. Louis.

In 1901 he was lured to the nascent American League by a large contract with the Boston Americans (later known as the Red Sox). He won the pitching Triple Crown in his first year in Boston by leading the AL in wins (33), earned run average (1.62), and strikeouts (158). In 1903 he helped the team win the inaugural World Series over the Pittsburgh Pirates. On May 5, 1904, he registered the first perfect game (no player reaching first base) of the modern era, for the Red Sox against the Philadelphia Athletics.

He also played for the Cleveland Indians (1909–11) in the AL and the Boston Braves (1911) in the NL before retiring. In each of 15 seasons during his 22-year career he won more than 20 games; in five of those years he won more than 30. Among his lifetime records are games started, 815; complete games, 749; and innings pitched, 7,356. His remarkably long career also produced a number of inglorious major league records: in addition to his career victory total, the sum of his defeats, 316, is also a record, as are his career totals of hits (7,092) and earned runs allowed (2,147).

Elected to the Baseball Hall of Fame in 1937, Young is commemorated in the Cy Young Award, instituted in 1956 to honour the best major league pitcher each year.

FANTASY BASEBALL

The term *fantasy baseball* was introduced to describe the Internet-based virtual baseball game. But it also can be loosely construed to mean a number of games that permit the fan to play either a virtual game or a virtual season of baseball. In all these fantasy games, the fans pose as both general manager and field manager of their team, building a roster through a draft and trades and making lineups in pursuit of the greatest statistical production. Game players use the batting averages, home runs, and other statistics posted by actual baseball players to determine the outcome of the fantasy games.

One of the earlier precursors of Internet-based fantasy baseball was a board game, introduced in 1951 by entrepreneur Dick Seitz, known as APBA (American Professional Baseball Association). A similar game called Strat-o-matic first appeared in the 1960s. Having purchased the APBA or Strat-o-matic board game, players annually ordered cards that listed the statistical data for the ballplayers from the prior season. A combination of data given on these cards and the rolling of dice determined the outcome of the player's "at-bat" or turn. In the 1990s computerized versions of these games permitted the statistics for a season from any baseball league in the world to be programmed in, as well as those from past major league seasons. The cult status that APBA and Strat-o-matic garnered carried over to rotisserie baseball.

Rotisserie baseball was invented in 1980 by author Dan Okrent and a group of baseball-minded friends who regularly met at the Manhattan restaurant Le Rotisserie Francais. They formed the core of the first rotisserie league. Unlike APBA, which is based upon a prior season's performance, rotisserie baseball and its later Internet-based fantasy variants are played during the course of the regular baseball season. Rotisserie baseball season begins with a player draft (sometimes done as an auction), with each team in the league selecting 23–27 players (with set quotas at each position) from major league rosters. The statistics that these players accumulate over the course of a season determine the winner of the rotisserie league. The statistics typically used in this game are batting average, home runs, runs scored, runs batted in, wins (pitching), saves, earned run average, and walks plus hits per innings pitched. As the season progresses, team managers can drop underperforming or injured players and acquire new ones.

What is now popularly called fantasy baseball developed from the rotisserie game and takes advantage of the capabilities of the Internet to share data with a dispersed group of people. Online fantasy baseball provides statistical management for small rotisserie leagues and also offers large-scale leagues in which multiple teams may own the same player.

The popularity of fantasy baseball spawned a new industry of statistical services and publications that analyzed players from a fantasy perspective and offered team management strategies. By the late 1980s, American gridiron football also had a fantasy version, and by the turn of the 21st century, nearly all team sports and many individual games had fantasy equivalents, most of which were played on the Internet. Fantasy games are now a global pastime wherever Internet access is available.

CHAPTER 3
PLAY OF THE GAME

Baseball is a contest between two teams of 9 or (if a designated hitter is allowed to take the pitcher's turn at bat) 10 players each. The field of play is divided into the infield and the outfield. Within the infield is a square area called the diamond, which has four white bases, one on each corner. The bases are 90 feet (27.4 metres) apart.

The teams alternate between being fielders (playing defense) and batters (playing offense). The nine fielders take up assigned positions in the playing field; one fielder, called the pitcher, stands on a mound in the centre of the diamond and faces the base designated as home plate, where a batter, holding a formed stick (a bat), waits for him to throw a hard leather-covered ball. The goal of the batter is to hit the ball out of the reach of the fielders and eventually (most often with the help of hits by subsequent batters) to run from base to base counterclockwise completely around the diamond, thus scoring a run. If a batter fails to advance in an appropriate manner (discussed later) to at least the first base, he is out; after three outs, the teams switch roles. When both teams have batted, an inning is completed. After nine innings, the team with the most runs wins the game. If there is a tie, extra innings are played.

GROUNDS

In major league playing fields, the distance to the fence from home plate along the foul lines (marking the official limits of the playing field) must be 250 feet (76.2 metres) or more. For fields built after 1958, however, the distance

Aerial view of a baseball diamond. Jupiterimages/Comstock/Thinkstock

along the foul lines should be at least 320 feet (98 metres), and the distance from home plate on a line through second base to the centre-field fence should be at least 400 feet (121.9 metres). The distance to the stands or fence behind home plate should be at least 60 feet (18.3 metres) but may taper off along the foul lines in the outfield. Coaches' boxes are in foul territory behind first and third base. On-deck circles, where the next batter up in the lineup waits for his turn at bat, are near the team benches.

The playing field is traditionally covered with grass, except for the pitcher's circle, or mound, the base paths, the adjacent infield from first to third base, and the home plate area. The use of an artificial turf, first known as astro-turf, was commonplace in the 1970s and '80s, and it is still used in some stadiums. Artificial turf fields are typically covered entirely by the turf, except for dirt areas around the pitcher's plate, home plate, and the bases. Because of the hardness of the artificial turf surface, play on such fields is very fast and balls bounce much higher than on natural grass. New types of artificial turf introduced in the late 1990s offered a softer, more grasslike experience and incorporated the dirt infield found on natural grass fields.

Canvas bags filled with soft material and attached to metal stakes driven into the ground mark first, second, and third base. Home plate is a flat, pentagonal, white slab of rubber embedded flush in the ground.

EQUIPMENT

The ball has a cork-and-rubber core, around which yarn is tightly wrapped; the cover consists of two snugly fitted pieces of white leather sewn together. The circumference is 9 to 9.25 inches (23 to 23.5 cm) and the weight between 5 and 5.25 ounces (142 and 149 grams). The bat is a smooth rounded stick of solid or laminated wood, not longer than 42 inches (107 cm) or thicker at the barrel end than 2.75 inches (7 cm), tapering to the handle end. (Usually, however, in major league baseball, players prefer a bat no longer than 35 inches [89 cm] that weighs about 30 ounces [850 grams] or less.) There is no weight restriction on the bat, but no metal or other reinforcement can be used in construction of the bat. (Amateur players, however, are permitted to use aluminum bats.) The handle may have tape and adhesive material, such as pine tar, applied to it to improve the grip (but such substances may not be applied more than 18 inches [46 cm] from the tip of the handle in major league play).

Baseball was originally played bare-handed. Beginning in 1860, catchers, who attempt to catch every pitch not hit, became the first to adopt gloves. First basemen, who take many throws for putouts (discussed later) from the infielders, soon followed, and finally all players adopted gloves. All gloves are constructed of leather with some padding. The catcher's glove, or mitt, presents a solid face except for a cleft between the thumb and index finger and is thickly padded except at the centre, where the pitched ball is caught. The glove cannot exceed 38 inches (96.5 cm) in circumference and 15.5 inches (39.4 cm) from top to bottom. The first baseman's glove is thinner and more flexible, a solid expanse of leather for the four fingers with a webbing connecting the thumb and index finger. All other players' gloves are finger gloves with leather straps connecting the thumb and index finger. Form-fitting batting gloves, designed to improve the grip, are now worn by most batters.

The catcher wears a helmet, a barred mask with a hanging throat guard, a padded chest protector, and lightweight guards covering the knees, shins, and ankles. The umpire behind home plate wears a similar chest protector and mask. At bat players wear a lightweight plastic batting helmet that flares down over the ears to protect the temples. Groin protection is also worn by male players.

UMPIRES

Umpires control the game. One behind home plate calls balls and strikes on the batter, determines whether a batter has been hit by a pitch or has interfered with the catcher (or vice versa), and calls runners safe or out at home plate. He and the other three umpires, stationed near first, second, and third base, may call hit balls foul (beyond the foul lines) or fair (or within the foul lines); the other three call runners safe or out at the first three bases. Any umpire may call an illegal pitching motion known as a balk (described in detail at the end of this chapter). An umpire may ask for help from his fellow umpires if he was out of position to see a play, and the first- or third-base umpire may be appealed to concerning whether a batter has taken a full swing for a strike call or instead checked his swing.

OFFENSE

The objective of the offense is to score runs by hitting fair balls out of the reach of the defense. Each team strives to advance its players around the bases to score as many runs as possible before the third out ends its half of the inning at bat.

THE BATTING ORDER

At the start of each game, managers from both teams submit a batting order to the umpire. The order lists the name and defensive position of each player in the game and the order in which they will hit. The order may not be changed during the course of the game. If a reserve player enters the game, he must take the spot in the batting order of the player he replaced. The first batter up for each side in the first inning is the first man in the batting order (known as the leadoff man). In succeeding innings, the first batter up is the man in the order who follows the last batter (with a complete at bat) from the previous inning. The leadoff man is typically a player who is fast afoot, makes frequent contact with the ball, and reaches base consistently. The second spot usually goes to a batter who seldom strikes out and has good bat skills (e.g., bunting, making contact with pitches, and driving the ball toward the right side of the field to advance a runner). The third batter is usually the best all-around hitter on the team, combing batting power and skill. Many of the greatest hitters of all time have been number three in their team's batting order—Ty Cobb, Babe Ruth, Ted

Williams, Willie Mays, Roberto Clemente, and Barry Bonds. Numbers four (known as the "cleanup" man) and five are the power hitters who are expected to consistently hit the ball into the outfield, allowing runners on base to score. The remaining positions in the batting order scale downward to players who, though not prolific hitters, are valued for their defensive contribution. Number nine is almost invariably the pitcher—except in the American League (AL), where since 1973 the pitcher does not bat. The pitcher was replaced in the batting order by a designated hitter (the DH), usually batting in one of the more likely run-producing positions. In interleague games the players follow the custom of the home ballpark, using a DH in American League parks and no DH in National League (NL) stadiums.

GETTING ON BASE

For a player to score a run in baseball, he must first get on base. There are seven ways in which a batter may reach base. The most common and productive way of doing so is by the hit. A hit is recorded when a batter successfully strikes the ball so that it cannot be caught—either before touching the ground in fair territory or soon enough after touching ground to be thrown to first or any other base before the batter or any other runner gets there. There are four kinds of hits: the single, which allows the batter to reach first base; the double, in which the batter reaches second; the triple, which sees the runner reach third base; and the home run, a hit that enables the batter to circle all the bases and score a run. A fair ball that flies over the outfield fence is an automatic home run (permitting the batter to leisurely "trot" around the bases). Hits also are described by the way the ball travels across the field.

WILLIE MAYS

(b. May 6, 1931, Westfield, Ala., U.S.)

Willie Mays is considered by many to have been the best all-around player in the history of baseball.

Both Mays's father and his grandfather had been baseball players. Willie Mays, who batted and fielded right-handed, played semiprofessional baseball when he was 16 years old and joined the Birmingham Black Barons of the Negro National League in 1948, playing only on Sunday during the school year. The National League New York Giants paid the Barons for his contract when he graduated from Fairfield Industrial High School in 1950. After two seasons in the minor leagues, Mays went to the Giants in 1951 and was named Rookie of the Year at the end of that season—one legendary in baseball. The Giants were far behind the Brooklyn Dodgers in the pennant race. With the great play of Mays and others, the Giants tied the Dodgers in the standings on the last day of the season, and a three-game playoff for the NL championship was won with a home run, known as "the shot heard 'round the world," hit by the Giants' Bobby Thomson.

Mays, who soon acquired the nickname "Say Hey Kid," became known first for his spectacular leaping and diving catches before he established himself as a hitter. He served in the army (1952–54), and upon his return to baseball in the 1954 season, when the Giants won the NL pennant and the World Series, Mays led the league in hitting (.345) and had 41 home runs. In 1966 his two-year contract with the Giants (who had moved to San Francisco in 1958) gave him the highest salary of any baseball player of that time. He was traded to the New York Mets midseason in 1972 and retired after the 1973 season. Late in his career he played in the infield, mainly at first base. His career home run total was 660 and his batting average .302. Mays had 3,283 hits during his career, which made him one of the small group of players with more than 3,000 career hits. He led the league in home runs in 1955, 1962, and 1964–65, won 12 consecutive Gold Gloves (1957–68), and appeared in 24 All-Star Games.

After retiring as a player, Mays was a part-time coach and did public relations work for the Mets. In 1979 Mays took a public relations job with a company that was involved in gambling concerns, with the result that he was banned from baseball-related activities just three months after being elected to the Baseball Hall of Fame. In 1985 the ban was lifted, and in 1986 Mays became a full-time special assistant to the Giants. His autobiography, *Say Hey* (1988), was written with Lou Sahadi.

A spectacular fly catch made by Willie Mays with the New York Giants during the All-Star Game, July 12, 1955. UPI

Driven balls are generally categorized as flies or fly balls (balls hit high into the air), ground balls (balls hit at a downward angle into the ground), and line drives (a ball that is close to and parallel to the ground). Another way the batter can reach base is through an error. An error occurs when a mistake by the fielder allows the batter to reach base on a play that would normally result in an out. The judgment of whether a play is a hit or an error is made by the official scorer. The final way in which a player may strike the ball in fair territory and reach base is by fielder's choice. This occurs when a fielder chooses to make a play on another base runner, allowing the batter to reach base safely.

There are several ways of reaching base without the batter making contact with bat and ball. The most common of these is the base on balls, also called a walk. Whenever the batter does not swing at a pitched ball and the ball does not cross the plate inside the strike zone (*see* Defense: The Putout), the umpire calls the pitch a ball. If four balls are thus called in a turn at bat, the batter is awarded a base on balls and walks to first base. The batter also can reach first base if a pitched ball at which he does not swing strikes any part of his person. Additionally the batter can reach first base if the catcher interferes with him by making contact with any part of his body or with the swing of his bat as the pitched ball is on its way to home plate. The umpire makes all hit-by-pitch and interference calls.

The seventh method of reaching base is the dropped third strike. If, with two men out or with first base unoccupied regardless of how many are out, the batter swings and misses the ball for his third strike or the umpire calls the third strike and if the catcher does not catch the pitched ball before it touches the ground, the batter is entitled to run for first just as if he had hit the ball in fair territory. The catcher must then get the ball and throw it to first ahead of the batter in order to put him out. If such a pitched ball rebounds off the catcher out into the infield, the pitcher or any infielder may make the pickup and throw to first, just as if it were an infield grounder.

ADVANCING BASE RUNNERS AND SCORING

Once a batter reaches base, the focus of the offense shifts to advancing the runner around the bases to score a run. A base runner who is at second or third base is said to be in scoring position, meaning that a base hit will likely score that runner. There are several tactics that a team might use to move runners into scoring position. Runners can advance with the benefit of a hit, walk, or batter hit by pitch or on an error by a fielder. A batter also can move the runner by hitting to the right side of the infield (forcing the defense to play in a direction opposite that of the runner) or by "sacrificing." A sacrifice occurs when the batter bunts the ball—that is, tries to tap it lightly with the bat to make it roll slowly along the ground in fair territory between the catcher and pitcher—so that one or more runners may be able to proceed to their next base while the ball is being fielded. The batter attempting a sacrifice expects to be thrown out at first base. Similar to a sacrifice, the squeeze play uses the bunt to score a runner from third base. The runner also may advance on a fly ball or line drive that is caught for an out. The runner may "tag up" (reestablish contact with the base) and, the moment the ball is caught, dash to the next base. The runner should be confident that the catch has put the fielder in a position where throwing him out will be difficult. When such a fly ball or line drive out allows a runner to score, it is called a sacrifice fly. Sacrifice plays and sacrifice flys can occur only with less than two outs.

One of the most exciting plays in baseball is the stolen base. A base runner may advance at his own risk on the bases at any time the ball is in play by stealing a base. To steal a base, a batter will take a "lead"—that is, advance a few steps off the base and toward the next base while the pitcher still holds the ball. When the pitcher begins his throw toward home plate, the runner breaks toward the next base. At this point the runner matches his speed against the strength and accuracy of the catcher's arm. As the runner nears the base, he goes into a slide (usually headfirst) in order to avoid a possible tag and to stop his forward momentum at the base. The base is stolen if the runner successfully makes it to the next base without being tagged out. Runners most often attempt to steal second base and third base. Stealing home is a rarity. A runner cannot steal first base. A stolen base attempt can be nullified if the batter fouls off the pitch, reaches base, or makes the final out of the inning.

SUBSTITUTIONS

The use of a substitute as an offensive tactic most commonly involves sending in a pinch hitter—that is, taking a hitter out of the lineup and substituting another player whose likelihood for driving the ball for a hit or a fly to the deep outfield is greater. Such a pinch hitter must be a player not already in the lineup or in the batting order at any previous time in the game. Except where there is a designated hitter, the pinch hitter most often substitutes for the usually weak-hitting pitcher. Pinch runners, players (usually with good base-stealing ability) who replace batters who have successfully reached base, also are used. Once a player is replaced, he cannot return to the game.

DEFENSE

To meet the offensive force of the team at bat, the rules provide the fielding team with ways of making outs. A putout removes the player from offensive play until his next turn at bat. The batting team's inning continues until three putouts are made; then it goes into the field and the opponent comes to bat.

OUTFIELDERS

The three outfielders are positioned so as to best be able to catch or field balls that are batted over or through the infield. The three outfield positions are left fielder, centre fielder, and right fielder. Outfielders must be able to judge the trajectory of flies and have enough speed to run to the point where the ball will come down. Batted or thrown balls that pass beyond the infielders along the ground must be run down and picked up by the outfielders. Outfielders adjust their positions in response to each batter's hitting tendencies. Strong throwing arms are essential, as is accuracy in throwing the ball to the right point in the infield. Right fielders typically have the strongest and most accurate throwing arms among outfielders. The centre fielder is chosen for his speed and expert judgment of fly balls. The centre fielder not only stations himself at a strategic point for each batter but often directs the playing positions of his outfield teammates. Almost invariably the most skillful defensive outfielders in baseball history, such as Tris Speaker, Joe DiMaggio, Willie Mays, and Ken Griffey, Jr., have been centre fielders.

TRIS SPEAKER

(b. April 4, 1888, Hubbard, Texas, U.S. — d. Dec. 8, 1958, Lake Whitney, Texas)

Player and manager Tris Speaker spent his 22-year career (1907–28) primarily with the Boston Red Sox and the Cleveland Indians. Speaker and Ty Cobb are generally considered the two greatest players of this period.

Tristram E. Speaker was perhaps the best centre fielder ever to play baseball. His speed allowed him to play a shallow centre field, which enabled him to catch many balls that would otherwise have been hits. His strong and accurate throwing arm prevented runners from taking an extra base, and he turned a record 139 double plays from the outfield over the course of his career. Speaker also holds the all-time career record for assists by an outfielder with 449. Today he is best remembered for his defense, but the left-handed-batting Speaker was also one of major league baseball's all-time great hitters. His .345 lifetime batting average is the fourth-best in the game. He also had 3,514 career hits — the fifth highest total by a major leaguer — and he recorded 200 or more hits in a season four times. Speaker's 792 doubles are the most in baseball history. Amazingly, he struck out only 220 times during his entire career.

The durable Speaker played in more than 100 games for 19 consecutive seasons. He began his career with the Boston Red Sox, whom he led to World Series championships in 1912 and 1915. In 1912 he won the Chalmers Award, the equivalent of today's Most Valuable Player. Speaker was traded to the Cleveland Indians in 1916 and was the Indians' player-manager between 1919 and 1926, a tenure that included a World Series championship in 1920. Speaker spent his last two seasons playing for the Washington Senators and then the Philadelphia Athletics. He was elected to the Baseball Hall of Fame in 1937.

INFIELDERS

The infielders form the inner ring of defense. They sometimes catch line drives on the fly, but mainly they pick up ground balls that roll toward the outfield or shoot swiftly across the grass on one or more bounces. When a batted ball strikes the ground, the play becomes a race between the batter running to first and an infielder trying to gain control of the ball and throw it. Like the outfielders, the four infielders shift position to guard against each batter's individual strengths. They have the additional responsibility of guarding the bases when occupied. When a ball is batted along the ground, only one infielder is called upon to gain control of it, but at least one other almost always covers a base to take the throw. Depending on the situation, sometimes two bases must be covered for a possible throw, sometimes all four. On a ball hit into the outfield, an infielder may need to position himself to receive a throw from an outfielder.

Each position has its special fielding requirements. Usually positioned to the left of second base, shortstop is the most difficult and demanding of the defensive positions, requiring outstanding agility, range, and a strong throwing arm. The throw from the shortstop to first base is the infield's longest and most difficult. The second baseman, who is typically positioned to the right of second base, does not require an exceptionally strong arm, but he does need as much range and agility as the shortstop. Together the shortstop and second baseman form the keystone of the defense, as both cover second base, take most of the throws from the outfield, and handle the majority of ground balls. Many of the game's greatest fielding players have been shortstops and second basemen, among them Honus Wagner, Pee Wee Reese, Dave Concepción, Ozzie Smith, and Omar Vizquel at shortstop and Nap Lajoie, Charlie Gehringer, Bill Mazeroski, Joe Morgan, and Roberto Alomar at second base.

The third baseman, playing to the right of third base and nearer the batter than the shortstop or second baseman, is not called on to cover as much ground, but his reflexes must be exceptional. The long throw across the

JOE MORGAN

(b. Sept. 19, 1943, Bonham, Texas, U.S.)

Joe Morgan won consecutive National League MVP awards in 1975–76, when he led the Cincinnati Reds to back-to-back World Series championships.

Joseph Leonard Morgan, a second baseman, played his first major league game at age 19. In 1965, his first full season, he was named the NL Rookie of the Year for the Houston Astros; he hit 14 home runs, scored 100 runs, and had a .271 batting average. He remained with the Astros through 1971, being named to the All Star team twice (1966 and 1970).

Morgan was one of eight players involved in a trade between the Astros and the Cincinnati Reds, and he played in the 1972 World Series his first year in Cincinnati. The Reds captured consecutive World Series titles in 1975 and 1976, while Morgan earned two MVP awards. In 1975 he had 17 home runs, 94 runs batted in (RBIs), 107 runs, and 67 stolen bases and hit .327. The following year he had 27 home runs, 111 RBIs, 113 runs, 60 stolen bases, and a .320 batting average. His slugging percentage of .576 was the league's best. He made the All Star team during each of his eight seasons with the Reds and received the Gold Glove Award five times (1973–77).

Morgan spent his final five seasons (1980–84) with four teams: the Houston Astros, the San Francisco Giants, the Philadelphia Phillies, and the Oakland Athletics. He played in his final World Series with the Phillies in 1983, finishing with 20 hits in 23 World Series games. In 22 seasons Morgan had 2,517 hits, 268 homers, 1,133 RBIs, 1,650 runs, 689 stolen bases, and a .271 batting average. He hit 266 of his home runs while playing second base, breaking Rogers Hornsby's record for most home runs by a second baseman. Ryne Sandberg later broke Morgan's record.

Morgan was elected to the Baseball Hall of Fame in 1990. After his retirement from professional baseball, he was a television analyst for network baseball broadcasts, as well as the owner of a beverage company.

infield requires a strong and accurate arm. First basemen are typically physically large in order to provide a big target for throws to first base. The first baseman's fielding of grounders is made easier by his position near the base toward which the batter is running. First basemen are often left-handed, an advantage in throwing from their position, and are generally among the most powerful hitters in the lineup.

THE BATTERY

The pitcher and catcher together are known as the battery or as batterymen. As a fielder, the pitcher may function as an emergency first baseman, and he fields bunts or other infield grounders hit his way. The ability of the pitcher to quickly transition from his pitching motion to a fielding stance can greatly improve his team's overall defense.

The "good hands" essential to every player are especially important for the catcher. Throughout the game he must catch the pitched balls not hit by the batter and sometimes catch pitches that strike the ground near the plate. The catcher also needs good agility behind the plate. He may need to move his body quickly to knock down an off-target pitch, chase a catchable foul ball, or pounce on a bunt. The catcher's throwing arm is a valuable element in his team's defense. Base runners are cautious of straying too far from their bases when the catcher has a quick and strong arm. Not surprisingly, a strong throwing arm has been the hallmark of baseball's greatest catchers, including Mickey Cochrane, Bill Dickey, Yogi Berra, Johnny Bench, and Iván Rodriguez.

Important as is his fielding, the catcher functions even more crucially as the counselor of the pitcher, as well as of the rest of the team. As the only player in the defensive lineup who has the whole game in front of him at all times, the catcher is best placed to advise teammates when necessary.

YOGI BERRA

(b. May 12, 1925, St. Louis, Mo., U.S.)

The idiosyncratic player, manager, and coach Yogi Berra established records (all since broken) for catchers of his era; he held the records for most home runs hit while playing in the position of catcher (313), most consecutive errorless games (148), and most consecutive chances handled (950; a chance constitutes any play in which a player can make a putout, an assist, or an error; when a chance is "handled," either a put out or an assist is the result).

As a boy in the Italian district of St. Louis, Missouri, Lawrence Peter Berra played softball, baseball, soccer, football, and roller hockey. He first played organized baseball with a YMCA team and later played American Legion baseball. He batted left-handed and, like most catchers, threw right-handed (the traditional reason for right-handed catchers predominating being that because most batters are right-handed and therefore stand to the left of home plate, a left-handed catcher is blocked from throwing out base runners). In 1942 Berra signed a contract with the New York Yankees. After a season in the minor leagues, he served in the United States Navy during World War II (1943–46) and played minor league baseball again in 1946. He moved up to the New York Yankees toward the end of the 1946 season and played with them as their regular catcher through 1963. Because Berra's catching was erratic, he played mostly in the outfield until 1949. His defensive and offensive playing then improved; he hit 20 or more home runs a season through 1958. He was named the American League's Most Valuable Player, an honour seldom bestowed on catchers, in 1951, 1954, and 1955. He played in 14 World Series (1947, 1949–53, 1955–58, and 1960–63), catching in more series games (75) than any other catcher. He hit a home run in his first World Series appearance; he hit 12 World Series home runs in all.

After retiring as a player, Berra managed the Yankees in 1964, winning the pennant and losing the World Series, and was fired. He was a coach for the New York Mets (1965–72) and then became team manager (1972–75). Thereafter he was a coach with the Yankees until 1983, when he was once again made their manager. He was fired during the 1985 season. Berra was one of the few men to manage

New York Mets manager Yogi Berra, 1973. John D. Hanlon/Sports Illustrated/Getty Images

pennant winners in both leagues, and he was elected to the Baseball Hall of Fame in 1972.

Berra was well known for amusing non sequiturs that are termed "Yogi-isms." Examples include statements such as "It's déjà vu all over again," "You can observe a lot by watching," and "Baseball is 90 percent mental, the other half is physical."

The Putout

The defense must collect outs to prevent the offense from scoring. There are a variety of ways in which the defense may "put out" or "force out" offensive players. A player also may be called out by an umpire for interfering with a defensive play.

Most putouts are made by (1) striking out the batter, (2) catching a ball on the fly, (3) throwing the batter out, or (4) tagging out a base runner.

The batter is allowed two strikes; a third strike results in an out, commonly called a strikeout. A strike occurs when a batter swings at a pitch and misses, when the batter does not swing at a pitched ball that passes through the strike zone, or when the ball is hit foul. A ball hit foul can count as only the first or second strike with one exception—a ball bunted foul can be called strike three. Umpires signal strikes and putouts with an emphatic movement of the right arm. The strike zone is a prescribed area in front of the batter and over home plate. Its upper limit is in line with the midpoint between the top of the shoulders and the top of the uniform pants, and the lower limit is in line with the bottom of the knees. The strike zone is thus an imaginary rectangular box 17 inches (43.2 cm) wide, with the length of its vertical sides dependent on the height of the batter. The perception of where the strike zone begins and ends may vary from umpire to umpire, leading to frustrated fans and irate batters, pitchers, catchers, and managers. Anyone who disputes an umpire's call of a ball or strike may be thrown out of the game.

A batter is put out if a fielder catches a batted ball before it touches the ground, whether it is a fair ball or foul. A foul tip, a pitched ball that the batter merely flicks slightly with his bat, however, counts only as a strike even if it is caught and held by the catcher, and it does not count as a putout unless it occurs on the third strike.

A member of the batting team is thrown, or forced, out if he bats a ball that touches the ground before being caught (usually by an infielder or the pitcher) and that is then thrown for the putout to the first baseman, who touches first base before the batter reaches the base.

A member of the offensive team is tagged out if, when running the bases and not in contact with a base, he is touched by the ball held by a member of the fielding team.

THE FORCE PLAY

Only one runner may occupy a base at any given moment. It is therefore possible for a runner to be thrown out at second base, third base, or even home plate without being tagged. The batter is entitled to try to reach first base safely the instant he hits a fair ball that strikes the ground. If a teammate is on first when the ball is hit, that base runner is no longer entitled to first base and must run to second. If runners are on first and second or on all three bases, they are all forced to run when the batter hits a fair ball that strikes the ground. Any base runner forced to run can be put out, or retired, by a fielder having the ball who can touch the next base before the runner reaches it.

This method of retiring base runners is called the force play. With first base occupied and the ball driven along the ground to the pitcher or an infielder, the ball often can be thrown first to second base for a force out of the man from first base, then relayed to the first baseman to retire the batter—two outs on one play, a double play. Although double plays can be initiated by force outs at home or third base, the second-to-first double play is the most common form.

A runner also can be thrown out without being tagged if he has left his base before a fly ball is caught. With the catching of the fly, the runner must return to the base he just left (known as tagging up) before being eligible to advance. If the player catching the fly throws the ball to that base before the runner returns and tags up, the runner is retired. On the other hand, after the catch the runner may attempt to reach the next base, where a tag is required to put him out.

The infield fly rule protects base runners from the deception of an infielder who may allow an infield fly ball to drop, thus setting up an easy force play. The rule applies only if both first and second are occupied by runners and there are fewer than two out. The batter is automatically out when the rule is invoked.

PITCHING

Until a batter hits the ball, the game is a duel between the pitcher (and catcher) and the batter, which is repeated with each at bat. Each batter that a pitcher strikes out or forces to hit a pop-up (pop fly, an easily caught fly) or easily fielded grounder is a gain for the defense, preventing runs and bringing the team closer to its turn at bat and a chance to score.

Until about 1870, the pitcher was merely a player assigned to put the ball in play by pitching it to the batter to hit. One man generally did nearly all the pitching for a club all season, only occasionally relieved by a "change" pitcher. This change pitcher was usually an outfielder, and

TOM SEAVER

Tom Seaver displaying classic pitching form as he throws for the New York Mets at Shea Stadium. Focus On Sport/Getty Images

(b. Nov. 17, 1944, Fresno, Calif., U.S.)

Tom Seaver was one of the game's dominant pitchers between the late 1960s and early 1980s.

During his 20-year career (1967–86), George Thomas Seaver, a right-handed pitcher, posted a record of 311 wins and 205 losses with a 2.86 earned run average (ERA). He won more than 20 games in a season five times, led the National League in victories and ERA on three occasions, and won the NL Cy Young Award three times. Seaver also led the NL in strikeouts five times, and his 3,640 career strikeouts rank sixth on the all-time list. His 61 career shutouts put him in a tie for seventh-best (with Nolan Ryan) in the history of major league baseball. Seaver was the NL Rookie of the Year in 1967 and was selected to the All-Star team 12 times.

Seaver was the catalyst in the transformation of the New York Mets franchise from an expansion team with a losing record in its first seven years of existence to World Series champions in 1969. In that season he won 25 games, lost 7, posted a 2.21 ERA, and won the Cy Young Award. He was elected to the Baseball Hall of Fame in 1992 — selected by 425 of the 430 sportswriters' votes (98.84 percent), the highest percentage in the history of the Hall of Fame.

the two would often merely exchange fielding positions without leaving the game. With the start of league baseball in the 1870s, the pitcher became more important in defensive play. His use of speed and location in delivering the pitch became a deciding element in competition.

Of the 25 players on a major league club's normal active roster, usually 11 to 12 are pitchers. The manager usually designates 5 of the 12 as starting pitchers, or the rotation starters. They take their turn every four or five days, resting in between. The remainder of the staff constitute the bullpen squad or the relief pitchers. When the manager or pitching coach detects signs of weakening on the part of the pitcher in the game, these bullpen pitchers begin warming up by throwing practice pitches. Since the early 1950s, relief pitching has grown in importance and become more specialized. Typically, one relief pitcher is designated as the "closer." Closers are usually used only when a team has a lead late in the game and have the job of "saving" the victory for the team by collecting the remaining outs.

THE PITCHING REPERTOIRE

Pitching demands more exact coordination of mental and muscular faculties and more continuous physical exertion than any other position in the game. On each pitch the pitcher is aiming at the strike zone, or a small part of it, 60 feet 6 inches (18.4 metres) away from the rubber on which his foot pivots in the act of pitching the ball. Pitchers use changes of speed, control (the ability to pitch to specific points in the strike zone), and different grips that affect the flight of the pitch in order to confound batters. The fastball is the basis of pitching skill. Good fastball pitchers are capable of throwing the ball 100 miles (160 km) per hour, but simply being fast is not enough to guarantee success. A fastball should not fly flat but have some

BOB FELLER

(b. Nov. 3, 1918, Van Meter, Iowa, U.S. — d. Dec. 15, 2010, Cleveland, Ohio)

A right-handed pitcher with a tremendous fastball, Bob Feller was a frequent leader in games won and strikeouts during his 18-year career with the Cleveland Indians of the American League.

Robert William Andrew Feller made his major league debut at age 17, when he joined the Indians mid-season in 1936, and he broke the AL single-game strikeout record in just his fifth start. The young hurler soon became a national sensation: his high school graduation was covered live by NBC radio, and he appeared on the cover of *Time* magazine before his second season. Initially Feller had control problems (his record of 208 bases on balls in 1938 stood into the early 1980s), but his pitching quickly improved, and for three consecutive years (1939–41) he led the league in innings pitched, wins, and strikeouts. In 1940 he also had the best earned run average in the AL, which, along with his registering the highest win and strikeout totals for the year, earned him that season's pitching Triple Crown.

Feller enlisted in the U.S. Navy in 1941 and served as a gunner on the USS *Alabama*; he missed three full seasons and most of a fourth during World War II. After his return to baseball he again led the league in strikeouts from 1946 through 1948, throwing 348, 196, and 194 strikeouts, respectively, in those years. In 1948, as a member of the most-storied team in franchise history, Feller also played a pivotal role in the Indians winning the World Series. He pitched three no-hit games, the first pitcher in the 20th century to do so, in 1940, 1946, and 1951. In his career he pitched 12 one-hit games.

After retiring in 1956, Feller continued to travel extensively to promote professional baseball, and he served briefly as a TV broadcaster for the Indians. An eight-time career all-star, he was elected to the Baseball Hall of Fame in 1962.

movement in order to get past a good hitter. An effective pitcher can throw the fastball high or low in the strike zone as well as in on the batter or away from him. Fastball pitchers of note include Walter Johnson, Satchel Paige, Bob Feller, Nolan Ryan, and Roger Clemens. An important pitch related to the fastball is the change-up, which is a deliberately slower pitch that can sneak past a batter expecting a fastball.

The fundamental, or regulation, curve is a swerving pitch that breaks away from the straight line, to the left (the catcher's right) if thrown by a right-handed pitcher, to the right if by a left-hander. Some pitchers also employ a curving ball that breaks in the opposite way from the regulation curve, a pitch known variously as the fadeaway (the curve thrown by Christy Mathewson), the screwball (thrown by Carl Hubbell), or some other name applied by the pitcher himself. In both curves and reverse curves, the ball reaches the batter at a slower rate of speed than the fastball, and the deception is almost as much a result of the slower ball's falling away from the bat as of its swerving from a straight trajectory.

A comparatively new pitch, called the slider, was first thrown by Hall of Famer Charles Bender and was popularized in the 1920s by George Blaeholder, who otherwise had an undistinguished major league career. The slider is a cross between the fastball and the curve and involves the best features of both. It is thrown with the speed and the pitching motion of the fastball, but, instead of the wide sweep of the conventional curve, it has a short and mostly lateral break; in effect, it slides away from the hitter.

Relatively few pitchers use the knuckleball, which lacks axial rotation, making it subject to air currents. The ball is wobbly as it approaches the batter and so is harder to hit solidly than a spinning ball. The knuckleball, however, is difficult to catch, and often it is missed by the catcher (a passed ball). The knuckler is thrown with an easy, almost lobbing motion, and, because of the minimal arm strain, knuckleball pitchers may have remarkable longevity.

In the 1970s relief pitcher Bruce Sutter introduced the split-fingered fastball, which broke downward at the plate in a motion often compared, with some exaggeration, to a ball rolling off a table.

In the early days of organized baseball, artificial aids were allowed that enabled the pitcher to throw what was called a spitball. Simple saliva, saliva produced by chewing tobacco or sucking on slippery elm, or sweat was applied to the ball. The ball thus treated dropped sharply at the

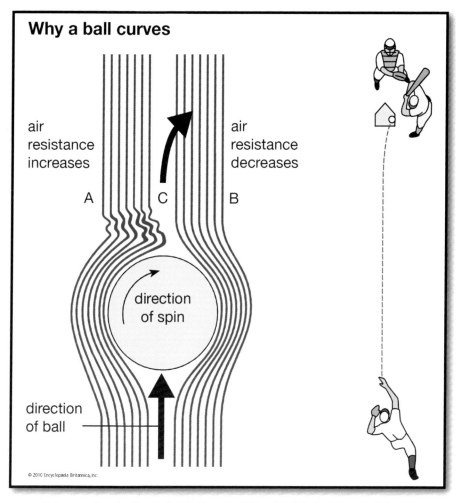

Why a ball curves

air resistance increases

air resistance decreases

A   C   B

direction of spin

direction of ball

© 2010 Encyclopædia Britannica, Inc.

Diagram showing how a baseball curves. The spin of the ball creates different levels of air resistance on either side of the ball, which then moves toward the direction of lower resistance. Encyclopædia Britannica, Inc.

plate. The pitch was outlawed in 1920, though pitchers then using it were allowed the pitch until they retired. Since then pitchers have from time to time been suspected of using it. Similar effects have been sought by those who illegally scar the surface of the ball with a sharp object such as a belt buckle or tack or with an abrasive tool such as a file or emery board.

Some batters, for their part, have looked for illegal advantage by drilling a hole down the barrel of a bat and filling it with cork or rubber balls; although this procedure lightens the bat, its effect on bat speed and "liveliness" is questionable.

PITCHING WITH MEN ON BASE

When an offensive player reaches base, a pitcher must change tactics in order to prevent the runner from scoring. The pitcher will alter his stance on the mound from the "windup," a stance that begins with the pitcher facing home plate, to the "stretch," a stance that begins with a left-handed pitcher facing first base or a right-handed pitcher facing third base. Pitching from the stretch allows for a shorter motion that gets the ball to the catcher more quickly and allows the base runner less time to steal a base. When a pitcher believes a runner is likely to attempt a steal, he will try to shorten the runner's lead or even "pick off" the runner (catch him off base) by making throws over to the runner's base. The pitcher attempting to pick off a runner must be careful not to commit a "balk." A balk occurs when (1) the pitcher, in pitching the ball to the batter, does not have his pivoting foot in contact with the pitching plate, (2) the pitcher does not hold the ball in both hands in front of him at chest level before starting his delivery or, once started, does not continue his motion, or (3) the pitcher starts to make a throw to first base when a runner is occupying that base but does not go through with the throw. When a balk is called by the umpire, all runners on base advance one base each.

Occasionally a pitcher will deliberately put a batter on base in order to improve the team's chances of getting outs. The pitcher will issue an intentional walk, four pitches intentionally thrown well outside the strike zone and away from the batter, for several possible tactical reasons: (1) to avoid a batter that is deemed particularly dangerous, (2) to set up a double play opportunity if first base is open with runners on base and less than two outs, or (3) to set up a force play.

SUBSTITUTIONS

Substitutions may be made at any point in the game when time has been called by the umpire. A player taken out of the lineup cannot return in the same game. Without making any substitution, the manager may at any time in the game shift his players from one fielding position to another. He may shift all nine positions in fielding, but he cannot change a player from one place to another in the batting order. Defensive substitutions are common in the late innings of a game when a team is protecting a lead. A fleet-footed outfielder, for example, will replace a slower player who is more valued for his hitting. The most frequent defensive substitution, however, is that of one pitcher for another.

CHAPTER 4
MAJOR LEAGUE
BASEBALL

Major League Baseball (MLB) is the umbrella organization that oversees the American and the National Leagues. The two leagues existed as separate legal entities for the vast majority of their respective histories, with the MLB only gaining complete control over major league professional baseball in the U.S. and Canada in 2000.

THE AMERICAN LEAGUE (AL)

The American League was founded as a minor league association in 1893 and was initially called the Western League. The Western League changed its name to the American League of Professional Baseball Clubs after the 1899 season, declared itself a major league in 1901 (the year now recognized as the league's first official season), and was granted equal status by the older National League in 1903. The American League consists of 14 teams (including one Canadian team) aligned in three divisions: the AL East, comprising the Baltimore Orioles, Boston Red Sox, New York Yankees, Tampa Bay Rays, and Toronto Blue Jays; the AL Central, comprising the Chicago White Sox, Cleveland Indians, Detroit Tigers, Kansas City Royals, and Minnesota Twins; and the AL West, comprising the Los Angeles Angels of Anaheim, Oakland Athletics, Seattle Mariners, and Texas Rangers.

AL EAST

BALTIMORE ORIOLES

Based in Baltimore, Md., the Orioles won World Series titles in 1966, 1970, and 1983.

The franchise that would become the Orioles was founded in 1894 as a minor league team based in Milwaukee, Wis., called the Brewers. The Brewers became a major league team in 1901 when their league—the renamed American League—was elevated to major league status. They moved to St. Louis, Mo., in 1902 and became known as the Browns. The St. Louis Browns featured Hall of Famers George Sisler and Bobby Wallace, but the team was not a success, reaching the World Series only once in their 52 years in St. Louis (1944, when they lost to their crosstown rivals, the St. Louis Cardinals). Possibly the most notable moment in Browns' history took place in a game against the Detroit Tigers on Aug. 19, 1951, when publicity-savvy owner Bill Veeck sent to the plate 3-foot 7-inch (1.09-metre) Eddie Gaedel, who walked on four straight pitches.

In 1954 the Browns moved to Baltimore, Md., and took on the traditional nickname of Baltimore baseball teams, the Orioles. In 1955 the team signed future 15-time All-Star Brooks Robinson, and—with the later additions of Boog Powell, Jim Palmer, Frank Robinson, and manager Earl Weaver—the Orioles entered into the first period of prolonged success in franchise history. Between 1963 and 1983 the club endured only one losing season, and they won eight division titles, six AL pennants, and three World Series. The Orioles drafted Cal Ripken, Jr., in 1978. Ripken went on to set a record for most consecutive games played (2,632) and became arguably the most popular player in the team's history.

In 1992 the Orioles started playing their home games in Oriole Park at Camden Yards. The baseball-only facility began a trend in the major leagues away from suburban multipurpose stadiums and toward ballparks located near the heart of a city. These new stadiums were meant to be evocative of the idiosyncratic ballparks of baseball's early years, and they contributed greatly to the record attendance at baseball games by the turn of the 21st century. Partly because of the increased revenue brought to the team by the popularity of Camden Yards and the team's subsequently larger payroll, the Orioles briefly returned to contention in the mid-1990s, but, following a series of questionable personnel changes, the team fell from baseball's top ranks in 1998, finishing no higher than third place in their division during the first decade of the 2000s. In 1999 the Orioles traveled to Cuba, where they became the first American baseball team in 40 years to play a game there, and defeated the Cuban national team.

BOSTON RED SOX

Based in Boston, the Red Sox are one of the most storied franchises in American sports and have won seven World Series titles and 12 AL pennants.

Founded in 1901, the franchise (then unofficially known as the Boston Americans) was one of the eight charter members of the American League. The team played at the Huntington Avenue Grounds from 1901 to 1911 and moved to Fenway Park in 1912. The oldest of all current major league ballparks, Fenway is known for its quirky features, the most famous of which is the 37-foot 2-inch (11.3-metre) left field wall known as the "Green Monster." The team officially took the name Boston Red Sox ("BoSox" or "Sox" for short) in 1908, adapting it from the Boston Red Stockings, the original name of Boston's first professional baseball team (now the Atlanta Braves).

Boston enjoyed immediate success with its superstar Cy Young, the premiere pitcher of his generation, and their talented third baseman and manager, Jimmy Collins. Boston won the very first World Series, in 1903, by defeating the Pittsburgh Pirates and continued its successful run in the 1910s, winning four more championships (1912, 1915, 1916, and 1918) with lineups that included centre fielder Tris Speaker (1907–15), pitcher Smokey Joe Wood (1908–15), and a young pitcher-turned-outfielder named Babe Ruth (1914–19).

The team's fortunes changed dramatically in 1920, however, with the notorious sale of Ruth to the New York Yankees by owner Harry Frazee. This was the genesis of the Red Sox–Yankees rivalry and of the supposed "Curse of the Bambino" ("Bambino" was one of Ruth's nicknames), cited by many Red Sox fans as the reason the team failed to win another World Series in the 20th century while the Yankees went on to become baseball's most successful franchise. After losing Ruth and other star players as well as their capable manager, Ed Barrow, to the Yankees, the Red Sox suffered through abysmal season after season over the next two decades.

Boston teams have featured some of the most talented hitters in baseball history, including Jimmie Foxx, Carl Yastrzemski, Carlton Fisk, Jim Rice, Manny Ramirez, and, most famously, Ted Williams, the left-handed outfielder considered by many to be the best pure hitter ever and the last player to bat above .400 in a season (.406 in 1941). Yet even with their great hitters and dominating pitchers—including Luis Tiant, Roger Clemens, and Pedro Martinez—the Red Sox were unable to win a championship between 1918 and 2004, often finding new and heartbreaking ways to lose crucial games. Making it to the World Series four more times (1946, 1967, 1975, 1986), the Red Sox lost each series in the seventh (and final)

The Boston Red Sox celebrate after winning their first World Series champion-ship since 1918, Oct. 27, 2004. Mike Ehrmann/WireImage/Getty Images

game. They also lost two AL pennant tiebreakers, both played at Fenway, to the Cleveland Indians (1948) and the Yankees (1978)—the latter after leading their division by 14½ games in July—and suffered a crushing play-off loss in 2003 to the Yankees.

Finally, in 2004, the Red Sox emerged triumphant after 86 years of frustration, winning the World Series in four games against the St. Louis Cardinals behind the pitching of Curt Schilling and the batting of Ramirez and David Ortiz. Just as important to Red Sox fans, they had vanquished their nemesis Yankees in the American League Championship Series, coming back from a 3–0 series deficit to win 4–3, the first team in baseball history to stage such a comeback in the postseason. The Red Sox—led by standout pitching performances by Josh Beckett, Jonathan Papelbon, and rookie Diasuke Matsuzaka—captured another World Series title in 2007, sweeping the Colorado

Rockies in four games. The Red Sox finished second to the Tampa Bay Rays in the AL East in 2008, but the team still qualified for the play-offs as the AL Wild Card winner (as owner of the best record for a non-division-winner in the AL), earning its fifth postseason berth in six seasons.

NEW YORK YANKEES

Based in the borough of the Bronx in New York City, the Yankees are one of the most famous and successful franchises in all sports. The team has won a record 27 World Series titles and 40 AL pennants.

The franchise began in 1901 in Baltimore, Md., competing as the Orioles in the AL for two seasons. The struggling Baltimore team was bought by Frank Farrell and Bill Devery in 1903 and brought to New York, initially to Hilltop Park (1903–12), one of Manhattan's highest points, which led to the name New York Highlanders. Local sportswriters often referred to the team as "Yankees" or "Yanks," because the team was in the American League. After the club moved to the Polo Grounds in 1913, the name Highlanders fell further into disuse, and the team was officially renamed the Yankees. The team has also been called the Bronx Bombers, the Pinstripers (due to the distinctive pinstripes on their home uniforms), and the Evil Empire (by opposing fans, particularly those of their archrival, the Boston Red Sox). They played at the Polo Grounds until 1922 and then moved to Yankee Stadium ("The House that Ruth Built," nicknamed after famed Yankees slugger Babe Ruth), where they played from 1923 to 2008. The team moved to a new ballpark, also named Yankee Stadium, in 2009.

The team was not a regular pennant contender during its first 18 years in New York. Its fortunes changed completely in 1920, however, with the acquisition of Ruth from the Red Sox for cash and a loan against Boston's Fenway Park—the most famous sale in baseball history.

JOE DIMAGGIO

(b. Nov. 25, 1914, Martinez, Calif., U.S.—d. March 8, 1999, Hollywood, Fla.)

Joe DiMaggio was an outstanding hitter and fielder and one of the best all-round players in the history of the game.

Joseph Paul DiMaggio was the son of Italian immigrants who made their living by fishing. He quit school at 14 and at 17 joined his brother Vincent and began playing baseball with the minor league San Francisco Seals. (In addition to Vincent, who would go on to play for several major league teams, including the Pittsburgh Pirates, a younger DiMaggio brother, Dominic, played for the Boston Red Sox.) Joe's contract with San Francisco was purchased by the New York Yankees, and he was brought up to the major leagues in 1936. In his rookie season with the Yankees he batted .323 during the regular season and .346 against the New York Giants during the World Series.

In 1937 DiMaggio—who was known as "Joltin' Joe" and the "Yankee Clipper"—led the American League in home runs and runs scored, and in 1939 and 1940 he led the American League in batting, with averages of .381 and .352. DiMaggio was a very consistent hitter; early in his career, during his 1933 season with the Seals, he had a hitting streak of 61 consecutive games. His consistency led to one of the most remarkable records of major league baseball—DiMaggio's feat of hitting safely in 56 consecutive games (May 15–July 16, 1941). The prior record for the longest hitting streak of 44 games was set in 1897 (and, at that time, foul balls did not count as strikes). With the exception of DiMaggio's streak, no player has hit in more than 44 consecutive games since. In addition to his fine hitting ability, DiMaggio had outstanding skill as a fielder, tying the American League fielding record in 1947 with only one error in 141 games. Indeed, he played his position in center field with such languid expertise that some ill-informed fans thought he was lazy—he rarely had to jump against the outfield wall to make a catch or dive for balls, he was simply there to catch them.

Between 1936 and 1951 DiMaggio helped the Yankees to nine World Series titles—in 1936, 1937, 1938, 1939, 1941, 1947, 1949, 1950, and 1951. During the same period the Yankees won 10 American League championships (the Yankees won the pennant but not the World Series in 1942.) DiMaggio missed three seasons (1943 through 1945) serving in the military during World War II.

Joe DiMaggio and Marilyn Monroe leaving San Francisco City Hall after their January 1954 marriage ceremony. AFP/Getty Images

DiMaggio received the Most Valuable Player (MVP) award for the American League in 1939, 1941, and 1947. He retired at the end of the 1951 season. He was elected to the Baseball Hall of Fame in 1955.

In 1954 DiMaggio married film star Marilyn Monroe, which only added to his iconic status in American culture. Though this marriage lasted less than a year, the couple remained close until her death in 1962. In his retirement he acted as a spokesman for commercial concerns and worked for charitable causes. The lustre of his career remained undimmed at his death; he was loved by fans as much for his integrity and dignity as for his phenomenal playing skills.

With the superstar pitcher-turned-outfielder leading the charge, the Yankees dynasty began to take shape during his second season with the team. It won three consecutive AL championships and the team's first World Series title (1923). The Yankees solidified their command throughout the 1920s and '30s, winning a total of 11 pennants and eight World Series championships, with contributions by such baseball legends as first baseman Lou Gehrig, outfielder Joe DiMaggio, and pitcher Waite Hoyt. In the mid-1920s the hard-hitting Yankees lineup—including Ruth, Gehrig, Tony Lazzeri, Bob Meusel, and Earle Combs—earned the nickname "Murderers' Row." The 1927 Yankees, distinguished by Ruth's 60 home runs (a record that stood for 34 years before being surpassed by that of another Yankee, Roger Maris, in 1961) and Gehrig's 175 runs batted in, are considered by many baseball enthusiasts to be the best team of all time.

Despite losing Gehrig to amyotrophic lateral sclerosis (better known as Lou Gehrig disease) and Ruth to retirement, the Yankees continued their dominance unabated in the 1940s, with three consecutive league pennants (1941–43) and two World Series championships (1941, 1943) by teams starring DiMaggio. This stretch was followed by five consecutive World Series titles (1949–53) under manager Casey Stengel, whose squads featured such illustrious greats as centre fielder Mickey Mantle, catcher Yogi Berra, shortstop Phil Rizzuto, and pitcher Whitey Ford. In 12 seasons as the team's manager, Stengel won 10 AL pennants and seven World Series. One of Stengel's World Series-winning squads was a part of arguably the most memorable moment in World Series history: in game five of the 1956 series, with the Yankees and their rival Brooklyn Dodgers tied at two wins apiece, unheralded pitcher Don Larsen threw the only perfect game in postseason history, retiring all 27 opposing batters without letting anyone on base.

Following another era of dominance in the late 1950s and early 1960s (featuring World Series championships in 1958, 1961, and 1962), the Yankees entered a period of relative decline. They failed to win another major league title until 1977, when they were managed by Billy Martin and led by the celebrated slugger Reggie Jackson, who had been signed in the previous off-season by the team's outspoken and controversial new owner, George Steinbrenner.

After two decades most notable for the multiple firings and rehirings of Martin by Steinbrenner, the Yankees returned to glory under the stewardship of Joe Torre (1996–2007), who managed the team to six AL championships and four World Series titles (1996, 1998–2000), with teams featuring star shortstop Derek Jeter, closer Mariano Rivera, seasoned pitcher David Cone, and veteran role players such as Tino Martinez and Paul O'Neill. In addition to their on-field success, the Yankees under Steinbrenner were notable for the vast amount of money the team spent on its payroll, which was routinely the highest in the league and occasionally neared 10 times the size of the smallest payroll in the sport. Steinbrenner's teams also had a propensity to make splashy acquisitions of superstar players, including pitchers Randy Johnson and Roger Clemens, outfielder Gary Sheffield, and third baseman Alex Rodriguez.

Over the years, Steinbrenner ceded the duties of overseeing the Yankees to his two sons, Hank and Hal, and in 2008 Hal was given control of the team, while George remained the nominal chairman until his death in 2010. In 2009 the Yankees returned to the World Series for the first time in six years under Joe Girardi, who had become the Yankees' manager in 2008. In six games the Yankees dethroned the Philadelphia Phillies, en route to winning their 27th World Series title.

Tampa Bay Rays

Based in St. Petersburg, Fla., the Rays began play in 1998 and were known as the Devil Rays until the end of the 2007 season.

In the years before the advent of the Rays, the Tampa–St. Petersburg area was often suggested as a relocation site for many struggling major league baseball teams. The region had been a centre for major league spring training since the Chicago Cubs moved their operation to Tampa in 1913, and many teams expressed interest in moving to a site with a well-established fan base. However, no teams relocated to the area, and Tampa Bay went without a major league franchise until it was granted an expansion team at the 1995 Major League Baseball owner meetings.

Months before their inaugural season began, Tampa Bay signed future Hall of Famer Wade Boggs, who grew up in Tampa and further spurred fan interest in the new team. However, the Devil Rays franchise did not have an auspicious beginning: it posted losing records in each of its first 10 seasons and finished last in its division in every year save one, when it finished second to last.

In 2008 the newly renamed Rays engineered one of the greatest turnarounds in professional sports history. Behind the leadership of manager Joe Maddon and the play of young stars Scott Kazmir, Matt Garza, Evan Longoria, and Carl Crawford, the Rays posted a 95–67 record—a 29-game improvement from their 2007 mark of 66–96—and qualified for the first play-off appearance in the franchise's history as AL East champions. In the American League Championship Series, the Rays bested the defending world champion Boston Red Sox in seven games to advance to the World Series. The Rays lost the World Series in five games to the Philadelphia Phillies, but their 2008 season still stood as one of the most dramatic one-year turnarounds in sports history.

TORONTO BLUE JAYS

Based in Toronto, the Blue Jays are the only franchise in Major League Baseball that plays in a city not in the United

States. The team has won two AL pennants and two World Series titles (1992, 1993).

The Blue Jays played their first game in 1977, after joining the AL alongside fellow expansion team the Seattle Mariners. Toronto finished at the bottom of the AL East in each of its first five seasons, which led to the hiring of manager Bobby Cox in 1982. Cox guided the "Jays" (as the team is sometimes known by its fans) to their first winning season in 1983—the beginning of an 11-year streak of years with a record over .500—and a franchise-record 99 wins and a division title in 1985. This meteoric Toronto rise stalled in the 1985 AL Championship Series (ALCS), which the team lost in seven games to the Kansas City Royals after holding a three-games-to-one series lead. Led by the play of outfielder George Bell and shortstop Tony Fernández, the Blue Jays finished near the top of the divisional standings throughout the remainder of the 1980s, including a second-place finish in 1987 in a play-off race that was decided only in the final weekend of the regular season.

In 1989 the Blue Jays began playing their home games in the Skydome—known as the Rogers Centre from 2005—which was the first stadium in the world to have a retractable roof. That season, with new manager Cito Gaston, Toronto again captured a divisional crown, but they were defeated by the eventual champion Oakland Athletics in the ALCS. The Jays again lost in the ALCS in 1991 (to the Minnesota Twins). In 1992 the team reached its first World Series, behind the play of first baseman John Olerud, outfielder Joe Carter, and second baseman Roberto Alomar, and Toronto defeated its former manager Cox's Atlanta Braves in six games. Toronto returned to the World Series the next year and beat the Philadelphia Phillies on Carter's series-winning home run in the ninth inning of game six, which was only the second such homer (after Bill Mazeroski's World Series winner in 1960) in major league history. In the following years, Jays pitcher Pat Hentgen became an AL Cy Young Award winner (as the best pitcher in the league), and the team acquired superstar pitcher Roger Clemens, but Toronto nevertheless began posting losing records for the first time in over a decade.

Between 1998 and 2007 the Blue Jays finished in third place in the AL East behind the dominant New York Yankees and Boston Red Sox teams eight times. The Toronto teams of this era featured slugger Carlos Delgado and pitching ace Roy Halladay, and they finished with winning records more often than not, but they were unable to overtake the two powerhouse franchises. Toronto rehired Gaston (who had been fired in 1997) in the middle of the 2008 season to try to recapture the team's past glory, but he retired at the end of the 2010 season after having led the Blue Jays to three straight fourth-place finishes.

AL CENTRAL

CHICAGO WHITE SOX

Based in Chicago, the White Sox have won three World Series titles, two in the early 1900s (1906, 1917) and the third 88 years later, in 2005. They are often referred to as the "South Siders," a reference to their location in relation to Chicago's other major league team, the Cubs.

The White Sox were originally known as the Sioux City (Iowa) Cornhuskers, and the team was founded as a minor league organization in 1894. The club was purchased by Charles Comiskey at the end of its first season and was relocated to St. Paul, Minn. The team moved to Chicago in 1900, and the renamed American League was elevated to major league status the following year, with Chicago taking the first league title in 1901. The Chicago incarnation of the franchise was known as the White Stockings until 1904, when they took on their current name.

The team's image was long tarnished by its appearance in the 1919 World Series, in which Chicago players conspired to fix the outcome in favour of the underdog Cincinnati Reds. Gambling connections were eventually linked to eight members of the team, including outfielder Shoeless Joe Jackson. In what became known as the Black Sox Scandal, evidence revealed that the men had intentionally lost the World Series in eight games, earning the players bans and damaging the reputation of the team and the sport. In the wake of the scandal, the White Sox struggled for the next 86 seasons, winning just one AL pennant—in 1959 with a hustling team nicknamed "the Go-Go Sox," though they also won a division championship in 1983 with a group of players remembered for "winning ugly."

While they did not have many successful teams during much of the 20th century, the White Sox featured a number of future Hall of Famers, including Eddie Collins, Luke Appling, Al Simmons, Luis Aparicio, and Nellie Fox, as well as fan favourites Minnie Miñoso and Harold Baines. In 1981 the Sox signed Carlton Fisk, an 11-time all-star (four with the White Sox) and one of the greatest catchers of all time. First baseman Frank Thomas played 16 years for the team and won back-to-back AL Most Valuable Player awards in 1993 and 1994.

In 2005 manager Ozzie Guillen led a veteran White Sox team to an unexpected championship, the team's first World Series title since 1917. The White Sox returned to the postseason in 2008 but failed to advance past the first round of the play-offs.

CLEVELAND INDIANS

Based in Cleveland, the Indians have won five AL pennants and two World Series titles, the first in 1920 and the second in 1948.

The Indians began as a minor league club based in Grand Rapids, Mich., and moved to Cleveland in 1900. The team was elevated to major league status in 1901 and was called the Cleveland Bluebirds, or Blues. They became the Cleveland Bronchos in 1902 before taking on the name "Naps" the following year in honour of their new star player, Nap Lajoie. In 1915 owner Charles Somers requested that local newspapers pick a new name for the franchise, and "Indians" was chosen. In 1916 the team traded for Tris Speaker, who led the Indians to their first World Series championship in 1920.

The Indians did not reach the postseason again for 28 years, but their return was memorable. The 1948 Indians were led by shortstop-manager Lou Boudreau, the AL's Most Valuable Player that year, one of five future Hall of Fame members on the team. The others were outfielder Larry Doby, the first African American to play in the AL, and three pitchers: Bob Feller, Bob Lemon, and 42-year-old rookie and former Negro league star Satchel Paige. (In 1975 the Indians made Frank Robinson the major league's first African American manager.) The Indians finished the 1948 regular season tied with the Boston Red Sox, whom they defeated in the first one-game play-off in major league history. Cleveland then bested the Boston Braves in six games to capture their second World Series title.

The Indians won 111 games in 1954 but were swept by the New York Giants in a World Series that produced one of baseball's most enduring images—Willie Mays's over-the-shoulder catch of Indian Vic Wertz's towering drive to deep centre field in the first game. Thereafter the Indians entered a long period of mediocrity, finishing with a losing record in 27 of the 34 seasons between 1960 and 1993. A popular legend attributes this period to the "curse of Rocky Colavito," visited on the Indians in 1960 when the team traded Colavito, the AL's leading home-run hitter, in 1959 to the Detroit Tigers for Harvey Kuenn, who had led the league in batting averages.

Under manager Mike Hargrove, the Indians reemerged and won five straight AL Central Division titles (1995–99), advancing to the World Series twice during their run. The success of these teams—which featured Manny Ramírez, Omar Vizquel, and Jim Thome, among others—in addition to the popularity of Cleveland's new ballpark, Jacobs Field, led to the Indians setting a record for consecutive sold-out home games, 455 between 1995 and 2001. With the exception of a postseason berth during the 2007 season (which ended in a dramatic seven-game loss to the Red Sox in the AL Championship Series), recent Indians teams have not matched the success of the late-1990s squads.

Over the years, the Indians have been the subject of several motion pictures—including *The Kid from Cleveland* (1949) and *Major League* (1989)—and for a period entertainer Bob Hope was a part-owner of the team.

Detroit Tigers

Based in Detroit, the Tigers have won four World Series titles (1935, 1945, 1968, 1984) and 10 AL pennants.

The Tigers were founded in 1894 as a minor league franchise, playing alongside organizations that would become the Chicago White Sox, the Cleveland Indians, and the Baltimore Orioles in the Western League (the Tigers are the only surviving member of the Western League to remain in its original city). The Western League was renamed the American League in 1900, and it was elevated to major league status in 1901.

HANK GREENBERG

(b. Jan. 1, 1911, Bronx, N.Y., U.S.—d. Sept. 4, 1986, Beverly Hills, Calif.)

Hank Greenberg won two AL Most Valuable Player awards (1935, 1940) and became the sport's first Jewish superstar.

After a standout high school baseball career, Henry Benjamin Greenberg was offered a contract by his hometown New York Yankees. He was put off by the prospect of having to oust the team's then first baseman, superstar Lou Gehrig, so he declined the offer and studied for a year at New York University before signing with the Detroit Tigers in 1929. The lanky 6-foot 4-inch (1.93-metre) Greenberg appeared in just one game for the Tigers in 1930 before being sent to the minors for seasoning. He played his first full major league season in 1933, and he quickly established himself as one of baseball's premier power hitters.

Playing in the Detroit of the notoriously anti-Semitic Henry Ford and the Rev. Charles E. Coughlin, Greenberg initially dealt with a largely hostile crowd at his home games as well as on the road. Additionally, he often encountered prejudice on the field from opposing players and managers. His stellar play and his off-field graciousness—probably best exemplified by his well-publicized refusal to play on Yom Kippur during the 1934 pennant race—eventually won him the respect and praise of the baseball world. Greenberg helped the Tigers win their first World Series title in 1935, earning the AL MVP award in the process. In 1938 he hit 58 home runs (2 home runs short of Babe Ruth's then record), and in 1940 he led the league in home runs, runs batted in, and doubles while registering a .340 batting average to again be named MVP.

Greenberg missed three full seasons and parts of two more while serving in the military in World War II. After his return to the Tigers in 1945, he hit a dramatic ninth-inning grand slam in the last game of the season to clinch the AL pennant for Detroit (which then went on to win its second World Series title). Greenberg was traded to the Pittsburgh Pirates in 1947, and he retired in 1948. He was part owner and general manager of the Cleveland Indians from 1950 until 1957 and held the same positions for the Chicago White Sox from 1959 to 1961. He left baseball at the end of his stint with the White Sox and embarked on a successful career as an investor on Wall Street. Greenberg was elected to the Baseball Hall of Fame in 1956. His story is recounted in the award-wnning film documentary *The Life and Times of Hank Greenberg* (1999).

Hank Greenberg. Arthur Griffin/Time & Life Pictures/Getty Images

The early Tiger teams were not a success until Detroit acquired outfielder Ty Cobb—one of the game's all-time greats—in 1905. In just his third season, Cobb led the team to its first pennant and berth in the World Series, which it lost to the Chicago Cubs. The Tigers returned to the World Series in each of the following two seasons, but lost on each occasion.

The Tigers dropped in the AL standings in 1910, finishing in third place. In 1912 they played their first game in Navin Field (later known as Tiger Stadium), which would be home to the team for 88 seasons and become one of the most venerated ballparks in the game. The new home stadium was no guarantee of success, however, and the Tigers finished no higher than second place in the AL (which they did on two occasions) until 1934. That season, the sterling play of catcher and manager Mickey Cochrane, first baseman Hank Greenberg, and second baseman Charlie Gehringer (all future Hall of Famers) propelled the Tigers to the World Series, in which the club's unfortunate streak continued as Detroit lost to the St. Louis Cardinals in seven games. In 1935 Detroit returned to the World Series and finally broke through to win its first championship, defeating the Cubs in six games. The Tigers won another World Series in 1945, but in the 1950s the team finished above fourth place just once. One high point of the 1950s took place in 1953, when the Tigers signed 18-year-old Al Kaline, an outfielder who would go on to play 22 seasons with the team and earn the nickname "Mr. Tiger." Detroit tied a team record with 101 wins in 1961 but finished second in the AL behind a dominant New York Yankees team. In 1968 the Tigers team that featured pitchers Denny McLain (winner of the Cy Young Award and 31 games, the highest single-season win total in baseball since 1931) and Mickey Lolich, along with Kaline and sluggers Norm Cash and

Willie Horton, won 103 games and ran away with the AL pennant before beating the Cardinals in the World Series.

With the exception of a berth in the AL Championship Series in 1972, the Tigers teams of the 1970s were mostly mediocre, although quirky rookie pitcher Mark "The Bird" Fidrych was a brief national media sensation in 1976. In 1979 Detroit hired Sparky Anderson as manager, and under his guidance the team returned to the upper echelons of the AL, including another World Series championship in 1984. Talented teams led by such notables as pitcher Jack Morris and shortstop Alan Trammell remained near the top of the standings until 1989, when the Tigers experienced a sudden plummet to last place in the AL. Detroit continued to play poorly throughout most of the following two decades, including an AL-record 119-loss season in 2003. In 2006, however, the Tigers—behind the play of a mix of veteran stalwarts like catcher Iván Rodriguez and young stars such as pitcher Justin Verlander—surged into the play-offs, ultimately reaching the World Series, which they lost to the St. Louis Cardinals.

Kansas City Royals

Based in Kansas City, Mo., the Royals have won two AL pennants and one World Series championship (1985).

The Royals were founded in 1969 as an expansion franchise that was granted by Major League Baseball after the Kansas City Athletics moved to Oakland the previous year. The Royals did not take long to overcome the usual trials of an expansion club; they finished in second place in the AL West three times in their first seven seasons. In an effort to cultivate prospects other franchises had missed, team owner Ewing Kauffman founded the Royals Baseball Academy in Sarasota, Fla., in 1970. The academy aimed to use technological innovations and advanced training techniques to develop baseball skills in overlooked prospects with raw athletic ability, and it produced 14 major leaguers from the 77 prospects that attended the academy in its four years of existence. In 1973 three key members of the Royals during the team's most successful era made their debut: second baseman Frank White (a member of the first Royals Academy class), outfielder and designated hitter Hal McRae, and future Hall of Fame third baseman George Brett. The trio anchored Royals squads that won three consecutive division titles between 1976 and 1978 but that were defeated by the New York Yankees in each of the AL Championship Series of those seasons. After another second-place finish in 1979, Kansas City won a fourth division crown in 1980, as well as its first AL pennant, which was followed by a loss to the Philadelphia Phillies in the World Series.

The Royals made the postseason the following year despite having an overall losing record, owing to a midseason player's strike that led to an idiosyncratic split-season play-off format. The team was quickly eliminated, and the next two years saw it finish second in its division. In 1984 the Royals once more advanced to the ALCS, where they were swept by a powerhouse Detroit Tigers squad. The team's postseason disappointment finally ended in 1985 when the Royals—with Cy Young Award-winning pitcher Brett Saberhagen and all-star closer Dan Quisenberry complementing an offense led by Brett—went to their second World Series, where they faced the cross-state rival St. Louis Cardinals. After trailing in the Series three games to one, the Royals won game five on the road to set up a game six that became notorious for a controversial ninth-inning decision by umpire Don Denkinger. In that game, the Cardinals led 1–0 in the bottom of the ninth when pinch-hitter Jorge Orta was called safe on an infield single that was shown to be an out on television replays. The Royals took advantage of the break and rallied to score two runs in the inning and force a deciding game seven, which they won handily to claim their first World Series title.

Kansas City's remarkable stretch of seven play-off appearances in 10 years proved to be short-lived, as the team entered into a long postseason drought beginning in 1986. The Royals added two-sport star Bo Jackson that year, bringing hope that the franchise would continue its winning ways, but a severe hip injury he sustained while playing football for the Los Angeles Raiders in 1991 effectively ended his promising career and began a trend of the team's failing to capitalize on its promising young players. While the team did boast all-star first baseman and designated hitter Mike Sweeney through the late 1990s and early to mid-2000s, the Royals of this time were notable for their propensity to acquire young talented players—such as outfielders Carlos Beltrán, Johnny Damon, and Jermaine Dye—only to trade them away before they reached their prime. This practice, combined with the financial difficulties of fielding a competitive "small-market" team in this period, resulted in the Royals' finishing with losing records for the vast majority of these two decades, including four 100-loss seasons between 2002 and 2006.

MINNESOTA TWINS

Now based in Minneapolis, Minn., the Twins originally played in Washington, D.C. (1901–60), and were known as the Senators before relocating to Minneapolis in 1961. The franchise has won three World Series titles (1924, 1987, 1991) and six AL pennants.

The Washington Senators were founded in 1901 as one of the eight original American League franchises. The early Senator teams were extremely unsuccessful, posting some of the lowest winning percentages in baseball history en route to last- or second-to-last-place finishes in nine consecutive seasons between 1903 and 1911. This run led one newspaperman to famously sum up the team with the bon mot, "Washington—first in war, first in peace, and last in the American League." The lone bright spot for these Senator squads was future Hall of Fame pitcher Walter Johnson, who amassed a cumulative 2.17 earned run average over the course of his 21-year major league career, which was spent entirely in Washington. Johnson was joined by slugger Goose Goslin in 1921, and the two led the Senators to their first pennant win and the World Series championship in 1924, a title that was won in dramatic fashion over the New York Giants in the 12th inning of the seventh game of the series. The Senators returned to the World Series again in 1925 and 1933, but they lost in both appearances. In 1954 the Senators added one of baseball's all-time great power hitters, Harmon Killebrew, but he was not enough to revive fan interest in a franchise that had returned to an annual spot at the bottom of the AL standings since its last play-off berth in 1933. The Senators were relocated to the burgeoning Minneapolis baseball market in 1961.

Renamed the Twins, the team quickly became contenders in their new home, advancing to the World Series in 1965, with outfielder Tony Oliva and pitcher Jim Kaat joining Killebrew as the team's stars. Minnesota signed future seven-time AL batting champion Rod Carew in 1967. Carew won the AL Rookie of the Year award in his first season with Minnesota, and he, Oliva, and Killebrew led the Twins to AL Central Division titles in 1969 and 1970. The Twins returned to mediocrity for the remainder of the 1970s and the early 1980s, but in 1987 first-year manager Tom Kelly guided the Twins to a seven-game World Series victory over the St. Louis Cardinals.

The Twins participated in an even more eventful "Fall Classic" in 1991 with the Atlanta Braves, who, like the Twins, had finished in last place in their division the previous year, which made both World Series participants co-owners of the first "worst-to-first" turnarounds in modern baseball history. The World Series featured four games that ended with a game-winning hit by the home team. Facing elimination, the Twins won games six and seven in extra innings, the former highlighted by Kirby Puckett's 11th-inning home run and the latter featuring a remarkably durable 10-inning complete-game shutout performance by Minnesota's starting pitcher, Jack Morris.

In 2001 the Twins—who were one of Major League Baseball's least-profitable franchises—were one of the two teams (with the Montreal Expos) proposed by commissioner Bud Selig for elimination from the major leagues in an effort to raise revenue throughout the sport. A 2002 court order forced the Twins to play out their lease at the Hubert H. Humphrey Metrodome, which effectively ended the threat of contraction and gave the franchise time to plan for the construction of a more- profitable baseball-only ballpark.

The Twins began a streak of three straight AL Central Division titles in 2002, and they won their fourth divisional championship of the early 21st century in 2006, but the team failed to advance to the World Series on each occasion. After a two-year postseason absence, the Twins won another division title in 2009, only to lose in the first round of the play-offs. The team again took the AL Central championship in 2010.

AL WEST

LOS ANGELES ANGELS OF ANAHEIM

Based in Anaheim, Calif., the Angels won a World Series title in 2002, their first appearance in the "Fall Classic."

The Angels began play in 1961 as one of two expansion teams (with the Washington Senators) awarded by Major League Baseball that season—baseball's first additions to either of the two major leagues in 60 years. The Angels were originally based in Los Angeles and were owned by "Singing Cowboy" Gene Autry. The team was renamed the California Angels in 1965. In 1966, after five seasons in Los Angeles—which included a winning year in just their second season of play—they relocated to nearby Anaheim.

Before the 1972 season, the Angels traded six-time All-Star shortstop Jim Fregosi for future Hall of Fame pitcher Nolan Ryan, who went on to throw four of his record seven career no-hitters in an Angels uniform and contributed to the team's first play-off berth in 1979 (on a team managed by Fregosi). The Angels made the play-offs again in 1982 and 1986, but the team failed to advance to the World Series each season after losing series leads of two games to none and three games to one, respectively. The Angels endured another notable collapse in 1995, squandering a record 11½-game divisional lead over the Seattle Mariners with six weeks left in the season.

In 2002 the team, then known as the Anaheim Angels, won their first play-off series as they advanced to the World Series: led by sluggers Garret Anderson, Tim Salmon, and Troy Glaus, the Angels won a dramatic seven-game series over the San Francisco Giants that featured four contests that were decided by one run. With the addition of perennial all-star Vladimir Guerrero in 2004, along with the continued development of young pitchers such as Francisco Rodriguez, the Angels became a yearly play-off contender—winning division titles in 2004, 2005, 2007, 2008, and 2009—and one of baseball's best teams, but they did not match the postseason success of the 2002 Angels squad in those seasons.

Oakland Athletics

Based in Oakland, Calif., the Athletics—who are often simply referred to as the "A's"—have won nine World Series championships and 15 AL pennants.

Founded in 1901 and based in Philadelphia, the A's were one of the original eight members of the AL. The first half century of the franchise's existence was dominated by the iconic Connie Mack, who managed the A's from the team's inaugural year to 1950. The A's posted winning records in their first seven seasons, including AL pennants in 1902 and 1905, the latter of which earned the team its first World Series berth, in which the A's came up on the short end of a five-game series with the New York Giants. The A's returned to the World Series in 1910 and 1911, winning on each occasion behind the pitching of Charles Bender and Eddie Plank, as well as the batting of third baseman Frank "Home Run" Baker, second baseman Eddie Collins, and the other members of the famed "$100,000 infield" (so called because of the purported combined market value of the foursome). This core advanced to two more World Series in 1913 and 1914 (a win over the New York Giants and a loss to the Boston Braves, respectively) before competition from the newly formed Federal League forced Mack to sell off his star players to other teams in order to keep the franchise solvent. As a result, the A's first period of dominance was immediately followed by a woeful stretch of seven consecutive last-place finishes from 1915 to 1921 (including a 117-loss season in 1916).

The year 1925 was extremely significant for the struggling franchise. In addition to the A's finishing that season with their first winning record in a decade, the year saw three future Hall of Famers—first baseman Jimmie Foxx, pitcher Lefty Grove, and catcher Mickey Cochrane—make their debuts with the team, joining a solid core that already featured all-time great outfielder Al Simmons. After finishing in second place behind the powerhouse New York Yankees in 1927 and 1928, the A's won both the AL pennant and the World Series title in 1929 and 1930. The A's lost in their third consecutive trip to the World

Series in 1931 (a seven-game defeat at the hands of the St. Louis Cardinals), which was followed by another slide back to the bottom of the AL. In the 20 seasons between 1935 and 1954, the A's never placed higher than fourth in the league, with 11 last-place finishes. The team's prolonged poor play, combined with the emergence of the crosstown Phillies of the National League, led to increased financial strain on the A's ownership and the sale of the team to an out-of-town businessman in 1954, who in turn moved the A's to Kansas City, Mo., in 1955.

The Athletics did not post a single winning season in their 13 years in Kansas City, and their tenure there was most notable for flamboyant businessman Charlie Finley's purchase of the team in 1960. Finley introduced a number of quirky innovations to the team and its ballpark in an attempt to stimulate attendance, but these failed to have much of an impact, and the resulting loss of income—combined with his clashes with local civic leaders—led Finley to move the team to Oakland in 1968. Propelled by such young greats as outfielder Reggie Jackson and pitchers Catfish Hunter, Vida Blue, and Rollie Fingers, the A's quickly turned the franchise's fortunes around in their new home, winning three consecutive World Series titles from 1972 to 1974. The small-market A's lost most of their big stars with the advent of free agency at the end of the 1976 season, and they entered yet another rebuilding period.

The A's of the 1980s and early 1990s showcased slugger Mark McGwire, closer Dennis Eckersley, and stolen base king Rickey Henderson, and they advanced to three consecutive World Series (1988–90), winning a Bay Area showdown in 1989 over the now-San Francisco Giants. The late 1990s saw the Athletics turn to a new management strategy that focused on acquiring cheaper, less well-known players by giving added weight to in-depth statistical analysis over traditional scouting methods, a strategy that became known by the term "Moneyball" (so named after the title of a best-selling book about A's general manager Billy Beane). Many other franchises began implementing variations of this strategy after Beane built teams that qualified for five postseason berths in a seven-year span (2000–06) while having one of the lowest payrolls in baseball. However, more recent Athletics teams have failed to duplicate this unexpected success.

SEATTLE MARINERS

Based in Seattle, the Mariners were founded in 1977 and posted losing records until 1991 (an all-time mark for the longest period before a franchise's first winning season). The team is one of two current organizations (along with the Washington Nationals) to have never played in the World Series.

Seattle had previously been home to a Major League Baseball franchise for one year in 1969, and when that team—the Pilots, now the Milwaukee Brewers—relocated, local governments sued the AL for damages. In 1976 the league promised an expansion franchise in return for dropping the suit, and the Mariners joined the league alongside the Toronto Blue Jays the next year. The early Mariner teams, featuring players such as 1984 AL Rookie of the Year Alvin Davis and two-time All-Star second baseman Harold Reynolds, struggled mightily and routinely finished near the bottom of the divisional standings.

The team's slow turnaround to respectability had its roots in the debut of centre fielder Ken Griffey, Jr., in 1989. Griffey quickly became the biggest star in the sport, and his ascendance sent fans to the ballpark and made the Mariners competitive. He joined with designated hitter Edgar Martinez, pitcher Randy Johnson, and right fielder Jay Buhner to lead Seattle to winning seasons in 1991 and 1993, but a postseason appearance eluded the team until 1995.

ICHIRO SUZUKI

(b. Oct. 22, 1973, Kasugai, Japan)

Ichiro Suzuki became the first nonpitcher to shift from Japanese professional baseball to the American major leagues when he joined the Seattle Mariners for the 2001 baseball season.

Suzuki played baseball from an early age. Upon finishing high school, he was drafted by the Orix Blue Wave of the Japanese Pacific League. He saw limited action during his first two seasons because his manager disliked the young player's unorthodox batting style—a sort of pendulum motion created by kicking the front foot back and then striding forward with the swing. In 1994 a new manager gave Suzuki a starting spot on the team and let him swing the way he liked. He responded in amazing fashion, lifting his batting average to .400 during the season and finishing at .385—the second best batting mark in the history of Japanese baseball. He collected 210 hits, a record for one season. Through 2000 he won seven consecutive Pacific League batting titles, posted a career average of .353, and led his team to two pennants. He was not a power hitter, but his speed and bat control were unmatched. He was also considered among the top outfielders, with the strongest, most accurate throwing arm in the league. Suzuki threw right-handed but batted left-handed.

By 2000 Suzuki had established himself as the best baseball player in Japan and had begun his quest for stardom in the United States. He spent two weeks in the Mariners' 1999 spring training camp as part of a U.S.-Japan player exchange. A Japanese player in an American lineup was no longer quite the rarity it once had been; several Japanese pitchers, most notably Hideo Nomo and Hideki Irabu, had crossed the Pacific to play in the major leagues. Suzuki became the first nonpitcher to make the transition when he signed a three-year contract with the Mariners in November 2000. Because pitchers in the United States threw harder than their Japanese counterparts, some observers believed that Japanese hitters would struggle at the plate.

Suzuki made his major league debut with the Mariners on April 2, 2001. He answered his critics with a stellar season, capturing the American League Rookie of the Year award and a Gold Glove. His batting average in the 2001 regular season was .350, and it was .421 in the postseason games. In 2004 Suzuki broke George Sisler's 84-year-old

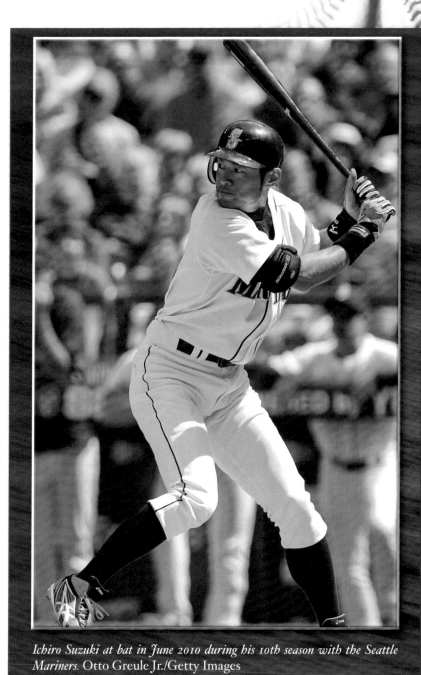

Ichiro Suzuki at bat in June 2010 during his 10th season with the Seattle Mariners. Otto Greule Jr./Getty Images

record for most hits in a single season, ending the year with 262 hits and a .372 batting average. Five years later, in 2009, he became the all-time leader in hits by a Japanese player, with 3,086 for his career in both Japan and the United States, and later in the year he recorded his 2,000th major league hit, reaching that plateau faster than any other player in history except Al Simmons. He collected more than 200 hits—and was named to the AL All-Star team—in each of his first 10 seasons with the Mariners. Not only did his 10 200-hit seasons tie Pete Rose's all-time record, they also set the mark for most consecutive years in which a player reached the 200-hit plateau.

That year, with the team threatened with relocation because of its substandard stadium and declining attendance, the Mariners rallied from an 11½-game deficit to the Anaheim Angels with six weeks left in the regular season to win the AL West title. In the first round of the play-offs, the Mariners staged a similarly dramatic comeback against the New York Yankees: they won the five-game series after having trailed two games to none, with Martinez hitting a two-run series-winning double in the 11th inning of the final game. The team's postseason run ended with a loss to the Cleveland Indians in the AL Championship Series (ALCS), but the renewed fan interest spurred county and state politicians to authorize the construction of a new baseball-only stadium, Safeco Field (which would open in 1999). In 1996 shortstop Alex Rodriguez emerged as yet another superstar in the Seattle lineup, but these talent-laden Mariner teams made just one brief play-off appearance in the next four years.

Seattle returned to the ALCS in 2000, where they lost to the Yankees in six games. In 2001 Japanese hitting sensation Ichiro Suzuki joined the team, and the Mariners—now playing without Johnson, Griffey, and Rodriguez—went on an unlikely run and posted an AL-record 116 wins, but their historic season ended with a second disappointing loss to the Yankees in ALCS. Mariners management then began making a series of poor personnel decisions that led Seattle back to the bottom of its division. In 2008 the Mariners reached an ignoble low as they became the first team to lose 100 games in a season in which they had a payroll of $100 million or more. This debacle led to the hiring of new on-field and general management, and the Mariners began to rebuild in 2009.

Texas Rangers

Currently based in Arlington, Texas, the Rangers began play in 1961 as the Washington (D.C.) Senators and have won one AL pennant (2010).

The Senators finished in last place or tied for last place in each of their first three seasons, and they lost at least 100 games in their first four seasons. Despite the addition of towering slugger Frank Howard before the 1965 season, the Senators did not greatly improve on their ignoble beginning. After the franchise's third last-place finish in 1968, Washington hired all-time great Ted Williams to become the team's manager, despite his never having coached baseball on any level before. Williams guided the Senators to their first winning season (with an 86–76 record) in his inaugural year at the helm, but the team regressed in each of its next two seasons. The Senators' continued subpar play contributed to years of poor attendance and insufficient revenue, and team ownership relocated the franchise to Arlington after the 1971 season.

Renamed in honour of the state's renowned military-cum-police force the Texas Rangers, the team had little more luck in its first year in Arlington than it had experienced in Washington. Not only did the Rangers lose 100 games but Williams—arguably the team's biggest attraction—retired. The Rangers brought in Billy Martin to manage the team toward the end of the 1973 season. The following year, led by recent acquisition Fergie Jenkins's expert pitching, Texas won 84 games and finished in second place in its division. However, the Rangers were never able to break through to a division title for the remainder of the decade.

In the early 1980s third baseman Buddy Bell blossomed into an all-star, but the Rangers did not have much team success, with five of the franchise's six seasons from 1980 to 1985 ending with losing records. Texas added more young talent, such as outfielder Ruben Sierra and second baseman Julio Franco, throughout the decade, but the team's long postseason drought continued into the 1990s. One bright spot of this time was future Hall of Fame pitcher Nolan Ryan, who played with the Rangers from 1989 to 1993 and who pitched his sixth and seventh career no-hitters during his tenure with the team. In 1989 the team was sold to an investment group that included future U.S. president George W. Bush, who would serve as the Rangers' managing general partner until 1994.

By the mid-1990s the Rangers had amassed a lineup full of powerful hitters, including catcher Iván Rodríguez, outfielder Juan Gonzalez, and first baseman Rafael Palmeiro, and they won three AL West titles (1996, 1998, 1999) in four years. Texas's first forays into the postseason were disappointments, however, as it lost decisively to the New York Yankees in the first round of the play-offs each year. In 2001 the team made headlines when star shortstop Alex Rodriguez signed for a then record $252 million over 10 years, despite the fact that the Rangers had finished a distant last place in their division the previous year. His presence failed to raise the Rangers out of the divisional cellar in his three seasons with the team, and Texas traded him to the Yankees in 2004 in order to begin a rebuilding process. Ryan was hired to serve as team president in 2008 (and became part of the team's ownership group in

2010), and a Rangers squad stocked with both promising prospects and established veterans such as third baseman Michael Young surged back into the postseason in 2010 after capturing the AL West title. The Rangers then ran off the first two play-off series wins in franchise history to capture the AL pennant and advance to the World Series, which they lost to the San Francisco Giants.

THE NATIONAL LEAGUE (NL)

The National League is the oldest existing major-league professional baseball organization in the United States. The league began play in 1876 as the National League of Professional Baseball Clubs, replacing the failed National Association of Professional Base Ball Players. The National League consists of 16 teams aligned in three divisions. In the NL East are the Atlanta Braves, Florida Marlins, New York Mets, Philadelphia Phillies, and Washington (D.C.) Nationals. In the NL Central are the Chicago Cubs, Cincinnati Reds, Houston Astros, Milwaukee Brewers, Pittsburgh Pirates, and St. Louis Cardinals. In the NL West are the Arizona Diamondbacks, Colorado Rockies, Los Angeles Dodgers, San Diego Padres, and San Francisco Giants.

NL East

Atlanta Braves

Based in Atlanta, the Braves are the only existing major league franchise to have played every season since professional baseball came into existence. They have won three World Series titles (1914, 1957, 1995) and 17 National League pennants.

The franchise was founded by Ivers Whitney Adams in 1871 as the Boston Red Stockings, one of nine charter members of the National Association of Professional Baseball Players, the forerunner of the NL. During its 82-year stay in Boston, the team was known by various nicknames, including Red Stockings, Red Caps, Rustlers, and Bees, finally settling on Braves. While in Boston, the team won 4 National Association pennants (1872–75), 10 NL pennants, and a memorable World Series championship in 1914 that came after a season in which the Braves were in last place as late as July 15—a turnaround that led to the nickname "Miracle Braves." In 1948 the Braves reached the World Series largely as a result of their two dominant pitchers, Warren Spahn and Johnny Spain, who inspired the slogan "Spahn and Spain and pray for rain."

After losing many of their fans to Boston's American League team (Red Sox) by the early 1950s, owing in part to the Braves posting a losing record in all but 12 of the 38 seasons since their World Series win, the franchise moved to Milwaukee, Wis., in 1953. Playing in Milwaukee County Stadium, the restructured team quickly improved, winning two pennants (1957, 1958) and a World Series (1957), behind the hitting of Hank Aaron and Eddie Matthews and the pitching of Spahn and Lew Burdette. The Braves finished with a winning record in each of their 13 seasons in Milwaukee, but their success could not prevent a precipitous decline in ballpark attendance in the 1960s, which led to the team moving to Atlanta after the 1965 season.

In 1976 the team was purchased by media entrepreneur Ted Turner, who began airing all the Braves' games to a national audience on his cable "superstation," WTCG (WTBS, or TBS, from 1979). While many criticized TBS's prominent coverage of the recently poor team with a mostly regional appeal as both unnecessary and overly biased—the station blithely billed the Braves as "America's Team"—the Braves' national profile was nonetheless raised by the broadcasts, and the team eventually became one of the more popular in the country. After suffering through many dreadful seasons and only making the play-offs twice (1969, 1982) in its first 25 seasons in Atlanta, the team was revitalized in the 1990s under the leadership of general manager John Schuerholz and manager Bobby Cox. This new Braves team was led by the young pitching trio of Greg Maddux, Tom Glavine, and John Smoltz—each of whom won at least one Cy Young Award with the Braves—and hitters such as David Justice and Chipper Jones. During the 1990s and early 2000s, the Braves had one of the most remarkable runs in U.S. sports history, winning an unprecedented 14 consecutive division titles from 1991 to 2005 (with the exception of the 1994 season, which was not finished owing to a labour dispute), playing in the World Series five times in the 1990s, and winning the organization's third World Series championship in 1995. In 2007 Time Warner (which had acquired the team in a 1996 merger with Turner Broadcasting System) sold the Braves, and TBS stopped its national broadcasts of the team's games.

FLORIDA MARLINS

Based in Miami, the Marlins have won two NL pennants and two World Series championships (1997, 2003).

Founded in 1993 as an expansion team alongside the Colorado Rockies, the Marlins, unsurprisingly, got off to a slow start, posting losing records in each of their first four seasons but improving each year. The Marlins had their first winning record in 1997 and qualified for the postseason as the NL wild card winner (as owner of the best record for a non-division-winning team in the NL). Led by the play of pitcher Livan Hernandez, outfielder Gary Sheffield, second baseman Luis Castillo, and catcher Charles Johnson, Florida defeated the San Francisco Giants and the Atlanta Braves in the NL play-offs to earn a berth in the World Series in just its fifth year of existence. The Marlins then beat the Cleveland Indians in a seven-game Series that was won by a single in the bottom of the 11th inning in the deciding game. Despite winning the Series, the Marlins claimed to be losing money, and a great number of the key players on the Series-winning squad were traded away by the middle of the following season, and the Marlins lost 108 games in 1998.

The Marlins continued to field low-payroll teams that struggled on the field through the beginning of the 21st century. In 2003 they again qualified for the postseason as the league's wild card entrant and advanced to the World Series. Young pitchers Josh Beckett and Brad Penny starred for the Marlins in their second Series, and the team defeated the favoured New York Yankees in six games to win a second title. Florida again cut its payroll after winning the championship, and, while the team's slide was not as precipitous as it was in 1998, the Marlins nevertheless missed the play-offs in 2004. Since 2003 the Marlins have been notable for cultivating talented young players, such as outfielder and third baseman Miguel Cabrera and shortstop Hanley Ramirez, but they have not yet been able to return to the postseason.

NEW YORK METS

Based in Flushing, Queens, N.Y., the Mets have won two World Series championships (1969, 1986) and four NL pennants.

The Mets trace their roots to the proposed Continental League, whose formation was announced in 1959 by New York attorney Bill Shea; a New York-based team was to be a charter member of the league. The league was abandoned in 1960 when it was promised two teams each in the American and National Leagues as part of professional baseball's expansion. The organization was formed in 1961, and the name Mets was chosen over several other suggestions because it was short and easy, similar to the corporate name (the New York Metropolitan Baseball Club Inc.), widely accepted by fans, and reminiscent of an earlier New York baseball team, the Metropolitans of the 19th century American Association (AA). The team, also known as the Amazin' Mets or the Amazins, began play in 1962 at the Polo Grounds; after two seasons they moved into the brand-new Shea Stadium.

Early Mets rosters were populated with popular New York ballplayers from a bygone era—over-the-hill veterans such as Gil Hodges, Duke Snider, and Yogi Berra—coached by Casey Stengel, the Yankees manager during their string of five consecutive World Series championships (1949–53). This nostalgic effort did not translate into success on the field, and the team earned the nickname "Lovable Losers," losing a record 120 games in its first season.

The 1969 team, with future Hall of Fame pitchers Tom Seaver and Nolan Ryan, won an improbable World Series championship, beating the favoured Baltimore Orioles in the World Series, and came to be known as the "Miracle Mets," having trailed the Chicago Cubs by 9.5 games in mid-August in the NL East. With famed centre fielder Willie Mays joining the team in 1972, the Mets returned to the World Series in 1973 but lost to the Oakland Athletics in seven games (the team's rallying cry that year—"Ya Gotta Believe!"—was coined by pitcher Tug McGraw in July when the team was well under .500). The rest of the decade the team posted a mediocre record.

In the 1980s the Mets were rejuvenated by a group of young pitchers including Dwight ("Doc") Gooden, Jesse Orosco, and Sid Fernandez and powerful hitters such as Darryl Strawberry and Gary Carter. In 1986 the team won 108 games and its second World Series, beating the Boston Red Sox in a legendary series, best remembered for first

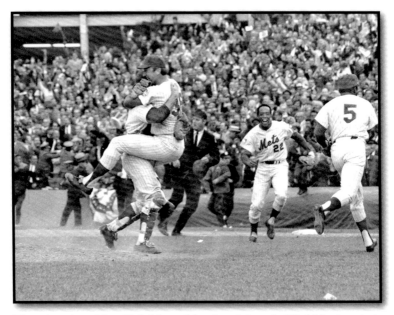

The triumphant New York Mets celebrating their 1969 World Series win in game five against the Baltimore Orioles. NY Daily News via Getty Images

baseman Bill Buckner's error in the 10th inning of game six that allowed the Mets to steal an improbable victory and then go on to claim the championship with another comeback win in game seven.

Substance abuse plagued some of the most talented young Mets stars (including Gooden and Strawberry), and, though the team won the NL East in 1988, it failed to reach the World Series in the rest of the 1980s or in the 1990s. The early 1990s saw the franchise fall on hard times; it lost 103 games in 1993, posting its worst season since 1965. By the late 1990s, however, the team became stronger, and in 2000 it reached the World Series, led by slugging catcher Mike Piazza, though the Mets lost to their crosstown rival, the Yankees, in what was named the "Subway Series." The Mets again made the play-offs in 2006, but the following year they missed the postseason after losing a seven-game lead with 17 games left in a dramatic late-season collapse.

In 2008 the Mets missed out once again on a play-off spot after leading their division for most of August, becoming the first team in major league history to be eliminated from postseason contention in consecutive years by losing their final regular-season game at home. One bright spot at this time was the opening of the team's new stadium, Citi Field, in 2009.

Philadelphia Phillies

Based in Philadelphia, the Phillies have won seven NL pennants and two World Series titles (1980 and 2008) and are the oldest continuously run, single-name, single-city franchise in American professional sports.

The Phillies were founded in 1883 and were informally known as both the Quakers and the Phillies (a shortened version of "Philadelphians") until they officially adopted the Phillies name in 1890. The team was not an early success and first qualified for the play-offs in 1915, behind the pitching of all-time great Grover Cleveland Alexander. Philadelphia traded Alexander after the 1917 season and entered into a period of prolonged failure that saw the team finish last or second to last in the NL in 24 of the 30 seasons from 1919 to 1947. In 1950 star outfielder Richie Ashburn and pitcher Robin Roberts led a Phillies team of "Whiz Kids" to their first berth in the World Series in 35 years, where they were swept by the New York Yankees.

The Phillies began another extended play-off drought after 1950, during part of which (1963–69) the unpredictable behaviour of temperamental slugger Dick Allen kept things interesting. The team began a turnaround in 1972, when future Hall of Famers Mike Schmidt and Steve Carlton made their Phillies debuts. Behind Carlton's dominant pitching and Schmidt's timely power hitting, the Phillies experienced the most prolonged period of success in franchise history, winning six NL East titles

STEVE CARLTON

(b. Dec. 22, 1944, Miami, Fla., U.S.)

In 1983 Steve Carlton became the second pitcher to surpass Walter Johnson's career record of 3,508 strikeouts (Nolan Ryan was the first).

Steven Norman Carlton pitched for Miami-Dade, a junior college in Florida, before the left-hander signed a contract with the St. Louis Cardinals in 1965. After a stint in the minor leagues, he moved up to the Cardinals in 1966. He was a three-time all-star in St. Louis, but a salary dispute with team management resulted in Carlton being traded to the Philadelphia Phillies after the 1971 season.

Carlton came into his own while pitching for the Phillies: he captured the pitching Triple Crown in his first season in Philadelphia—leading the National League in earned run average (1.97), wins (27), and strikeouts (310)—and won the NL Cy Young Award as the league's best pitcher. He went on to lead the league in strikeouts four more times (1974, 1980, 1982, 1983) and placed in the top 10 in NL strikeouts 16 times over the course of his 24-season career. A workhorse pitcher, Carlton also finished atop the league in innings pitched on five occasions. He won the NL Cy Young Award three more times (1977, 1980, 1982) before he left the Phillies in 1986.

Although he announced his retirement in 1986 after recording his 4,000th strikeout (while with the San Francisco Giants), Carlton continued to play, pitching for several teams until 1988. His 329 wins were the ninth highest total in major league history at the time of his retirement. Carlton amassed 4,136 strikeouts during his career, an amount exceeded only by Nolan Ryan, Randy Johnson, and Roger Clemens. Carlton was inducted into the Baseball Hall of Fame in 1994.

between 1976 and 1983. Though the team advanced to the World Series only twice in those years, it won the franchise's only world championship, in 1980. In 1993 the Phillies returned to the World Series only to lose to the Toronto Blue Jays on Joe Carter's dramatic series-winning home run in game six.

The Phillies set an ignoble mark in 2007, when they became the first franchise in sporting history to lose its

10,000th game. The 2007 season ended on a bright note, however, as the Phillies won their first NL East title in 14 years. The Phillies repeated as division champions in 2008, and they advanced to the World Series behind the dominant pitching of Cole Hamels and Brad Lidge. There they defeated the Tampa Bay Rays in five games to win the franchise's second World Series title in its history. In 2009 the Phillies won their second consecutive NL pennant but lost to the New York Yankees in the World Series.

WASHINGTON NATIONALS

Based in Washington, D.C., the Nationals are one of two current major league franchises—along with the Seattle Mariners—to have never played in the World Series.

The franchise was based in Montreal and known as the Expos (after Expo 67, the world's fair held in the city in 1967) for the first 36 years of its existence. Founded in 1969, the Expos were one of four teams to join Major League Baseball that year. Montreal lost 110 games in its first season to finish at the bottom of its division and tie for the worst record in the major leagues (with the San Diego Padres), and the team continued to finish in the lower half of the NL East throughout its first decade. During this time the franchise's most beloved player was outfielder Rusty Staub (the first Expo to have his number retired), whose red hair earned him the nickname "Le Grand Orange." In 1979, under the guidance of future Hall of Fame manager Dick Williams, the Expos posted their first winning season and finished only two games out of a division title. Behind star players such as catcher Gary Carter and outfielders Andre Dawson and Tim Raines, the Expos advanced to their first postseason appearance two years later during the strike-shortened 1981 season. That year they won their first-round series against the Philadelphia Phillies before losing to the eventual world champion Los Angeles Dodgers as the result of a ninth-inning home run in the deciding fifth game of the NL Championship Series.

For the remainder of the 1980s, Montreal fielded teams that usually finished their seasons with winning percentages within a few games of .500. In the early 1990s the Expos amassed a roster filled with young talent—such as outfielders Moises Alou, Marquis Grissom, and Larry Walker, as well as pitcher Pedro Martínez—that led to a rapid ascent toward the top of the divisional standings. After finishing the 1993 season three games out of first place, Montreal posted a league-best 74–40 record in 1994 only to have the remainder of the season canceled over a labour dispute, cutting short the team's best chance to win a division title. By the time Major League Baseball renewed play in 1995, Montreal had lost much of its young talent through free agency or trades in the off-season, and the Expos ended the year at the bottom of the NL East standings. In 1996 the team called up future all-star slugger Vladimir Guererro, but his late-season addition was not enough to push the Expos past the Atlanta Braves in their division. The Expos then began a prolonged period of subpar play that coincided with a decrease in home-game attendance and complaints by team ownership about the Expos' home stadium, which led to questions about the stability of the team's tenure in Montreal.

In 2001 the Expos were one of two teams (with the Minnesota Twins) that commissioner Bud Selig proposed for elimination from the major leagues in an effort to raise revenue throughout the sport. The team was then sold to MLB in 2002. A Minnesota court order effectively ended the threat of contraction in the major leagues, so MLB pursued relocating the franchise. The Expos played a handful of their "home" games in San Juan, P.R., in 2003 and 2004 while MLB courted suitors from different North

American cities. In 2005 the Expos moved to Washington, D.C., and became known as the Nationals. The Nationals have routinely fielded some of the worst teams in the NL, including one that posted a 102-loss season in 2008.

NL Central

Chicago Cubs

Based in Chicago, the Cubs have won 10 NL pennants and two World Series titles (1907, 1908). Despite their limited success, the Cubs—who are also known as the "North Siders" in reference to their home stadium's location on Chicago's north side—have one of the most loyal fan bases and are among the most popular franchises in baseball.

The team, originally known as the Chicago White Stockings, was a charter member of the NL in 1876 and had quick success. Led by Cap Anson, the team won 6 of the NL's first 11 championships. Before adopting the name Cubs in 1903 (the Cubs name was first associated with the team the previous year), the team was known by a variety of names, including the Colts and the Orphans. The Cubs' best season came in 1906, when they won 116 games and posted a .763 winning percentage, although they lost to the crosstown rival Chicago White Sox in the World Series. However, the 1907 and 1908 World Series titles were captured by the Cubs—the first team to win consecutive World Series.

In 1916 the Cubs moved into Weeghman Park (opened 1914), which in 1926 was renamed Wrigley Field and is today the second oldest baseball stadium still in use (Boston's Fenway Park opened in 1912). During the 1910s and '20s the team enjoyed limited success, winning NL titles in 1910 and 1918. From 1929 to 1938 the Cubs dominated the NL, winning four pennants (1929, 1932,

1935, and 1938) behind the strong play of centre fielder Hack Wilson, catcher Gabby Hartnett, and second baseman Rogers Hornsby. The 1932 World Series produced one of baseball's legendary moments—Babe Ruth's "called shot," when the New York Yankees slugger allegedly pointed to centre field and promptly hit a home run to that very spot.

After the 1938 season the Cubs had only one winning year until 1945, when they won the NL pennant. That year's World Series launched what has become known as the "Curse of the Billy Goat" (versions of the story vary). In the fourth game of the World Series, tavern owner Billy Sianis was forced to leave Wrigley Field after showing up with his goat; upon his ejection, Sianis cursed the franchise. Since 1945 the Cubs have failed to return to the World Series.

Post-1945 Cubs history is distinguished primarily by disappointment on an epic scale. In 1969 the Cubs were first in their division (then the NL East) throughout most of the season, leading it by as many as eight and a half games in mid-August before collapsing at the end of the season and falling to eight games behind the New York Mets, who went on to win the World Series. In 1984 the Cubs looked set to break their World Series drought, but, with the Cubs leading in the fifth and decisive game of the National League Championship Series (NLCS) against the San Diego Padres, a ground ball went through first baseman Leon Durham's legs, helping the Padres defeat the Cubs. In 2003 the Cubs again appeared to be headed for a World Series, leading three games to two over the Florida Marlins in the NLCS. Five outs away from making it to the World Series, the Cubs missed the chance at another out when fan interference blocked an attempted catch by outfielder Moises Alou of a pop foul near the stands (the so-called Bartman incident).

HARRY CARAY

Harry Caray leads the crowd in singing "Take Me Out to the Ballgame" at Chicago's Wrigley Field. Vincent Laforet/AFP/Getty Images

(b. March 1, 1914, St. Louis, Mo., U.S.—d. Feb. 18, 1998, Rancho Mirage, Calif.)

The sportscaster Harry Caray gained national prominence for his telecasts of Chicago Cubs baseball games on Chicago-based superstation WGN during the 1980s and 1990s.

After failing to become a professional baseball player out of high school, Harry Christopher Carabina sold gym equipment before turning his eye to broadcasting. In 1943 he got his first job calling minor league games for a radio station in Joliet, Ill. He moved on to Kalamazoo, Mich., where he started using his famous home run call, "It might be...it could be...it is! A home run!" Having changed his name to the more radio-friendly Caray, he started his major league broadcasting career in 1945 with the St. Louis Cardinals. After working for 25 years with the Cardinals, he had a brief one-year stint with the Oakland Athletics in 1970 before moving to Chicago, where he broadcast for the Chicago White Sox for 11 seasons and then with the Chicago Cubs from 1982 until 1997. Caray broadcast more than 8,300 baseball games in his 53-year career.

Wearing oversized thick-rimmed eyeglasses and using the expression "Holy cow" to begin his description of on-the-field plays that caught his attention, Caray became extremely popular throughout the United States. At the Cubs home park, Wrigley Field, he led the fans in singing "Take Me Out to the Ballgame" during the seventh-inning stretch. This tradition was actually started in 1976 during Caray's tenure with the White Sox. His unique style included unintentionally mispronouncing players' names, making outrageous comments that were often unrelated to the action on the field, and being both an outspoken critic and an unabashed fan of the home team. In 1989 Caray was presented with the Ford C. Frick Award and was enshrined in the broadcasters wing of the Baseball Hall of Fame. Both Caray's son Skip and his grandson Chip followed in his footsteps as baseball play-by-play announcers.

The Cubs ended up losing the game—and the series. Despite these disappointments, in 2008 the Cubs became only the second team in major league baseball history to record 10,000 wins. The Cubs won their second straight NL Central Division title in 2008, marking the first time in 100 years that the team qualified for the play-offs in two consecutive seasons.

The Cubs franchise has produced numerous Hall of Famers, including the double-play combination of shortstop Joe Tinker (1902–12, 1916), second baseman Johnny Evers (1902–13), and first baseman Frank Chance (1898–1912). Other notable Hall of Famers are infielder Ernie Banks ("Mr. Cub"), who spent his entire career (1953–71) with the team, hitting 512 home runs; outfielder Billy Williams (1959–74); second baseman Ryne Sandberg (1982–94, 1996–97); and pitcher Ferguson ("Fergie") Jenkins (1966–73, 1982–83). Ron Santo, the team's third baseman from 1960 to 1973, is among the most popular Cubs players not inducted into the Hall of Fame.

Among the most hallowed traditions at Wrigley Field home games is the seventh-inning stretch. Famed sports broadcaster Harry Caray led the singing of "Take Me Out to the Ballgame" from 1982 until 1997 (he died in February 1998); guest "conductors" now lead the crowd.

CINCINNATI REDS

Based in Cincinnati, Ohio, the Reds were founded in 1882 and have won five World Series titles (1919, 1940, 1975, 1976, 1990) and nine NL pennants.

The city of Cincinnati lays claim to hosting the first truly professional baseball team, called the Red Stockings, which began play in 1869 and was undefeated in its first 81 games against amateur clubs. Another Cincinnati-based team by the same name was one of the founding members of the NL in 1876, but this team was expelled from the league in 1880 for playing games on Sunday and allowing liquor on the grounds of its ballpark. While 1882—the year a Red Stockings club that featured a few members of the banned NL squad joined the newly formed American Association—is officially recognized by Major League Baseball as the current franchise's first year, most Cincinnatians nevertheless consider the Reds the oldest franchise in baseball, and the Reds organization itself includes these earlier clubs in the team history.

The Red Stockings finished atop the AA in their first season and posted winning records in most of their eight years in the league. The team moved back to the NL in 1890, which was the same year it shortened its nickname to "Reds." Cincinnati fielded a number of mediocre teams through the end of the 19th century and the beginning of the 20th, never finishing higher than third place in the NL until 1919. The 1919 squad won 96 games behind outfielder Edd Roush and pitcher Dolf Luque on its way to the franchise's first World Series berth. The Reds won the World Series five games to three over the Chicago White Sox, but their championship was tarnished when eight of Chicago's players were accused of having taken bribes to throw the series. Cincinnati's success was short-lived, however, and in the mid-1920s the team returned to the bottom of the NL for a long stretch, including four straight last-place finishes from 1931 to 1934.

In 1938 the Reds' young star pitcher Johnny Vander Meer became the only player in baseball history to throw

The Cincinnati Red Stockings, lithograph, 1869. Library of Congress, Washington,D.C. (digital file no. 3g01291u.)

no-hitters in consecutive starts. Vander Meer was a part of a nucleus of players that also included future Hall of Fame catcher Ernie Lombardi and that led the Reds to NL pennants in 1939 and 1940, as well as a World Series win in the latter season. By the middle of the decade, the Reds again found themselves routinely finishing in the bottom half of the NL.

Fearing association with communism at the height of the Red Scare in the United States, the team officially changed its nickname to "Redlegs" from 1954 to 1959. During this period one of the Reds' few bright spots was Ted ("Big Klu") Kluszewski, a power-hitting first baseman who famously cut the sleeves off his uniform to free his huge biceps. In 1956 Cincinnati called up outfielder Frank Robinson from the minor leagues, and he quickly became one of the biggest stars in the game. Robinson led the Reds to a pennant in 1961 (which was followed by a loss to the New York Yankees in the World Series), but in 1965 he was traded to the Baltimore Orioles for three players of relatively little consequence in what is considered by many observers to be one of the worst trades in the history of the game.

Baseball in the 1970s was dominated by Cincinnati teams known as the "Big Red Machine," which had left behind Crosley Field, with its distinctive left field terrace, for a new home, Riverfront Stadium. Boasting a regular lineup that featured three future Hall of Famers (catcher Johnny Bench, second baseman Joe Morgan, and first baseman Tony Pérez) as well as all-time major league hits leader Pete Rose, the Big Red Machine—under the guidance of manager Sparky Anderson—won five division titles in the first seven years of the decade. The Machine's first two trips to the World Series ended in disappointment, however, as it lost to Robinson's Orioles in 1970 and the Oakland Athletics in 1972, which was followed by a surprising loss to the underdog New York Mets in the 1973 NL Championship Series. The years of frustration ended in 1975, when the Reds won a remarkable 108 games and beat the Boston Red Sox for the franchise's first World Series title in 35 years. While the 1976 Reds won six fewer games than their 1975 counterparts, they led major league baseball in all the major offensive statistical categories and swept both teams they faced in the postseason en route to a second consecutive championship, leading a number of baseball historians to claim that they were the second greatest team ever, after the famed 1927 Yankees.

The Reds closed out the 1970s with two second-place divisional finishes and an NL Championship Series loss in 1979, but they missed out on the postseason in each season of the following decade. The team's most notable event of the 1980s was the 1989 lifetime ban from baseball of then manager Rose for gambling on the sport.

In 1990 the Reds surprisingly rebounded from their turbulent 1989 by winning their division after having never fallen out of first place for the entire season, the first time the feat had occurred in NL history. Behind first-year manager Lou Piniella, all-star shortstop Barry Larkin, and a motley crew of relief pitchers known as the "Nasty Boys," the Reds swept Oakland to win the franchise's fifth World Series.

Cincinnati fielded a few competitive teams through 1999, but the Reds of the first decade of the 21st century finished most of their seasons with losing records. In 2003 the Reds got a new home, the Great American Ball Park.

In 2010 the Reds ended a 15-year play-off drought— and surprised most baseball observers—by winning a divisional title after having placed no higher than third in their division in the previous nine seasons.

HOUSTON ASTROS

Based in Houston, the Astros won an NL pennant in 2005.

The team was founded in 1962 and was initially known as the Houston Colt .45s, taking its name from the famous sidearm of the American West. The team was at first fairly poor, as it finished among the bottom three positions in the NL in its first seven seasons. Perhaps the most notable occurrence during this period was the 1965 opening of the team's new home stadium, the Astrodome, named for Houston's role as a centre for the National Aeronautics and Space Administration. The Astrodome was the world's first multipurpose domed sports stadium, and it was billed as the ballpark of the future. Its opening was a national media sensation, and the team adopted its current nickname to become more readily identified with the newly famous stadium.

In 1970 the Astros called up outfielder César Cedeño, who went on to earn All-Star honours four times and become the team's first superstar (though fans of the early Houston teams might argue the case of diminutive power hitter Jimmy ["the Toy Cannon"] Wynn). He was joined by fellow All-Star outfielder José Cruz in 1975, but the Astros remained relatively unsuccessful throughout the 1970s, finishing higher than third in their division on just one occasion in the decade (second place in 1979). In 1980 the Astros signed pitching ace Nolan Ryan, who helped the team to its first postseason berth the following autumn. Houston was eliminated that year by the eventual champion Philadelphia Phillies in a dramatic five-game NL Championship Series that featured four extra-inning contests, including the deciding game. The Astros returned to the play-offs in the following strike-shortened 1981 season, but they fell to the Los Angeles Dodgers in another series that extended to the maximum five games. Future Cy Young Award winner Mike Scott was acquired in 1983, and he teamed with Ryan to give the Astros one of the most formidable pair of starting pitchers in the NL. In 1986 Houston earned another berth in the NLCS, where it was defeated by the New York Mets in six games. The series was notable for its LCS-record 16-inning game six, as well as for the fact that Scott was named Most Valuable Player of the series despite having played for the losing side.

Houston was a middle-of-the-pack team for the remainder of the 1980s and the early 1990s. But starting in 1993, it posted seven consecutive winning seasons and made three postseason appearances, led by the play of first baseman Jeff Bagwell and catcher–second baseman Craig Biggio, a pair known by Houston fans as "the Killer B's." The Astros were eliminated in the opening round of each of their three play-off appearances in 1997–99, and even after the team added a third star "B" in 1999—outfielder (and later first baseman) Lance Berkman—it remained unable to progress any farther until the mid-2000s. The team left the Astrodome in 2000 to begin play in Enron Field (later Minute Maid Park). In 2004 the Astros advanced to the NLCS, where they lost a seven-game series to the St. Louis Cardinals. The team finally met with a modest amount of play-off luck the following year as it defeated the Cardinals in an NLCS rematch to earn a place in the first World Series in franchise history. The Astros were swept by the Chicago White Sox in the 2005 Series, and, despite often fielding competitive teams, have not returned to the postseason since.

MILWAUKEE BREWERS

Based in Milwaukee, Wis., the Brewers spent their first 29 seasons (1969–97) in the American League.

The team that would become the Brewers was founded in 1969 in Seattle as the Pilots. After an inaugural season that was unsuccessful both financially and on the baseball diamond, the franchise was moved to Milwaukee (which had been home to the Braves baseball franchise from 1953 to 1965), where it took on the name of a long-standing local minor league team, the Brewers. The Brewers struggled initially, posting a losing record in each of their first eight seasons in Milwaukee. The arrival of future Hall of Fame shortstop Robin Yount in 1974 heralded the beginning of a slow turnaround for the Brewers, which was further bolstered in 1978 by the debut of another future Hall of Famer, infielder–designated hitter Paul Molitor. The Brewers ran off three consecutive winning seasons before claiming their first division title in 1981. They won their only AL pennant the following year, advancing to the World Series, where they lost to the St. Louis Cardinals in seven games.

After their World Series appearance, the Brewers entered a period of sustained mediocrity, during which they finished no higher than third in their division for nine straight seasons. In 1992 the Brewers won 92 games and finished second to the eventual-champion Toronto Blue Jays in the AL East, but 12 consecutive losing seasons followed. With the addition of two expansion teams in 1998, Major League Baseball asked the Brewers to switch from the AL to the NL, and Milwaukee became the first team in the 20th century to change leagues. The team began playing in a new stadium, Miller Park, in 2001. In 2008 the Brewers—led by sluggers Prince Fielder and Ryan Braun and dominant pitchers CC Sabathia and Ben Sheets—won 90 games and qualified for the postseason as the NL Wild Card (as owner of the best record for a team that did not win its division title), the team's first play-off appearance since 1982.

PITTSBURGH PIRATES

Based in Pittsburgh, Pa., the Pirates are among the oldest teams in baseball and have won the World Series five times (1909, 1925, 1960, 1971, 1979).

The team that would become the Pirates was founded as the Pittsburgh Alleghenys in 1882 and played in the American Association before moving to the National League in 1887. League officials accused the Alleghenys of using "piratical" tactics to steal talented players from opposing teams, and the ball club embraced the label and in 1891 officially adopted the name Pirates.

Shortstop and Pittsburgh-area native Honus Wagner was among the team's early standouts, playing with the Pirates from 1900 to 1917. The winner of eight batting titles and a member of the first group of players inducted into the Baseball Hall of Fame, Wagner led the Pirates to three straight pennants at the turn of the 20th century and to an appearance in the first World Series (1903), which Pittsburgh lost to the Boston Red Sox in eight games.

The Pirates won their first World Series title in 1909, but the team struggled in the 1910s before returning to the World Series to defeat the Washington Senators in 1925. They reached the World Series again in 1927 but lost to a standout New York Yankees squad that featured Babe Ruth and Lou Gehrig.

Less successful years followed, but the Pirates, led by future Hall of Fame member Roberto Clemente, won the 1960 World Series dramatically with Bill Mazeroski's game-winning home run in the ninth inning of the seventh game. In the 1970s the Pirates left Forbes Field, their home for more than 60 years, to play in Three Rivers Stadium, where the power hitting of Willie Stargell and Dave Parker helped them clinch the NL East six times and win World Series championships in 1971 and 1979. In the mid-1980s the Pirates acquired sluggers Barry Bonds and Bobby Bonilla, and the team finished atop the NL East three consecutive seasons (1990–92) but failed to advance to the World Series each year. Bonds signed with the San Francisco Giants as a free agent after the 1992 season, and

HONUS WAGNER

(b. Feb. 24, 1874, Mansfield [now Carnegie], Pa., U.S.—d. Dec. 6, 1955, Carnegie, Pa.)

Honus Wagner was one of the first five men elected to the Baseball Hall of Fame (1936). He is generally considered the greatest shortstop in baseball history and is regarded by some as the finest all-around player in the history of the National League.

A right-handed batter and thrower, John Peter Wagner had a bulky physique for his era—he stood about 6 feet (1.83 metres) tall and weighed 200 pounds (91 kg)—and had unusually long arms. He was, however, very fast as a base runner and as a defensive player. Wagner played for the short-lived Louisville Colonels franchise from 1897 through 1899, when he was traded to the Pittsburgh Pirates. He topped the NL in extra-base hits in his first season in Pittsburgh and posted a league-leading and career-high .381 batting average. Wagner went on to lead the NL in batting average seven more times, and he hit at least .330 in each season between 1899 and 1909. In 1901 he led the Pirates to the first of three consecutive NL pennants, the last of which gave the Pirates a berth in the first World Series, a loss to the Boston Red Sox. Wagner helped the Pirates to the first World Series title in their franchise history in 1909.

He retired in 1917, finishing his 21-year career with a lifetime batting average of .328 and 3,420 hits. Playing at the height of the "dead-ball" era, he never amassed large home run totals (his career high, which he reached twice, was 10), but he was a prodigious power hitter for the time, leading the league in slugging percentage on six occasions. Wagner's total of 252 triples is the greatest ever attained by an NL player. He also retired with 722 stolen bases, which was the second highest total in major league history at the time. Wagner managed the Pirates briefly in 1917, was a coach on the team from 1933 to 1951, and remained a popular figure in Pittsburgh.

the Pirates (who began playing in PNC Park in 2001) have not fielded a winning team since his departure. In 2009 the Pirates had their 17th straight losing season, a record for a professional franchise in the four major North American sports leagues.

St. Louis Cardinals

Based in St. Louis, Mo., the Cardinals were founded in 1882, and they have won 10 World Series titles and 21 league pennants. Second only to the New York Yankees in World Series championships, St. Louis is the oldest major league team west of the Mississippi River and one of baseball's most consistently successful franchises.

Originally known as the Brown Stockings (1882) and the Browns (1883–98) and playing in the American Association, the franchise met with almost immediate success, winning four consecutive AA pennants from 1885 to 1888. In 1892 the team moved to the NL, where it struggled, finishing in last or second to last place in five of their first seven seasons in the new league. In 1900 the franchise became known as the Cardinals after one year with the nickname "Perfectos." The team continued to play poorly through the first two decades of the 20th century, but in 1915 it added future Hall of Fame infielder Rogers Hornsby, who sparked a Cardinals turnaround. In 1926 Hornsby guided the team to its first pennant in 38 years and a berth in the World Series, where the "Cards" defeated the New York Yankees in seven games. Another all-time great infielder, Frankie Frisch, led the Cardinals to three World Series appearances between 1928 and 1931, including one series win (1931). In 1934 future Hall of Fame pitcher Dizzy Dean (born Jay Hanna Dean) won 30 games (and his brother Paul won 19) for a charismatic World Series-winning Cardinals team with a rough-and-tumble style that earned it the nickname "the Gashouse Gang."

In 1941 Stan Musial joined the club. Musial became arguably the Cardinals' most beloved star, playing 22 seasons in St. Louis and leading the team during the most

Dizzy Dean. Encyclopædia Britannica, Inc.

successful period in franchise history. The Cardinals teams of the 1940s finished first or second in the NL standings in every year of the decade save one. They appeared in four World Series over that span and won three of them (1942, 1944, 1946), the last of which was famous for outfielder Enos Slaughter breaking an eighth-inning tie with the Boston Red Sox in the deciding seventh game by scoring from first base on a line drive over the shortstop's head—a tremendous demonstration of hustle that became known as the "Mad Dash."

After a period of relative decline in the 1950s, the 1960s brought another Cardinals renaissance. Led by the dynamic pitching of Bob Gibson and the speedy Lou Brock, the Cardinals played in three seven-game World Series in the decade, with their series wins in 1964 and 1967 coming against the Yankees and the Red Sox, respectively. The Cardinals' 1964 championship was notable for ending the Yankees' remarkable mid-century dynasty that saw the New York team win 14 pennants in 16 seasons. In 1966 the team moved into Busch Memorial Stadium (renamed Busch Stadium in 1982), which would serve as the franchise's home until 2005. In 1970 the Cardinals traded away outfielder Curt Flood, who then sued Major League Baseball to challenge the club's ability to trade him without his permission, which later led to the establishment of free agency. The outstanding defensive shortstop Ozzie Smith joined the team in 1982 and helped them win the World Series in his first year in St. Louis. Smith's Cardinal teams returned twice more to the World Series in the 1980s, losing both times.

In 1996 the Cardinals hired manager Tony La Russa, who would go on to become the winningest manager in team history. The following year, St. Louis added slugger Mark McGwire, whose chase of the single-season home run record in 1998 made him a local icon (though allegations of steroid use would later damage his reputation among Cardinal fans). Superstar slugger Albert Pujols joined the team in 2001 and led them to a return to the World Series in 2004, which was a sweep at the hands of the resurgent Red Sox. In 2006 an underdog Cardinals squad advanced to the World Series, where it easily defeated the favoured Detroit Tigers to become the champion with the lowest regular-season winning percentage in baseball history, after having posted a win-loss record of 83–79.

NL West

Arizona Diamondbacks

Based in Phoenix, the Diamondbacks won the World Series in 2001, only their fourth season in Major League Baseball.

The Diamondbacks (or "D-backs") were founded in 1998 as an expansion franchise, along with the Tampa Bay Devil Rays (now known as the Tampa Bay Rays). In their first season the Diamondbacks unsurprisingly finished last in their division. The team added free agent pitcher Randy Johnson before the 1999 season, and he—along with another new acquisition, Luis Gonzalez, and holdover third baseman Matt Williams—led the Diamondbacks to a rapid improvement as they won 100 games and earned a postseason berth (a first-round loss to the New York Mets). When Curt Schilling went to the team during the 2000 season and joined Johnson in the starting rotation, the Diamondbacks boasted arguably the top pair of pitchers in baseball, and the twosome were at their most dominant in 2001. That year Johnson and Schilling finished first and second in voting for the Cy Young Award (given annually to the league's best pitcher) while leading Arizona to its second division title. The team then advanced to its first

World Series, where it defeated the New York Yankees in a dramatic seven-game series behind co-Most Valuable Player performances by the two star pitchers.

The Diamondbacks again advanced to the postseason in 2002, but this success was followed by a quick descent into the divisional cellar as Arizona posted a 51–111 record in 2004. The team traded away both Schilling (2003) and Johnson (2005; though he returned to Arizona from 2007 to 2008) and rebuilt around young position players and dominant pitchers such as Brandon Webb and Dan Haren. Recent Diamondbacks teams have had varying success— including a second trip to the NL Championship Series in 2007—as the franchise has tried to duplicate the remarkable accomplishments of its early years.

COLORADO ROCKIES

Based in Denver, the Rockies have never won a divison title, but they advanced to the 2007 World Series after gaining a play-off berth as the NL wild card entrant (as owner of the best record for a non-division-winning team in the NL).

The team began play in 1993, along with the Florida Marlins, as an expansion team. The Rockies were immediately notable for the high scores of their home games, which were largely a result of the relative lack of resistance to batted balls in the thin air at Denver's high elevation and the effects of the dry climate on the balls' leather covering. The team capitalized on these unique conditions, and early Rockies clubs were highlighted by sluggers such as first baseman Andres Galarraga, third baseman Vinny Castilla, and outfielders Dante Bichette and Larry Walker. Colorado made a surprise run to a postseason appearance in just its third year of existence, earning the NL wild card in 1995, which was followed by a first-round play-off loss to the Atlanta Braves. The Rockies posted a respectable

83–79 record in each of the next two seasons, but they failed to build any lasting success in the aftermath of the franchise's impressive first few years.

Colorado struggled through the start of the 21st century: it finished no better than second to last in its division from 1998 to 2006. In 2002 the Rockies began storing their baseballs in a humidor to mitigate the effects of their homefield advantage, as the leather on balls kept in the dry Denver air constricted, making the balls significantly lighter. The change was instantaneous, as Coors Field—the team's stadium—became a statistically average ballpark and the Rockies began boasting some of the better pitchers in the NL.

In 2007 a reconfigured Rockies team led by outfielder Matt Holliday, first baseman Todd Helton, and all-star relief pitcher Brian Fuentes went on a remarkable late-season run, winning 14 of their final 15 games to win the franchise's second NL wild card. Their hot streak extended to the play-offs, where the Rockies swept both the Philadelphia Phillies and the Arizona Diamondbacks en route to their first NL pennant. At the World Series, however, the Rockies were themselves swept by the Boston Red Sox.

Los Angeles Dodgers

Based in Los Angeles, the Dodgers have won six World Series titles and 21 NL pennants.

Founded in 1883, the Dodgers were originally based in Brooklyn, N.Y., and were known as the Atlantics. The team joined the American Association in 1884 and won the league pennant in 1889. Brooklyn was one of four American Association teams to join the NL the following year, and they won their first NL pennant in their inaugural season in the league. Brooklyn developed a natural rivalry with Manhattan's New York Giants following their move to the NL, which became one of the game's most renowned and enduring feuds, even after each team's relocation to California in 1958. In 1913 the team moved into Ebbets Field, an intimate ballpark that served as the home of the Dodgers until 1957. The team was known as the Grays, the Bridegrooms, the Superbas, and the Robins before they settled on the name Dodgers in 1932.

The Dodgers won NL pennants in 1941, 1947, 1949, 1952, and 1953 but lost the World Series to the crosstown New York Yankees each time, earning the Dodgers the affectionate nickname "Dem Bums" and precipitating their fans' famous annual lament, "Wait 'til next year." In the midst of this run, the Dodgers made history in April 1947 by calling up African American third baseman Jackie Robinson (who had been signed to a minor league contract by the pioneering Dodgers general manager Branch Rickey two years earlier), shattering major league baseball's long-standing colour barrier. In 1955 the Dodgers finally bested the Yankees and won the franchise's first World Series title behind a lineup led by future Hall of Famers Robinson, Roy Campanella, Pee Wee Reese, and Duke Snider. Despite the team's enduring popularity in Brooklyn—they finished first or second in NL attendance in seven of the nine seasons between 1949 and 1957—team owner Walter O'Malley moved the franchise to Los Angeles in 1958 in order to capitalize on the financial windfall that was likely to come from major league baseball's expansion to West Coast markets.

An instant success in their new home, the Dodgers set numerous NL attendance records at Dodger Stadium, which was located in scenic Chavez Ravine, a few miles outside downtown Los Angeles. The Dodgers won World Series championships in 1959, 1963, and 1965 behind the clutch pitching of stars Sandy Koufax and

SANDY KOUFAX

(b. Dec. 30, 1935, Brooklyn, N.Y., U.S.)

Despite his early retirement due to arthritis, Sandy Koufax is ranked among the sport's greatest pitchers. A left-hander, he pitched for the Brooklyn Dodgers in the National League from 1955 to 1957, continuing, after they became the Los Angeles Dodgers, from 1958 to 1966.

Born Sanford Braun, he was given his stepfather's surname when his mother remarried. The young Koufax first excelled in basketball, which earned him a scholarship to the University of Cincinnati. There he earned a spot on the school's varsity baseball team, and his pitching prowess led to tryouts with a number of professional teams. Koufax was signed by the Dodgers, and he left school after one year to immediately join the team's major league roster.

Koufax pitched sparingly in his first two seasons with the Dodgers, and his performance was pedestrian in the following four: through his first six seasons as a professional, he had a cumulative record of 36–40 and an earned run average (ERA) of 4.10. His breakthrough came in 1961, when—after changing his pitching technique in spring training—he won 18 games, was named an NL all-star for the first of six consecutive times, and broke Christy Mathewson's 58-year-old NL strikeout record with 269. From 1962 through 1965 Koufax had the lowest ERA in the NL, winning the NL Most Valuable Player award in 1963 and the NL Cy Young Award in 1963 and 1965. He led the Dodgers to World Series titles in both 1963 and 1965, winning World Series MVP honours on both occasions. The devoutly Jewish Koufax famously refused to pitch in game one of the 1965 World Series, which fell on Yom Kippur, but he returned to pitch in games two, five, and seven, throwing complete-game shutouts in the latter two contests. In his last season, 1966, he won 27 games and posted a 1.73 ERA, both career bests, and he took home his third Cy Young Award. On Sept. 9, 1965, he pitched his fourth no-hit game, a major league record (until 1981); the fourth no-hitter, against the Chicago Cubs, was also a perfect game (no player reached first base).

During his career Koufax struck out 2,396 batters in 2,324 innings; his average of more than one strikeout per inning is a rare accomplishment. In each of three seasons—1963, 1965, and

Sandy Koufax. Focus On Sport/Getty Images

1966 — he struck out more than 300 hitters; his 382 strikeouts in 1965 set a major league record that remained unbroken until 1973. Twice he struck out 18 batters in a nine-inning game. After his playing career ended, Koufax worked as a television broadcaster and as a minor league pitching coach and adviser for the Dodgers. He was elected to the Baseball Hall of Fame in 1971, the first year that he was eligible.

Don Drysdale and the speed of base-stealing sensation Maury Wills. The team won three NL pennants in the 1970s (1974, 1977, and 1978) but failed to capture a World Series title in that decade. Toward the end of the 1976 season, manager Walter Alston—who had guided the team to each of its first four world championships—retired abruptly and was replaced by a fellow future Hall of Famer, Tommy Lasorda.

In 1981 the Dodgers acquired pitcher Fernando Valenzuela, who became the first player to win both Cy Young and Rookie of the Year awards in the same season, on his way to leading the Dodgers to their fifth World Series win, in 1981. Veteran slugger Kirk Gibson joined NL Cy Young Award-winning pitcher Orel Hershiser in 1988. At the end of that season the Dodgers defeated the Oakland A's in the World Series, which featured a dramatic game-winning pinch-hit home run by Gibson in game one. Despite the presence of such popular stars as Mike Piazza and Hideo Nomo in subsequent years, the Dodgers have not won an NL pennant since 1988; the current streak is the franchise's longest in more than 60 years. In 2008 the Dodgers finished the major league season as one of the hottest teams in baseball, as first-year manager Joe Torre and mid-season acquisition Manny Ramirez rallied the team to a late-season surge that resulted in the Dodgers' winning the NL West title. Los Angeles lost in the NL Championship Series in both 2008 and 2009, and Torre and Ramirez both left the team in 2010.

SAN DIEGO PADRES

Based in San Diego, the Padres were founded in 1969 and have won two NL pennants (1984, 1998).

The franchise came into existence alongside three other expansion teams in 1969. The Padres lost 110 games in their first season to place at the bottom of their division and tie for the worst record in the major leagues, with the Montreal Expos. They continued to finish last in the NL West for the next five seasons, and the team threatened to move to Washington, D.C., before McDonald's Corporation magnate Ray Kroc purchased the franchise in 1974 to keep it in San Diego. The Padres had their first winning season in 1978 behind the play of future Hall of Famer members Dave Winfield and Gaylord Perry, the latter of whom won the 1978 NL Cy Young Award (at age 39) for outstanding pitching. The winning was short-lived, however, as the Padres posted losing records in each of the following three seasons.

The 1982 season brought two significant figures to San Diego: manager Dick Williams, who had guided the Oakland Athletics to two World Series titles in the 1970s, and outfielder Tony Gwynn, who would go on to become the face of the franchise in his 20 seasons with the Padres. The duo helped the team to a 40-win increase from the previous year, and the Padres finished 1982 with a .500 winning percentage. In 1984 Gwynn and fellow allstars Steve Garvey and Rich ("Goose") Gossage led the Padres to their first division title, which they followed with a five-game victory over the Chicago Cubs in the NL Championship Series to earn their first World Series berth. At the World Series the Padres faced off against a Detroit Tigers team that was one of the most dominant squads in baseball history, and San Diego lost in five games. The Padres returned to the middle of the NL West pack the following year, and the team entered into another long postseason drought.

After two last-place finishes in 1993 and 1994, the team hired former Padres player Bruce Bochy to manage the squad. Bochy would go on to lead the team for a club-record 12 seasons, and his positive impact on the team was almost immediate: the Padres rocketed to a division title in 1996 behind the play of NL Most Valuable Player Ken Caminiti. San Diego was swept out of the play-offs by the St. Louis Cardinals that year, but the team was more successful in its return to the postseason in 1998, when it defeated the Houston Astros and the Atlanta Braves on its way to another World Series berth. Once again, the Padres had the misfortune of playing a remarkably accomplished team in the Series, a New York Yankees squad that had won 114 games in the regular season (an American League record at the time) and that swept San Diego. The Padres were a last-place or second-to-last-place team for the following five seasons. In 2005 the Padres won the first of two consecutive division titles, led by the pitching of starter Jake Peavy and Trevor Hoffman (who became the league's all-time save leader in 2006), but each postseason appearance ended with a loss in the first round of the play-offs. A disgruntled Bochy left the Padres after the 2006 season to manage the divisional rival San Francisco Giants, and his departure was soon followed by both Hoffman's and Peavy's as the Padres began a rebuilding effort.

San Francisco Giants

Based in San Francisco, the Giants have won six World Series titles and 21 NL pennants.

The franchise that would become the Giants was established in 1883 in New York City and was initially known as the Gothams. In 1885 the team changed its name to the Giants, which was supposedly inspired by a description of the squad by its proud manager in the wake of an extra-inning victory. The Giants won their first pennant in 1888—as well as an early and unofficial version of the World Series against the champions of the American Association—and they repeated as NL champions the following year. The team's 1889 "World Series" win was notable because it came over the American Association's Brooklyn Bridegrooms (later Dodgers, now the Los Angeles Dodgers), who, after joining the NL in 1890, began a storied rivalry with the Giants franchise that extends to the present day.

New York soon entered into a less competitive period and only returned to the top of the NL with the hiring of manager John McGraw in the middle of the 1902 season. McGraw's Giants won the NL pennant in his second full season with the team, but he refused to play the champion of the supposedly inferior American League, so the official World Series was not held in 1904. The Giants won another pennant the following season and agreed to play in the World Series, in which they defeated the Philadelphia Athletics in five games behind the stellar pitching of future Hall of Famers Christy Mathewson and Joe McGinnity, who combined to allow no earned runs in the series.

McGraw would guide the Giants to four World Series berths between 1911 and 1917, but the team lost on each occasion. New York broke through to win a World Series title in 1921 and repeated the feat the following season. By the end of the 1920s, the Giants added three future Hall of Fame players: first baseman Bill Terry, outfielder

Mel Ott, and pitcher Carl Hubbell. McGraw retired midway through the 1932 season and was replaced by Terry, who served as a player-manager until 1936 and as manager only until 1941. Terry led his team to a World Series win in his first full season managing the Giants, as well as Series losses to the dominant New York Yankees in 1936 and 1937.

During the 1940s the Giants never finished higher than third place in the NL. The team made a bold move by hiring manager Leo Durocher away from the Dodgers during the course of the 1948 season. His acquisition paid off with trips to the World Series in 1951 and 1954, with the Giants winning the title in 1954. Additionally, these two postseason appearances were noteworthy for involving two of the greatest plays in baseball history: Bobby Thomson's dramatic pennant-winning home run (known as the "shot heard 'round the world") in 1951 and Willie Mays's famed over-the-shoulder catch during the 1954 World Series.

Despite these high points, attendance at the Giants' now legendary home, the Polo Grounds, lagged as the team continued to play in the Yankees' shadow, so the franchise relocated to San Francisco in 1958, at the same time that the Dodgers moved from Brooklyn to Los Angeles. The San Francisco Giants featured a number of prominent young players that brought fans to the team's new stadium, Candlestick Park, in droves. In addition to Mays—who is considered one of the greatest all-around players in baseball history—the Giants boasted a lineup with first basemen/outfielders Orlando Cepeda and Willie McCovey and pitcher Juan Marichal. However, this star-studded team was not the foundation of great on-field success: the Giants played in only one World Series (a loss in 1962) during the team's first 29 years in the Bay Area.

BARRY BONDS

(b. July 24, 1964, Riverside, Calif., U.S.)

A great all-around baseball player, Barry Bonds broke the major league home run records for both a career (with his 756th home run, in 2007) and a single season (with 73 home runs in 2001).

Bonds was born into a baseball family. His father, Bobby Bonds, was an outfielder for the San Francisco Giants. His cousin was baseball great Reggie Jackson. His godfather was the legendary Willie Mays, who was a teammate of Bobby Bonds. Barry Bonds excelled at baseball from early childhood. The San Francisco Giants drafted him out of high school, but he turned down the contract the team offered him and instead chose to play college baseball for Arizona State University. Bonds was drafted by the Pittsburgh Pirates in 1985 and joined the Pirates' major league roster in 1986.

Bonds garnered numerous Gold Glove awards for his play in left field but was best known as an extremely productive hitter. In 2004 he became only the third major leaguer to hit more than 700 home runs in his career, and he became the major league all-time walks leader, surpassing Rickey Henderson. He compiled a career batting average of .300 and was such a dangerous hitter that opposing managers routinely walked him intentionally when men were on base. Bonds was also an excellent base runner, reaching the plateau of 500 career stolen bases in 2003. He was voted the National League's MVP seven times (1990, 1992, 1993, 2001, 2002, 2003, and 2004), the first player in either league to win the award more than three times.

Bonds became a free agent in 1992 and signed with the San Francisco Giants, with whom he continued to have record-breaking seasons. He completed the 2001 season with 73 home runs, breaking Mark McGwire's 1998 record of 70 home runs on October 5. In 2005 Bond's personal trainer pleaded guilty to distribution of banned steroids, leading to speculation that Bonds may have used the performance-enhancing drugs; however, Bonds testified before a grand jury in 2003 that he had never knowingly used steroids or received injections from his personal trainer. On Aug. 7, 2007, Bonds hit his 756th home run—off Washington Nationals pitcher Mike Bacsik in San Francisco—to surpass Hank Aaron's career record. At the end of the season, however, Bonds became a free agent after the

Giants elected not to offer him a new contract. In November 2007 he was indicted on charges of perjury and obstruction of justice for his 2003 grand jury testimony. In April 2011 Bonds was found guilty of obstruction of justice, but the jury was unable to reach a verdict on the perjury charges.

While the Giants' return to the World Series in 1989 did not feature much memorable on-field play—the team was swept in four games by the Oakland A's—it was noteworthy for a 7.1-magnitude earthquake that struck the Bay Area shortly before game three of the series was scheduled to begin. The event was made even more prominent by the fact that many television stations were broadcasting live from Candlestick Park before the game, so images of the earthquake and its aftermath were instantly carried to households across the country.

In 2010 the Giants, behind a strong pitching staff led by young star Tim Lincecum, returned to the postseason for the first time since 2003. The team then advanced to the World Series, where they defeated the Texas Rangers in five games to capture the franchise's first championship since their move to California.

THE WORLD SERIES

The postseason play-off series known as the World Series pits champions of the American League against the National League champions.

The World Series began in 1903 after the cessation of hostilities between the NL and the newly formed AL. Boston (AL) defeated Pittsburgh (NL) five games to three in a best-of-nine-game series. Attendance was just over 100,000, and the players' shares of receipts were slightly more than $1,000 each. In 1904 the New York Giants (NL) refused to play Boston, again the AL champion; but the series resumed in 1905 and continued annually until 1994, when a prolonged players' strike forced its cancellation that year. A seven-game format has been standard since 1922. Beginning in 1955, one player has been voted the Most Valuable Player of each series, a great honour in baseball. Montreal and Toronto were granted major league teams in 1969 and 1977 respectively—the first Canadian teams in major league baseball; Toronto's World Series win in 1992 was the first victory for a non-U.S. team. The New York Yankees of the AL have won the most series.

The World Series name has been applied to several baseball championships of lesser import, including the Junior World Series, played between champions of the International League and the American Association (both American professional minor leagues), and the Little League World Series, an annual event with international representation for teams of boys and girls 9 to 18 years old.

CHAPTER 5
SELECTED HALL OF FAMERS, 1936 THROUGH 1965

The National Baseball Hall of Fame and Museum (popularly known as the "Baseball Hall of Fame") is a museum and honorary society based in Cooperstown, N.Y. The origins of the hall can be traced to 1935, when plans were first put forward for the 1939 celebration of the supposed centennial of baseball. The first vote for players to be admitted into the hall was held in 1936, the date sometimes given for the hall's establishment. Dedication ceremonies took place in June 1939.

Selections to the Hall of Fame are made annually by two groups: the Baseball Writers' Association of America (BBWAA) and the Baseball Hall of Fame Committee on Baseball Veterans. For the period 1971–77 a special committee inducted nine players from the Negro leagues into the Hall of Fame.

Players are selected by members of the BBWAA who have been active for 10 years and by a few honorary members of the BBWAA. Approximately 450 writers participate each year. To be eligible for selection, the prospective player must have been active in the major leagues at some time during a period beginning 20 years before and ending 5 years prior to election. (When, however, Roberto Clemente was killed in an airplane crash in late 1972, the 5-year waiting period was waived so that he could be immediately inducted in 1973. Later in 1973 the election rules were changed to permit selection of a player six months after his death.) Further rules stipulate that a player must have played at least 10 years in the major leagues and is required to receive 75 percent of the votes to be elected. There is no set number of players elected each year. No write-in votes are permitted, and the ballot is formed of those players who received a vote on a minimum of 5 percent of the ballots cast in the preceding election or those who are eligible for the first time and are nominated by any two of the six members of the BBWAA Screening Committee.

In 1953 the Baseball Hall of Fame Committee on Baseball Veterans was established. It holds elections each year to select players, managers, umpires, and executives no longer eligible for selection by the BBWAA.

Memorabilia of all eras of the game and an extensive baseball library are also housed in the hall and museum.

This chapter contains biographies of Hall of Fame players (arranged chronologically by year of induction) who were elected to the Hall during its first 30 years of existence.

TY COBB

(b. Dec. 18, 1886, Narrows, Ga., U.S. – d. July 17, 1961, Atlanta, Ga.)

Ty Cobb is considered one of the greatest offensive players in baseball history and generally regarded as the fiercest competitor in the game.

During his 24-season career in the American League, Tyrus Raymond Cobb set the record for runs scored of 2,245, a test that was not surpassed until 2001 by Rickey Henderson. Cobb's mark of 892 stolen bases was surpassed only in 1979 by Lou Brock (and in 1991 it was Henderson who beat Brock's record for stolen bases as well). Finally,

Ty Cobb. New York Times Co./Archive Photos/Getty Images

Cobb's lifetime batting average of .366 was unequaled through the 20th century. (It should be noted that there is disagreement among sports statisticians as to the exact figure for Cobb's lifetime batting average and runs batted in.) Cobb led the American League in batting 12 times, winning nine batting titles in a row (1907–15). Three times his batting average topped .400 (1911, .420; 1912, .410; and 1922, .401), and for 23 straight years he batted at least .300.

Cobb, who was also known as the "Georgia Peach," became a major league player with the Detroit Tigers of the American League in 1905, when he was 18. He spent 22 seasons as an outfielder with the Tigers (1905–26) and also managed the team from 1921 through 1926. A member of the Philadelphia Athletics when he retired in 1928, Cobb hit .323 in his last season. He batted left-handed and threw right-handed, stood about 6 feet 1 inch (1.9 metres), and weighed 175 pounds (79.4 kg). In the first election to the Baseball Hall of Fame, in 1936, Cobb received the most votes. He invested his baseball earnings shrewdly and amassed a comfortable fortune.

His autobiography, *My Life in Baseball* (ghostwritten by sportswriter Al Stump), was published in 1961. Stump amended the record in 1994 with *Cobb: A Biography*, which presents a far more honest view of the great player. Cobb's racism, misogyny, and volatile and violent personality are covered in Stump's second book, which was the basis of a 1994 film, *Cobb*.

WALTER JOHNSON

(b. Nov. 6, 1887, Humboldt, Kan., U.S.—d. Dec. 10, 1946, Washington, D.C.)

Walter Johnson had perhaps the greatest fastball in the history of the game. A right-handed thrower with a sidearm delivery who batted right as well, Johnson pitched for the Washington Senators of the American League (AL) from 1907 through 1927.

Johnson played semiprofessional baseball in Idaho after graduating from high school. Upon his arrival in Washington, D.C., he was immediately hailed as one of the hardest-throwing pitchers in the major leagues, and his fastball helped earn him the nickname "Big Train." In his fourth season, at age 22, Johnson led the AL in complete games, innings pitched, and strikeouts. His performance improved progressively until in 1913 he won 36 games, posted a 1.14 earned run average, and won the Chalmers Award, the equivalent of today's Most Valuable Player (MVP). He won a second MVP award in 1924 and also led the Senators to their first World Series title—shutting out the New York Giants over the final 4 innings of the 12-inning seventh game to earn the win.

In 21 seasons he struck out 3,508 batters, a major league record that would stand until 1983, when it was broken by three pitchers: Nolan Ryan, Steve Carlton, and Gaylord Perry. Johnson's record for shutout victories (110) still stands. His record for games won (417) is second only to that held by Cy Young.

Johnson was nonplaying manager of the Washington club (1929–32) and of the Cleveland Indians (1933–35). A popular player, he was elected to the Baseball Hall of Fame in 1936.

CHRISTY MATHEWSON

(b. Aug. 12, 1880, Factoryville, Pa., U.S.—d. Oct. 7, 1925, Saranac Lake, N.Y.)

Christy Mathewson is regarded as one of the greatest pitchers in the history of the game.

Christopher Mathewson was one of the first "college men" to enter the major leagues, having played football and baseball at Bucknell University in Lewisburg, Pa. After pitching for teams in various independent leagues during the summers following his freshman and sophomore years, his contract was purchased by the New York Giants of the National League (NL), and Mathewson made his major league debut at age 19 in July 1900. He appeared in only six games during his first season, but he entered the Giants' starting pitching rotation in 1901, when he placed sixth in the NL in both earned run average (ERA) and wins.

Mathewson won more than 20 games in each of 13 seasons (12 consecutive, 1903–14) and 30 or more on four occasions. His landmark season came in 1905, when he won his first pitching Triple Crown by leading the NL in wins (31), ERA (1.28), and strikeouts (206). But Mathewson was even more impressive in the 1905 World Series, in which he pitched three complete-game shutouts, striking out 18 total batters while allowing just one base on balls as the Giants defeated the Philadelphia Athletics in a five-game series. In 1908 he recorded 37 victories (11 of them shutouts), had a 1.43 ERA, and struck out 259 batters to win his second Triple Crown. He also led the league in ERA in 1909, 1911, and 1913, but his skills had eroded by 1916. Realizing that his playing days were numbered, Mathewson requested a trade to the Cincinnati Reds. Although he only pitched one game for the Reds before retiring as a player in 1916, Mathewson served as the team's manager until 1918.

He won 373 regular-season games in his career—tying Walter Johnson for the third highest total in major league history—while losing only 188. A right-handed thrower and batter, Mathewson was a master of the fadeaway pitch, later called the screwball. Testifying to the pitcher's exceptional control, a Giants' catcher said he could "catch Matty in a rocking chair." Mathewson was an intelligent, proud, reticent man with great powers of concentration. From 1923 until his death he was president of the Boston Braves in the National League. Mathewson was one of the first five players chosen for the Baseball Hall of Fame in 1936.

NAP LAJOIE

(b. Sept. 5, 1874, Woonsocket, R.I., U.S.—d. Feb. 7, 1959, Daytona Beach, Fla.)

One of the game's best hitters and an outstanding fielder, Nap Lajoie had a .338 career batting average, the 2nd highest ever for a second baseman, with 3,242 hits, the 13th highest total in major league history.

Napoleon Lajoie began his career with the National League's Philadelphia Phillies in 1896, and after five seasons he moved over to the Philadelphia team—the Athletics—in the new American League. His .426 batting average with the Athletics in 1901 is the highest ever recorded in the American League. A lawsuit was filed to keep Lajoie from leaving the National League, and in 1902 the Pennsylvania Supreme Court barred him from playing with any team other than the Phillies. A compromise was reached, and Lajoie was allowed to play for another American League team, the Cleveland Bronchos, but he was required to stay out of the lineup when Cleveland played in Philadelphia. Lajoie's performance in 1902 rejuvenated the Cleveland team, and the next season the club was renamed the Naps in tribute to Lajoie. He played more than half of his 21-year career with Cleveland before returning to the Philadelphia Athletics for two seasons (the injunction against him playing in Philadelphia was lifted in 1903).

In 1910 the popular Lajoie was involved in a race for the batting title with the relatively disliked Ty Cobb. Lajoie and Cobb were neck and neck for much of the year, and there was confusion in the process of determining batting averages. Cobb, assuming he had won the title and the new car that accompanied it, did not play in the last two games of the year. Lajoie did play and had eight hits in nine at-bats, although six were bunts with the opposing team's third baseman ordered to play deep. Even so, Cobb officially won the title by .001, but both players were given cars in an attempt to limit controversy. Over 70 years later, it was discovered that two hits were incorrectly credited to Cobb in 1910, but attempts to award the batting title to Lajoie were rejected by commissioner Bowie Kuhn. Lajoie was elected to the Baseball Hall of Fame in 1937.

CONNIE MACK

(b. Dec. 22/23, 1862, East Brookfield, Mass., U.S.—d. Feb. 8, 1956, Philadelphia, Pa.)

A manager and team executive, Connie Mack was the "grand old man" of the major leagues in the first half of the 20th century. He managed the Philadelphia Athletics (A's) from 1901 through 1950, during which time they won nine American League championships and five World Series (1910–11, 1913, 1929–30). He was president of the club from 1937 through 1953.

Cornelius Alexander McGillicuddy played, chiefly as a catcher, in about 700 major league games with Washington (1886–89), Buffalo (1890), and Pittsburgh (1891–96). While a player, he shortened his name so that it would fit on a scoreboard. Mack also managed Pittsburgh from Sept. 3, 1894, through the 1896 season.

In 1897 Mack joined the Milwaukee club in the Western League (renamed the American League in 1900) as playing manager. In 1901 he became manager and part owner of the Philadelphia A's and helped establish the American League as a major league. In his 53 years of managing in the big leagues, his teams won 3,776 games and lost 4,025, both all-time records. In 1937 he was elected to the Baseball Hall of Fame.

GROVER CLEVELAND ALEXANDER

(b. Feb. 26, 1887, Elba, Neb., U.S. — d. Nov. 4, 1950, St. Paul, Neb.)

One of the finest right-handed pitchers in the history of the game, Grover Cleveland Alexander is also frequently considered the sport's greatest "control" pitcher. From 1911 to 1930 he won 373 major league games and lost 208. Alexander pitched for three National League teams during his major league career: the Philadelphia Phillies (1911–17, 1930), the Chicago Cubs (1918–26), and the St. Louis Cardinals (1926–29).

Alexander grew up on a farm, where his daily labours helped him develop the strength and endurance that were to become hallmarks of his pitching. He defied his father's wishes that he study law and instead took a job as a telephone lineman so he could play baseball on the weekends. In 1909 Alexander began playing semiprofessionally, and his stellar pitching drew the attention of the Phillies, who brought him to the major leagues in 1911.

In his first season Alexander won a league-leading 28 games. In his first seven seasons the workhorse pitcher led the NL in innings pitched six times and in complete games five times. In 1915 he won the first of three career pitching Triple Crowns — the others came in 1916 and

Grover Cleveland Alexander. Photo File/Hulton Archive/Getty Images

1920 — by topping the league in earned run average (1.22), strikeouts (241), and wins (31) as he helped the Phillies capture the first NL pennant in their team history. For three consecutive years (1915–17) he won 30 or more games; in 1916, when he achieved 33 victories, 16 were shutouts, a major league record. (His career total of 90 shutouts is second only to Walter Johnson's 110.) Fearing that they would lose Alexander to the army once the United States entered World War I, the Phillies traded him to the Cubs after the 1917 season.

Not only did Alexander miss the majority of the 1918 season because of wartime service, but, as a result of his time at the front, he lost hearing in one ear, began experiencing epileptic seizures, and developed a drinking problem. Barring his standout triple-crown-winning 1920 season, Alexander's postwar pitching was of a decidedly lower quality. Cubs management grew weary of his alcoholism over the years and traded him to their rivals in St. Louis early in the 1926 season. However, the most dramatic performance of Alexander's career came in the 1926 World Series. In the seventh and deciding game, he came in as a relief pitcher in the seventh inning with the Cardinals leading the New York Yankees 3 to 2 and with the bases loaded. With two out, he struck out future Hall of Famer Tony Lazzeri. He then pitched scoreless eighth and ninth innings to clinch the title for the Cardinals. Alexander spent three more seasons with the Cardinals and one with the Phillies before he was released in 1930. He then played for the House of David team (a team fielded by a communal Christian religious sect) until 1935.

Alexander's alcoholism worsened after he left the sport, and he spent his last years in reduced circumstances. He was elected to the Baseball Hall of Fame in 1938.

EDDIE COLLINS

(b. May 2, 1887, Millerton, N.Y., U.S.—d. March 25, 1951, Boston, Mass.)

Eddie Collins was one of the most proficient hitters and base stealers in the sport's history.

Edward Trowbridge Collins, Sr., was raised in affluent circumstances in the suburbs north of New York City. He attended Columbia University, where he was the quarterback of the football team as well as the shortstop of the baseball team. While still in college, Collins began playing semiprofessional baseball under an assumed name. When his side job was uncovered by Columbia, he forfeited his senior year of eligibility. His moonlighting paid dividends, however, when a vacationing Philadelphia Athletics player saw Collins play and raved about him to Athletics manager Connie Mack. Mack signed Collins to a contract, and the young infielder played abbreviated seasons with the Athletics in 1906 and 1907 before joining the team full-time in 1908 after graduating from Columbia.

Nicknamed "Cocky"—not for any arrogance but for his supreme self-confidence in his abilities—Collins switched his primary position to second baseman in 1909, and his career subsequently flourished. In 1910 he had a .324 batting average and stole a league-high 81 bases. That season he helped the Athletics win their first World Series championship by batting .429 in the team's five-game victory over the Chicago Cubs. The Athletics repeated as champions in 1911, with Collins batting .365 during the regular season. The Athletics captured a third title in 1913, and the following season Collins won the Chalmers Award, the equivalent of today's Most Valuable Player award, after leading the Athletics to their fourth American League pennant in five years (the team was denied a fourth championship by the Boston Braves in the 1914 World Series). After the 1914

Eddie Collins, c. 1911. Bain News Service/Library of Congress, Washington, D.C. (digital file no. 11526r)

season the financially troubled Mack began selling off his star players, and Collins was sent to the Chicago White Sox.

In his third year in Chicago, Collins helped the White Sox to their first 100-win season in club history and to a World Series victory over the New York Giants. In 1919 the White Sox won another AL pennant but were infamously defeated in the World Series by the Cincinnati Reds, as eight Chicago players—not including Collins—conspired to lose the series in what is known as the Black Sox Scandal. Collins batted a career-high .372 in 1920 and finished second in the balloting for the League Award, the successor to the Chalmers Award, in 1923 and 1924. However, his team successes were limited during the early to mid-1920s. He was a player-manager for the White Sox for part of the 1924 season and for the entirety of the following two seasons, but he was fired in 1926 after failing to guide the team to any place higher than fifth in the AL and was released as a player soon thereafter. Collins then signed with the Athletics, for whom he played sparingly (often as a pinch hitter) and primarily served as a coach until his final game appearance in 1930.

At the time of his retirement, his 3,315 career hits was the fifth highest total in baseball history, and his 741 stolen bases was the fourth best career total. He spent two seasons as a full-time coach for the Athletics (1931–32) before serving as the general manager of the Boston Red Sox from 1933 to 1947. Collins was inducted into the Baseball Hall of Fame in 1939.

LOU GEHRIG

(b. June 19, 1903, New York, N.Y., U.S.—d. June 2, 1941, Bronx, N.Y.)

Lou Gehrig was one of the most durable players in baseball history and one of its great hitters. From June 1,

Baseball cards, often sold with bubble gum, have been a staple of American memorabilia since the 1930s. Here, baseball great Lou Gehrig is featured on a 1934 card. Transcendental Graphics/Archive Photos/Getty Images

1925, to May 2, 1939, Gehrig, playing first base for the New York Yankees, appeared in an unprecedented 2,130 consecutive games, which led to his famous nickname "the Iron Horse." (His record stood until it was broken on Sept. 6, 1995, by Cal Ripken, Jr.) A quiet, gentle man, Gehrig was somewhat overshadowed by his colourful teammate Babe Ruth, whom he followed in the Yankees' batting order.

Born Ludwig Heinrich Gehrig, he attended Columbia University before joining the Yankees organization. In each of seven major league seasons, he batted in 150 or more runs, and in 1931 he established the American League record of 184 runs in a season. On June 3, 1932, he hit four consecutive home runs in one game, becoming the first player of the 20th century to do so. In 1934 he won the Triple Crown, leading his league in batting average (.363), home runs (49), and runs batted in (RBIs; 165). He hit 49 home runs again in 1936.

In 1939, Gehrig was diagnosed with a rare nervous system disorder, amyotrophic lateral sclerosis (ALS); this disease has come to be known as Lou Gehrig's disease. On May 2, he took himself out of the Yankees' lineup, and he never played baseball again. He left baseball with a career batting average of .340, with 493 home runs and 1,990 runs batted in, all during regular season play. In seven World Series (34 games), he batted .361, hit 10 home runs, and drove in 35 runs.

On July 4, 1939, Lou Gehrig Appreciation Day was held in his honour. It was at this event that Gehrig made the memorable speech featured in the film version of his life, *The Pride of the Yankees* (1942), in which he claimed to be "the luckiest man on the face of the earth." The then-standard one-year waiting period after retirement for election into the Baseball Hall of Fame was waived for Gehrig, and he entered the Hall of Fame in late 1939.

ROGERS HORNSBY

(b. April 27, 1896, Winters, Texas, U.S.—d. Jan. 5, 1963, Chicago, Ill.)

Generally considered the game's greatest right-handed hitter, Rogers Hornsby had a career batting average of .358, which is second only to Ty Cobb's .367.

Hornsby made his major league debut with the St. Louis Cardinals in 1915 at age 19. After playing a number of positions early in his career, in 1920 he moved to second base, which became his primary position for the remainder of his career. Hornsby led the National League in batting for six consecutive seasons, 1920–25, hitting over .400 in three of those seasons (1922, 1924–25). His 1924 average of .424 was the highest attained in the major leagues in the 20th century. In addition to his outstanding ability to hit for average, Hornsby had great power: during his six-year reign as the NL's batting champion, he also led the league in slugging percentage each season and in home runs twice (1922, 1925). He captured the League Award (a precursor to the Most Valuable Player award) in 1925. In 1926, as the Cardinals' playing manager, he led the team to its first World Series victory, a seven-game triumph over the New York Yankees.

The outspoken Hornsby demanded a new contract after the Cardinals' championship, but he was instead traded to the New York Giants. The following season he was traded again, to the Boston Braves, for whom he again led the league in batting average in 1928. Hornsby was traded for a third time in three years before the 1929 season, to the Chicago Cubs. He won another League Award in his first season with the Cubs, and he batted over .300 in each of his first three seasons in Chicago. His play fell off dramatically in his fourth year with the club, however, and he was released 19 games into the 1932 season.

He played sparingly with the Cardinals (1933) and the St. Louis Browns (1933–37) before retiring in 1937.

Hornsby served as a player-manager during select seasons with the Braves (1928) and Cubs (1930–32), as well as during his entire tenure with the Browns. In addition, he was a full-time manager for part of the 1952 season with the Browns and part with the Cincinnati Reds, whom he also managed in 1953. He also served as a scout and coach for a number of major league teams after his playing days ended. Hornsby was elected to the Baseball Hall of Fame in 1942.

LEFTY GROVE

(b. March 6, 1900, Lonaconing, Md., U.S.—d. May 22, 1975, Norwalk, Ohio)

Lefty Grove was the most dominant pitcher of the 1920s and one of the greatest left-handed pitchers in history.

Robert Moses Grove grew up in a mining town and worked odd jobs when his formal education ended after the eighth grade. Grove did not play organized baseball until age 19. He began his professional career in 1920, winning 108 games for the minor league Baltimore Orioles of the International League before his contract was bought by Connie Mack of the AL Philadelphia Athletics in 1924 for $100,600, a record sum at the time. Grove debuted for the A's the following year at age 25 and led the league in strikeouts, the first of seven consecutive seasons in which he topped the AL in that category.

Not until he mastered control of his pitches, however, did he become a star pitcher of his era. From 1927 through 1933 Grove won at least 20 games each season, and he led the league in earned run average on five occasions as an Athletic (1926, 1929–32). In 1931 he was 31–4 with a career-low 2.06 ERA and won the AL Most Valuable Player award. In addition to his standout individual accomplishments, Grove was a key contributor on two A's World Series championship teams (1929–30).

Mack was forced to sell Grove to the Boston Red Sox in 1934. After a disappointing and injury-plagued first season in Boston, Grove regained a good measure of his original form and led the AL in ERA four times (1935–36, 1938–39) in his eight seasons with the team. He retired in 1941 with career totals of 300 wins, 141 losses, a 3.06 earned run average, and 2,266 strikeouts. In 1947 Grove was elected to the Baseball Hall of Fame.

JIMMIE FOXX

(b. Oct. 22, 1907, Sudlersville, Md., U.S.—d. July 21, 1967, Miami, Fla.)

Jimmie Foxx was the second man in major league history to hit 500 home runs. (Babe Ruth was the first.) A right-handed hitter who played mostly at first base, he finished with a total of 534 home runs. His career batting average was .325.

James Emory Foxx was a sensational schoolboy athlete, playing with a semiprofessional baseball team in the summer after his junior year of high school. He was so successful that the Philadelphia Athletics of the American League purchased his contract, and Foxx left high school during his senior year to join the team at spring training. He played sparingly from 1925 to 1927 before becoming a regular in the team's lineup in 1928.

The next season, Foxx had the first of his 13 years with at least 100 runs batted in: he drove in 113 runs as the Athletics ran away with the AL pennant en route to a World Series title. Philadelphia won a second championship in 1930, which was highlighted by Foxx hitting the game-winning home run in the top of the ninth inning of game five. In 1932 he hit 58 home runs, his highest single-season output, batted a career-high .364, led the league with 169 RBIs, and won his first Most Valuable Player award. Foxx won the Triple Crown in 1933 by leading the AL in batting average (.356), home runs (48), and RBIs (163), which resulted in another AL MVP award. His strong play continued through the next two years, but struggling Philadelphia traded him to the Boston Red Sox soon after the 1935 season.

Foxx played with Boston from 1936 to mid-1942. His best season with the team came in 1938, when he hit 50 home runs, drove in 175 runs, and was named MVP for a third time. In 1940 he hit his 500th career home run, but his play quickly deteriorated after his last all-star-quality season in 1941. Foxx was let go by Boston and then claimed by the Chicago Cubs early in the 1942 season. He announced his retirement at the end of the year after batting .205 in 70 games with the Cubs, but he returned to the sport for short stints with the Cubs and the Philadelphia Phillies in 1944 and 1945, respectively, before permanently retiring in 1945.

Foxx's post-baseball life was plagued by alcoholism and financial troubles, and he held a number of odd jobs in addition to several positions as a minor league coach until his death at age 59. He was elected to the Baseball Hall of Fame in 1951.

CHAPTER 6
SELECTED HALL OF FAMERS, 1966 THROUGH THE PRESENT

With a few exceptions, the individuals who have been inducted into the Hall of Fame since 1966 starred in the years following World War II, a time when baseball, through the proliferation of television, came into America's living rooms. As a result, these Hall of Famers (arranged chronologically by year of induction) are among the most iconic figures in the sport's history, able to be recognized by even casual fans simply by nicknames like "the Splendid Splinter," "Hammerin' Hank," and "the Mick."

TED WILLIAMS

(b. Aug. 30, 1918, San Diego, Calif., U.S.—d. July 5, 2002, Inverness, Fla.)

Variously known as "the Splendid Splinter" and "Teddy Ballgame," Ted Williams compiled a lifetime batting average of .344 as an outfielder with the American League Boston Red Sox from 1939 to 1960. He was the last player to hit .400 in Major League Baseball (.406 in 1941).

Theodore Samuel Williams was an excellent ballplayer as a child and later led his high school team to the state championships. He batted left-handed but threw right-handed, baseball's most desirable combination. Williams was signed by a minor league team in the Pacific Coast League, and after several seasons in San Diego and

Ted Williams in the spring of 1955, back on deck for the Boston Red Sox. Hy Peskin/Sports Illustrated/Getty Images

Minneapolis he was brought up to the Red Sox major league team in 1939. He had a fine rookie season with a batting average of .327.

His sophomore season in 1940 was more difficult. Although he batted .344 for the year, he was in something of a hitting slump in the early months. The criticism and heckling that arose from the sporting press and the fans soured Williams's attitude; thus began a career-long feud between Williams and the media and a love-hate relationship with Boston fans. Williams began refusing to acknowledge cheering fans—for the rest of his career he would never again tip his cap to the crowd.

In 1941 Williams hit for a season average of .406. His battle with the media continued, however. He had requested a draft deferment in 1942 because he was his mother's sole support. Although many other players played baseball instead of enlisting in 1942 (Joe DiMaggio, for example), the press called Williams's choice unpatriotic and derided him for it. He decided to enlist in the U.S. Navy and entered active duty in November 1942. In that same year he won the first of two Triple Crowns (in which a player has the best batting average, most home runs, and most runs batted in [RBIs] during a single season).

Williams missed the baseball seasons of 1943–45 training and serving as a Navy flyer, but he saw no combat. Upon his return to baseball in 1946 he had lost none of his skill, hitting .342 in 1946 and in 1947 winning his second Triple Crown. In 1952 he was once again called up for military service, and for most of the '52 and '53 seasons he served as a pilot during the Korean War, this time in combat. (He batted .400 and .407 respectively for these years, but because he played only 43 games the records are not for complete seasons and therefore are not counted.)

Williams hit a career total of 521 home runs, even though he lost five prime years of his career to military service. He won the American League batting title in 1958 (at age 40) with a .328 average, the oldest player ever to do so. Concerning his abilities as a hitter, Williams once said, "A man has to have goals—for a day, for a lifetime—and that was mine, to have people say, 'There goes Ted Williams, the greatest hitter who ever lived.'" In 1960 he announced that he would retire at the end of the year. During the final home game of the season he hit a home run in his last at bat. The fans cheered and called for him but Williams still refused to come out of the dugout and recognize them (an incident that author John Updike famously described with the line "gods do not answer letters").

Williams returned to the major leagues from retirement in 1969 to manage the Washington Senators, and in his first year he was named American League Manager of the Year. He left the franchise in 1972, after it had become the Texas Rangers. After his retirement as a manager, he occasionally worked as a batting coach and became a consultant for a line of fishing equipment (he was an avid fisherman).

Williams was elected to the Baseball Hall of Fame in 1966. His autobiography, written with John Underwood, *My Turn at Bat*, was published in 1969. Other works written by Williams and Underwood are *The Science of Hitting* (1971) and *Ted Williams' Fishing "The Big Three": Tarpon, Bonefish, and Atlantic Salmon* (1988). In 1991, to commemorate his .400 season, the Boston Red Sox hosted a Ted Williams Day. After a brief speech, Williams tipped his cap to the cheering Boston fans.

BRANCH RICKEY

(b. Dec. 20, 1881, Stockdale, Ohio, U.S.—d. Dec. 9, 1965, Columbia, Mo.)

Branch Rickey was a baseball executive who devised the farm system of training ballplayers (1919) and hired the first black players in organized baseball in the 20th century.

Wesley Branch Rickey started his professional playing career while studying at Ohio Wesleyan University, spent two seasons (1906–07) in the American League as a catcher, and graduated from the University of Michigan Law School in 1911. After serving as field manager of the American League St. Louis Browns (1913–15), he began a long association with the National League St. Louis Cardinals—as club president (1917–19), field manager (1919–25), and general manager (1925–42).

Dismayed at the inability of the Cardinals to bid successfully for promising minor league players, he persuaded club owner Sam Breadon to buy stock in the Houston (Texas) and Fort Smith (Arkansas) minor league teams

Jackie Robinson (left) *and Branch Rickey during a contract signing session in the offices of Ebbets Field, Brooklyn, NY, 1950.* Transcendental Graphics/Getty Images

so that St. Louis would have first choice of their players. The Cardinals won nine league championships with players signed during Rickey's tenure. He left the Cardinals to become president and general manager of the Brooklyn Dodgers of the National League (1943–50).

In the spring of 1945, Rickey founded the United States League for black players, whom unwritten law excluded from organized baseball, and he was criticized for encouraging continued segregation in sports. There are no records indicating that the league ever played any games; however, it served as a front that allowed Rickey to quietly scout black ballplayers for one who could lead the desegregation of the major leagues. In October 1945 he signed infielder Jackie Robinson for the Dodgers' minor league organization. Robinson's success with the Dodgers from 1947 led other owners to seek black talent. Rickey later was vice president, general manager (1950–55), and chairman of the board (1955–59) of the Pittsburgh Pirates.

Rickey was inducted into the Baseball Hall of Fame in 1967.

STAN MUSIAL

(b. Nov. 21, 1920, Donora, Pa., U.S.)

In his 22-year playing career with the St. Louis Cardinals, Stan Musial won seven National League (NL) batting championships and established himself as one of the game's greatest hitters.

Stanley Frank Musial was a phenomenal schoolboy athlete in both baseball and basketball, and he signed his first professional baseball contract while in high school. A left-handed batter and thrower, Musial began his career as a pitcher but developed a sore arm and switched to the outfield while still in the minor leagues.

He quickly worked his way up through the Cardinals' minor league system and made his major league debut in 1941. The following year Musial became a full-time player for St. Louis, where he teamed with Terry Moore and Enos Slaughter to form what would become one of the finest offensive and defensive outfield combinations in baseball history and played a significant role in the team's 1942 World Series victory.

Musial's breakthrough year came in 1943, as he led the NL in hits (220) and batting average (.357) and won the league's Most Valuable Player (MVP) award at just age 22. After leading the Cardinals to another World Series title in 1944, he enlisted in the U.S. Navy for service during World War II. Returning to baseball in 1946, he won a second MVP award after batting .365 as the Cardinals captured their third World Series championship in five years. Musial had his greatest season statistically in 1948 as he posted career-high (and league-leading) totals in batting average (.376), hits (230), runs (135), and runs batted in (131), which resulted in a third NL MVP award. In the 1950s the Cardinals had little success as a team, but Musial thrived as an individual, leading the league in batting average four times (1950–52, 1957), in runs three times (1951–52, 1954), and in hits once (1952).

He retired after the 1963 season with a career batting average of .331. At the time of his retirement, his totals of times at bat (10,972), hits (3,630), and runs scored (1,949) were second only to those of Ty Cobb, and his total of runs batted in (1,951) was exceeded only by Babe Ruth and Lou Gehrig; all were records for the NL (since surpassed). Musial also set a major league record with 1,377 extra-base hits (broken by Hank Aaron in 1973). When his career as a player ended, Musial became an executive of the Cardinals, which included a one-year stint as the team's general manager in 1967, when he oversaw a World Series championship. A 20-time NL all-star, he was elected to the Baseball Hall of Fame in 1969.

SATCHEL PAIGE

(b. July 7, 1906?, Mobile, Ala., U.S.—d. June 8, 1982, Kansas City, Mo.)

Satchel Paige was a pitcher whose prowess became legendary during his many years in the Negro leagues; he finally was allowed to enter the major leagues in 1948 after the unwritten rule against black players was abolished. A right-handed, flexible "beanpole" standing more than 6 feet 3 inches (1.91 metres) tall, Paige had considerable pitching speed, but he also developed a comprehensive mastery of slow-breaking pitches and varied deliveries. He is rated as one of the greatest players in the history of baseball.

Leroy Robert Paige, who received his distinctive nickname as a young railroad porter, honed his baseball skills while in reform school. He entered the Negro leagues playing for the Chattanooga Black Lookouts in 1926. He was a pitcher for various teams in the Negro Southern Association and the Negro National League. Wearing a false red beard, he also played for the House of David team (a team fielded by a communal Christian religious sect that forbade its male members to shave or cut their hair). A true "iron man," he pitched in the Dominican Republic and Mexican leagues during the northern winter. As a barnstormer, he would travel as many as 30,000 miles (48,000 km) a year while pitching for any team willing to meet his price. He is reputed to have pitched a total of 2,500 games during his nearly 30-year career, winning 2,000 of them.

Paige was a colourful and larger-than-life figure in the Negro leagues, prone to stunts such as sending the infield players into the dugout while he pitched or deliberately loading the bases before pitching to Josh Gibson, a hitter of great renown. His showmanship and popularity caused white baseball fans to take greater notice of the players in the Negro leagues, which perhaps hastened the integration of baseball. Despite the colour bar, Paige faced the best major league players in exhibition games before 1948. He once struck out Rogers Hornsby, probably the greatest right-handed hitter in baseball history, five times in one game. In Hollywood in 1934 Paige scored a spectacular 1–0 victory in 13 innings over Dizzy Dean, who won 30 games for the St. Louis Cardinals that year.

In his later years Paige derived much amusement from the controversy about his age; his birth date is sometimes placed as early as Dec. 18, 1899. He was surely well past his prime in 1948 when team owner Bill Veeck signed him for the Cleveland Indians; whatever his exact age, he was the oldest rookie ever to play in the major leagues. He helped to spark that team to American League pennant and World Series victories that year. When Veeck purchased the St. Louis Browns, Paige joined that team, and he was its most effective relief pitcher from 1951 through 1953. He also pitched three scoreless innings for the Kansas City Athletics in 1965, which made him the oldest to pitch in the major leagues.

Paige was famous for his pithy remarks. One well-known quotation on on "How to Stay Young" reads:

> *1. Avoid fried meats, which angry up the blood. 2. If your stomach disputes you, lie down and pacify it with cool thoughts. 3. Keep the juices flowing by jangling around gently as you move. 4. Go very light on the vices, such as carrying on in society. The social ramble ain't restful. 5. Avoid running at all times. 6. Don't look back. Something might be gaining on you.*

Paige was elected to the Baseball Hall of Fame in 1971. His autobiography, *Maybe I'll Pitch Forever* (1962), written with David Lipman, was revised in 1993.

ROBERTO CLEMENTE

(b. Aug. 18, 1934, Carolina, P.R.—d. Dec. 31, 1972, San Juan)

An idol in his native Puerto Rico, Roberto Clemente was one of the first Latin American baseball stars in the United States.

Clemente was originally signed to a professional contract by the Brooklyn Dodgers in 1954. He was given a $10,000 bonus—very high by the standards of the times—but was sent to the minor leagues for the 1954 season. Because of a major league rule that stipulated that any player given a bonus of more that $4,000 had to be kept on the major league roster for his entire first season or be subject to a draft from other clubs, the Dodgers lost Clemente. Pittsburgh, which had finished last in the National League in 1954, selected him; Clemente made his major league debut on April 1, 1955, and spent his entire career with the Pittsburgh Pirates. For 18 seasons Clemente delighted fans with his hitting ability, daring base running, and strong throwing arm. His outstanding arm was perhaps his greatest physical asset. He won 12 Gold Gloves, the award given to the best fielding player in each position in the league. Baseball's most talented outfielders are still compared to Clemente. He was also a very good hitter, winning four National League batting titles while compiling a lifetime average of .317. In 1972 Clemente got his 3,000th base hit on his very last at bat as a player. At the time, only 10 other players had reached this mark.

While Clemente amassed a mountain of impressive statistics during his career, he was often mocked by the

Roberto Clemente. Focus On Sport/Getty Images

print media in the United States for his heavy Spanish accent. Clemente was also subjected to the double discrimination of being a foreigner and being black in a racially segregated society. Although the media tried to call him "Bob" or "Bobby" and many of his baseball cards use "Bob," Clemente explicitly rejected those nicknames, stating in no uncertain terms that his name was Roberto. There was also confusion over the correct form of his surname. For 27 years the plaque at the National Baseball Hall of Fame read "Roberto Walker Clemente," mistakenly placing his mother's maiden name before his father's surname. Only in 2000 was it changed to its proper Latin American form, Roberto Clemente Walker.

Perhaps equally as important as Clemente's accomplishments on the field was his role as an advocate for equitable treatment of Latin baseball players, in which he took great pride. Near the end of his career, Clemente commented, "My greatest satisfaction comes from helping to erase the old opinion about Latin Americans and blacks." A close friend of Clemente's, Spanish-language sportscaster Luis Mayoral, added, "Roberto Clemente was to Latinos what Jackie Robinson was to black baseball players. He spoke up for Latinos; he was the first one to speak out."

In the off-season, Clemente returned to his homeland, playing winter baseball in the Puerto Rican League, providing baseball clinics to young players, and spending time with his family. He headed relief efforts in Puerto Rico after a massive earthquake hit Nicaragua in late December 1972. When Clemente received reports that the Nicaraguan army had stolen relief supplies meant for the people, he decided to accompany the next supply plane. Shortly after takeoff from the San Juan airport on

Dec. 31, 1972, the plane crashed, killing Clemente. The Baseball Hall of Fame waived the rule requiring a five-year wait after retirement (or death) before a player could be elected to the Hall, and in July 1973 Clemente was the first player born in Latin America to be inducted into the national baseball shrine. The award presented annually to a Major League Baseball player for exemplary sportsmanship and community service was renamed the Roberto Clemente Award in 1973.

WARREN SPAHN

(b. April 23, 1921, Buffalo, N.Y., U.S.—d. Nov. 24, 2003, Broken Arrow, Okla.)

Warren Spahn was one of the sport's biggest stars in the years immediately following World War II, and his total of 363 major-league victories established a record for left-handed pitchers. His feat of winning 20 or more games in each of 13 seasons also was a record for left-handers. He set still another mark by striking out at least 100 batters each year for 17 consecutive seasons (1947–63). At the time of his retirement, in 1965, his career total of 2,583 strikeouts was the third highest in baseball history.

Spahn, the son of a former semiprofessional baseball player, signed with the Boston Braves (later the Milwaukee Braves) of the National League in 1940 and pitched his first major league game in 1942. Drafted into the army the following year, he saw extensive combat service during World War II and received a Bronze Star and Purple Heart. In 1946 Spahn returned to professional baseball, and his fluid, high-kick delivery and pinpoint accuracy soon established him as one of the game's leading pitchers. In 1957 he helped the Braves win the World

Series. A wiry, finely conditioned athlete, Spahn pitched two no-hit games at age 39 and 40. He was also one of the best hitters among pitchers, and his 35 career home runs set a record for pitchers in the NL. In 1965, his last season, he played for the New York Mets and the San Francisco Giants. Spahn was a 14-time All-Star and the recipient of the Cy Young Award (1957). In 1973 he was inducted into the Baseball Hall of Fame.

MICKEY MANTLE

(b. Oct. 20, 1931, Spavinaw, Okla., U.S. — d. Aug. 13, 1995, Dallas, Texas)

One of the most iconic players in the history of the New York Yankees (1951–68), Mickey Mantle was a powerful switch-hitter (right- and left-handed) who hit 536 home runs.

Mantle began playing baseball as a Little League short-stop at Commerce (Okla.) High School. A football injury sustained in 1946 led to osteomyelitis, a bone-tissue infection, which required five operations before the disease was controlled.

Mantle played as an outfielder on Yankee farm clubs (1949–50) and joined the Yankees in 1951. He played with them mainly as an outfielder until he went to first base in 1967. He played much of his career heavily taped because of his earlier bone disease. He led the league in home runs for four seasons (1955–56, 1958, and 1960), and in 1961, when his teammate Roger Maris broke Babe Ruth's season home run record, Mantle hit a season high of 54. He led the league six times in runs scored (1954, 1956–58, 1960–61) and in runs batted in in 1956, the year he won the league Triple Crown for home runs, RBIs, and batting average (.353). In the 1980s his career 536 home runs placed him sixth among home-run hitters. He played in 12 World Series (1951–53, 1955–58, 1960–64), hitting a record 18 home runs in them. He was voted the American League's Most Valuable Player in 1956, 1957, and 1962.

After his retirement as a player Mantle (who was often simply known as "the Mick") coached for the Yankees and sold life insurance. In 1983 the baseball commissioner barred him from any connection with professional baseball because he had taken a public-relations position with an Atlantic City (N.J.) gambling casino. The ban was lifted in 1985. Mantle was elected to the Baseball Hall of Fame in 1974.

BOB GIBSON

(b. Nov. 9, 1935, Omaha, Neb., U.S.)

A right-handed pitcher, Bob Gibson was at his best in crucial games. In nine World Series appearances, he won seven games and lost two, and he posted an earned run average (ERA) of 1.92.

At Omaha (Neb.) Technical High School, Pack Robert Gibson was a star in basketball and track, as well as a baseball catcher. He also played basketball and baseball at Creighton University (Omaha). After playing professional basketball with the Harlem Globetrotters for one season, Gibson signed with baseball's St. Louis Cardinals in 1957 and played with their minor league teams until 1959.

A member of the Cardinals' starting pitching rotation from 1961, Gibson broke onto the national stage at the 1964 World Series, where he pitched complete-game victories in games five and seven to earn World Series

Most Valuable Player honours and clinch the title for the Cardinals. He outdid this effort in the 1967 World Series, winning all three of his starts—including the decisive seventh game—en route to again being named World Series MVP. Gibson's 1968 season is regarded as one of the finest pitching campaigns in the history of baseball. That year he completed 28 of his 34 starts, led the league in shutouts (13) and strikeouts (268), and had an ERA of 1.12, the lowest single-season ERA since 1914. Gibson won both the NL Cy Young and NL MVP awards for 1968. Two years later he added a second Cy Young Award after posting a league-high 23 wins with a 3.12 ERA and a career-high 274 strikeouts.

Gibson pitched quickly, and his best pitches were a fastball and a slider. He also had a reputation as one of the game's most menacing pitchers because of his nearly perpetual glower when on the mound and his tendency to brush batters off the plate by throwing inside. A tremendous fielder, he won nine Gold Glove awards over the course of his 17-year career. Gibson amassed 3,117 total strikeouts, the first pitcher to accumulate more than 3,000 since Walter Johnson in the 1920s.

The eight-time NL all-star retired as a player in 1975. He later worked as a pitching coach for the New York Mets and Atlanta Braves, and in 1996 he became a special instructor for the Cardinals. Gibson was elected to the Baseball Hall of Fame in 1981.

HANK AARON

(b. Feb. 5, 1934, Mobile, Ala., U.S.)

During his 23 seasons in the major leagues (1954–76), Hank Aaron surpassed batting records set by some of

Hank Aaron. Focus On Sport/Getty Images

the greatest hitters in the game, including Babe Ruth, Ty Cobb, and Stan Musial.

Henry Louis Aaron, a right-hander, began his professional career in 1952, playing shortstop for a few months with the Indianapolis Clowns of the Negro American League. His contract was bought by the Boston Braves of the National League, who assigned him to minor league teams. In 1954 he moved up to the majors, playing mostly as an outfielder for the Braves (who had moved to Milwaukee, Wisconsin, in 1953). In 1956 he won the league batting championship with an average of .328, and in 1957, having led his team to victory in the World Series, he was named the league's Most Valuable Player. By the time the Braves moved to Atlanta at the end of 1965, Aaron, whose homer-hitting prowess earned him the nickname "Hammerin' Hank," had hit 398 home runs. In Atlanta on April 8, 1974, he hit his 715th, breaking Babe Ruth's record, which had stood since 1935. After the 1974 season, Aaron was traded to the Milwaukee Brewers, who were at that time in the American League. Aaron retired after the 1976 season and rejoined the Atlanta Braves as an executive. He was elected to the Baseball Hall of Fame on Jan. 13, 1982. In 2010 the Hank Aaron Childhood Home and Museum opened on the grounds of Hank Aaron Stadium, the home of Mobile, Alabama's minor league baseball team.

Aaron's batting records include totals of 1,477 extra-base hits and 2,297 runs batted in. His home run record of 755 was broken by Barry Bonds in 2007. Aaron's other career statistics include 2,174 runs scored (second to Ty Cobb) and 12,364 times at bat in 3,298 games (second to Pete Rose). His hits (3,771) were exceeded only by those of Ty Cobb and Pete Rose. Aaron's lifetime batting average was .305.

FRANK ROBINSON

(b. Aug. 31, 1935, Beaumont, Texas, U.S.)

A Hall of Fame baseball player, Frank Robinson is also known for becoming the first black manager in Major League Baseball in 1975.

As a youth, Robinson played sandlot and American Legion Junior League baseball in Oakland, Calif., and at McClymonds High School, where he also played football and basketball. The right-hander played third base and pitched occasionally. After graduation he was signed by the National League Cincinnati Reds and played with their minor league teams (third base and outfield) until he joined the parent club in 1956, the year he was awarded Rookie of the Year honours. Robinson won an NL Most Valuable Player award in 1961, and he batted more than .300 in 5 of the 10 years before he was traded to the American League Baltimore Orioles in 1966. In his first season with Baltimore he won the Triple Crown—leading the league in home runs (49), runs batted in (122), and batting average (.316)—and he was named the 1966 AL MVP, becoming the first to win the award in both leagues. He remained with Baltimore through 1971 and then played with the NL Los Angeles Dodgers (1972) and the AL California Angels (1973–74) and Cleveland Indians (1974–76). With 586 career home runs, Robinson ranked fourth in home runs hit, after Hank Aaron (755), Babe Ruth (714), and Willie Mays (660) when he retired in 1976.

Robinson began managing the Indians in 1975, the first African American to manage a major league team. He had begun his managing career in winter baseball for the Santurce team in the Puerto Rican League in 1968 and had also coached at Baltimore and in the minor leagues for the International League. In 1981 he became manager of the NL San Francisco Giants. In 1984 Robinson returned to the Orioles, working as a coach, as a manager (he was named AL Manager of the Year in 1989), and in the front office for the team's upper management. He stayed with the Orioles until the end of the 1995 season. In 2000 Robinson was put in charge of discipline as a vice president of Major League Baseball, meting out fines and suspensions in controversial imbroglios. In 2002 he became manager of the Montreal Expos (from 2005 known as the Washington Nationals); he was fired by the franchise in 2006. Robinson was elected to the Baseball Hall of Fame in 1982.

JOHNNY BENCH

(b. Dec. 7, 1947, Oklahoma City, Okla., U.S.)

In 17 seasons with the Cincinnati Reds, Johnny Bench established himself as one of the game's finest catchers. He won 10 consecutive Gold Glove Awards (1968–77) and had an exceptional throwing arm. Bench was a master at blocking home plate from base runners, and he popularized the now-standard style of catching one-handed.

Bench was signed to a contract with the Reds in 1965 and played with its minor league teams until he moved up to the Reds late in the 1967 season. From 1968, when he was chosen National League Rookie of the Year (the first catcher ever so named from either league), he was the team's regular catcher, though in the early 1980s he caught less and finally switched to playing third base. Bench led the league in runs batted in (1970, 1972, and 1974) and in home runs (1970 and 1972). Together with Pete Rose and Joe Morgan, he helped lead the Reds to four World Series (1970, 1972, 1975, and 1976), two of which the Reds

Johnny Bench, 1975. Tony Tomsic/Getty Images

won (1975 and 1976). Bench's greatest performance was in the 1976 series, in which he batted .533. At his retirement in 1983, he held the record for the most home runs by a catcher, 327, a mark subsequently broken by Carlton Fisk. (Bench's career total for home runs is 389, but only 327 of those runs were hit while he was catching.) Bench was inducted into the Baseball Hall of Fame in 1989.

MIKE SCHMIDT

(b. Sept. 27, 1949, Dayton, Ohio, U.S.)

One of the finest all-around third basemen in history, Mike Schmidt spent his entire career with the Philadelphia Phillies.

Michael Jack Schmidt played college baseball in Ohio and was drafted by the Phillies in 1971. After playing for their minor league team, he was brought up to the major leagues in 1972. He struggled with hitting in his first seasons, but by 1974 he led the league in home runs and began to have some consistency as a batter. In 1980 Schmidt hit 48 home runs, breaking the existing record for home runs in a season by a third baseman. He led the National League in home runs eight times, and, by the conclusion of his 18-year career, he had amassed 548 home runs (then ninth on the all-time list) and had 1,595 runs batted in.

His defensive skills were easily equal to his offense, and he was awarded 10 Gold Gloves (1976–84 and 1986) during his career, more than any other third baseman except Brooks Robinson. During Schmidt's tenure the Phillies won two National League pennants (1980 and 1983) and a World Series championship (1980). Schmidt was voted Most Valuable Player on three occasions (1980, 1981, and 1986). He was elected to the Baseball Hall of Fame in 1995.

SPARKY ANDERSON

(b. Feb. 22, 1934, Bridgewater, S.D., U.S.—d. Nov. 4, 2010, Thousand Oaks, Calif.)

Sparky Anderson was a baseball manager who had a career record of 2,194 wins and 1,834 losses and led his teams to three World Series titles.

George Lee Anderson spent six years playing in baseball's minor leagues before being called up to the majors to play second base for the Philadelphia Phillies in 1959. He returned to the minor leagues the following year, where he played another four seasons. Realizing his opportunities for returning to the big leagues were limited, Anderson began to explore a career as manager: between 1964 and 1968 he managed five different minor league clubs. In 1969 he returned to the major leagues as a coach for the San Diego Padres.

Anderson was named manager of the Cincinnati Reds in 1970 and led the team to the National League title in his first season. In his nine years with the Reds, his teams won five National League pennants and two World Series championships (1975 and 1976). During this period, Cincinnati's "Big Red Machine" featured future Hall of Fame members Joe Morgan, Tony Perez, and Johnny Bench, as well as the major league's career hits leader, Pete Rose. The Reds were one of the dominant teams of the 1970s, and the 1975 team is considered one of the best of all time. Anderson was fired at the end of the 1978 season after the Reds placed second in the NL West in consecutive seasons.

In 1979 Anderson moved to the American League to manage the Detroit Tigers, whom he led for 17 seasons before retiring in 1995. In 1984 the Tigers won 104 games and the World Series, and Anderson became the first manager in the history of baseball to win a World Series championship in both the National and American leagues. Anderson was selected as a Manager of the Year on four occasions: twice for the NL (1972 and 1974) and twice for the AL (1984 and 1987). He was elected to the Baseball Hall of Fame in 2000.

TONY GWYNN

(b. May 9, 1960, Los Angeles, Calif., U.S.)

Noted as one of the sport's all-time best singles hitters, Tony Gwynn is considered the greatest player in the history of the San Diego Padres franchise.

Anthony Keith Gwynn attended San Diego State University (Calif.) on a basketball scholarship, where he set a school record for assists as the team's point guard. He also excelled at baseball and was drafted in 1981 by both the San Diego Clippers (later the Los Angeles Clippers), of the National Basketball Association, and by the San Diego Padres, of Major League Baseball. He chose the Padres, and during the 1982 season he was called up from their minor league team to play. He played his entire career as an outfielder with the Padres.

In 1984 he hit .351 and helped his club reach the World Series. In the 1994 strike-shortened season he hit .394, the best batting average since Ted Williams hit .406 in 1941. Although the Padres lost to the New York Yankees in the 1998 World Series, Gwynn hit .500 (8 for 16), with 1 home run and 3 runs batted in.

Gwynn's career highlights include tying the National League record for most consecutive seasons hitting .300 or better (17), tying the NL record for most batting titles (8), being the 22nd player to reach 3,000 hits, and winning the Golden Glove award (for fielding) 5 times. He retired from professional baseball at the end of the 2001 season, and in 2002 he became the head baseball coach at San Diego State University. Gwynn was elected to the Baseball Hall of Fame in 2007.

CAL RIPKEN, JR.

(b. Aug. 24, 1960, Havre De Grace, Md., U.S.)

In his 21-year major league career, Cal Ripken, Jr., established himself as one of the most durable athletes in professional sports history. On Sept. 6, 1995, Ripken played his 2,131st consecutive game for the Baltimore Orioles and thereby broke Lou Gehrig's major league record of consecutive games played. Gehrig's record had stood for more than 56 years.

Ripken joined the Orioles' major league team in 1982 after having spent a few seasons in their minor league system. Ripken's original position was third base, but he switched to shortstop in 1982. He was named American League Rookie of the Year in that year, when he hit 28 home runs and had 93 runs batted in. He holds the record for most career home runs by a shortstop, 345.

Ripken was voted Most Valuable Player in 1983, when he led the Orioles to a World Series title. He also won the MVP award in 1991. His father, Cal Ripken, Sr., was an Orioles coach for 15 years and briefly managed the team. In 1987 Cal, Sr., became the first father ever to manage two sons in a major league game: Cal, Jr., and Billy, an infielder.

It is the streak of consecutive games played, however, that characterized Ripken's career. Gehrig's mark of 2,130 consecutive games played was thought by some baseball experts to be unreachable in modern times. Ripken not only surpassed Gehrig's record but extended his streak to 2,632 games before he removed himself from the lineup before the final game of the 1998 season, the first time he had sat out a game in almost 18 years. He retired from baseball at the end of the 2001 season. He was elected to the Baseball Hall of Fame in 2007.

Ripken's biography, *The Only Way I Know* (1997), was written with Mike Bryan.

RICKEY HENDERSON

(b. Dec. 25, 1958, Chicago, Ill., U.S.)

One of the greatest leadoff hitters in the sport's history, Rickey Henderson set a record for the most stolen bases in major league baseball in 1991, and in 2001 he set a record for the most career runs scored.

Henderson was an All-American running back in football as a high school athlete in Oakland, California. He chose to play baseball over football, however, and competed in the minor leagues for four seasons. Henderson's career in the major leagues began with the Oakland Athletics in June 1979. In 1980, his first full season, he became one of only three players ever to have stolen 100 bases, breaking Ty Cobb's American League record of 96 bases. It was the first of seven consecutive seasons in which Henderson led the American League in stolen bases. In 1982 he broke Lou Brock's single-season record of 118 stolen bases, set in 1974, with 130 stolen bases. Henderson added 108 stolen bases the following year.

Henderson was traded to the New York Yankees after the 1984 season but was traded back to Oakland midway through the 1989 season and helped the Athletics win the World Series. In 1990 Henderson—having hit 28 home runs, scored 119 runs, stolen 65 bases, and batted .325— was selected American League Most Valuable Player. He set the American League career stolen-base record that

Rickey Henderson celebrating the 939th stolen base of his career in this 1991 game against the New York Yankees. Focus On Sport/Getty Images

year with his 893rd steal, again breaking a mark set by Cobb. Henderson stole the 939th base of his career in 1991, breaking Brock's major league record.

Henderson played for numerous teams in the 1990s. His frequent trades to different teams were fueled in part by contract disputes and the perception that he was not a team player.

The 2001 season was a landmark for Henderson. On April 25, while a member of the San Diego Padres, he broke Babe Ruth's lifetime record for bases on balls (walks). When Ruth retired from baseball in 1935, he had 2,062 bases on balls, a testament to his ability to judge pitches and intimidate pitchers, and it was thought that the record would never be broken. Ted Williams (with 2,019) had been the only other player to even top 2,000 walks until Henderson, who ended the 2001 season with 2,141 walks. (The career walk record was broken again by Barry Bonds in 2004.) Henderson continued his record-breaking season on October 4, setting the all-time record for runs scored. His 2,246th run broke the career record for runs held by Ty Cobb, which had stood since Cobb's retirement in 1928. On October 7, the last day of the 2001 regular season, Henderson became only the 25th player in major league history to have recorded 3,000 hits.

He last appeared in a major league game in September 2003, but he continued to play for independent minor league teams over the following two years. Henderson officially retired from baseball in 2007. Two years later he was elected to the Baseball Hall of Fame. His autobiography, *Off Base: Confessions of a Thief*, was published in 1992.

CHAPTER 7
OTHER BASEBALL GREATS

The biographies in this chapter (which are arranged alphabetically) portray recent greats who are not yet eligible for the Hall of Fame, such as Ken Griffey, Jr.; past stars who have been banned from that shrine, such as Shoeless Joe Jackson; or players who—owing to the ongoing controversy over performance-enchancing drug use—walk the line between those two categories, such as Roger Clemens and Mark McGwire.

ROGER CLEMENS

(b. Aug. 4, 1962, Dayton, Ohio, U.S.)

One of the most successful power pitchers in history—thus earning the nickname "Rocket"—Roger Clemens was the first pitcher to win the Cy Young Award seven times.

William Roger Clemens was raised in Texas and played college baseball for the University of Texas Longhorns before being drafted in 1983 by the Boston Red Sox. After only one year in the minor leagues, Clemens made his major league debut in 1984. In 1986 he had a record of 24 wins and 4 losses and helped the Red Sox to the American League (AL) pennant. He was awarded his first Cy Young Award and was also voted the American League's Most Valuable Player (MVP), a rare double honour for a pitcher. Clemens went on to win two additional Cy Young Awards (1987 and 1991) while playing with the Red Sox.

Clemens left Boston to play with the Toronto Blue Jays in 1997 and once again won the Cy Young Award for a season with more than 20 wins. In 1998 he won 20 games and lost 6 for the Blue Jays to earn his fifth (and his second consecutive) Cy Young Award. He was traded to the New York Yankees in 1999 and finally won a World Series championship. He had respectable seasons in 1999 and 2000, but he was back in top form in 2001, earning 20 wins and an unprecedented sixth Cy Young Award. In 2004 he pitched for the Houston Astros, posting 18 wins and earning his seventh Cy Young Award (and his first in the National League [NL]). After three seasons with the Astros, Clemens returned to the Yankees in 2007.

Clemens twice struck out 20 batters in a single game (in 1986 and 1996—at that time no pitcher had reached this record even once) and passed the 4,000-strikeout mark in 2003, the same year he picked up his 300th career win. Clemens suffered from shoulder problems during the latter stages of his career, but he remained a feared pitcher despite his age and the decreased velocity of his fastball.

In December 2007 Clemens was prominently mentioned in the report on steroid use in baseball by former U.S. senator George J. Mitchell. In it Clemens was alleged to have taken performance-enhancing drugs during the 1998, 2000, and 2001 baseball seasons; Clemens denied the allegations. In 2010 he was indicted by a federal grand jury on charges of perjury and making false statements to Congress for allegedly lying to a U.S. House of Representatives committee in 2008, when he denied having used performance-enhancing drugs.

KEN GRIFFEY, JR.

(b. Nov. 21, 1969, Donora, Pa., U.S.)

One of the dominant power hitters of the 1990s, Ken Griffey, Jr., also ranked among the best defensive outfielders of all time.

In 1987 George Kenneth Griffey, Jr., was the first player selected by the Major League Baseball draft and was signed by the American League Seattle Mariners. He made his major league debut in 1989. His father, outfielder Ken Griffey, Sr., was playing for the Cincinnati Reds in that year, and the Griffeys thus became the first father and son ever to play in the major leagues at the same time. Griffey, Sr., arranged to be traded to the Mariners late in the 1989 season, and the two formed a sentimental duo in the lineup until his retirement in 1991.

Griffey, Jr., soon began to prove his worth as both a centre fielder and a hitter. He was injured in his rookie season, but in 1990 he won his first Gold Glove Award, had a batting average of .300, and played in the All-Star Game. He went on to win the American League Gold Glove Award for the years 1991–99 with his spectacular fielding. In 1997, when Griffey hit 56 home runs and batted in 147 runs, he was a unanimous selection for the American League's Most Valuable Player award.

At the close of the 1999 season, Griffey—who had come to dislike playing in the Mariners' new pitcher-friendly stadium and wanted to work closer to his family's home in Orlando, Fla.—requested a trade from Seattle. In February 2000 he was traded to Cincinnati, which he considered his hometown and where his father worked as a coach. Griffey struggled with a series of injuries in Cincinnati. When he was on the field, he remained a dangerous left-handed hitter. In 2004 he became the 20th major league player to hit 500 home runs, and he was named to the National League All-Star team in 2000, 2004, and 2007. In 2008, after hitting his 600th career home run, Griffey joined Barry Bonds, Hank Aaron, Babe Ruth, Willie Mays, and Sammy Sosa as the only players in major league history to accomplish that feat. Griffey was traded to the Chicago White Sox in July 2008.

He became a free agent for the first time in his career at the end of the 2008 season, and he signed with the Mariners again in February 2009. Griffey's return to Seattle was a boon for the Mariners' attendance figures, but his deteriorating on-field play and subsequent lack of playing time led him to abruptly retire from baseball in June 2010.

SHOELESS JOE JACKSON

(b. July 16, 1888, Greenville, S.C., U.S. — d. Dec. 6, 1951, Greenville)

Shoeless Joe Jackson was by many accounts one of the greatest players in baseball history, but he was ultimately banned from the game because of his involvement in the 1919 Black Sox Scandal.

Born into extreme poverty, Joseph Jefferson Jackson began work in a cotton mill when he was barely six and never went to school. He survived a sickly childhood caused by the lint-filled air in the mill, then grew tall and gangly, with exceptionally long, strong arms. At age 13 he was an extraordinary ballplayer, the youngest ever to play on a mill team. He acquired his nickname when nursing blistered feet from a new pair of spikes (baseball shoes). Playing without them, he hit a base-clearing triple that provoked an opposing fan to cry out, "You shoeless bastard, you!" Even his bat became part of his growing legend—Black Betsy, a locally hewn piece of hickory 36

Shoeless Joe Jackson, 1919. Library of Congress Prints and Photographs Division

inches (91 cm) long, weighing 48 ounces (1.4 kg), 12 ounces (340 grams) heavier than modern bats, and stained by countless splatters of tobacco juice.

In 1908 Connie Mack, owner of the Philadelphia Athletics (A's), bought Jackson's contract with the Greenville Spinners for $325, but the 19-year-old Shoeless Joe, homesick for his 15-year-old wife, Katie, and embarrassed by his hayseed illiteracy, got off the train at Richmond, Virginia, to catch the first train back to Greenville.

The following season Mack sent Jackson to Savannah, Georgia, where he hit a league-leading .358. When recalled to the A's in Philadelphia, he was humiliated by the relentless hazing of veteran teammates. Mack offered to hire a tutor to teach him to read and write, but Shoeless Joe wanted none of it. In 1910 he was traded to the Cleveland Naps (later the Indians), where he hit an astonishing .407 in his first full season as a big league player. He liked the city, developing a taste for fine food and nice clothes. In an amusing irony, he loved expensive shoes. Fans liked his pleasant, easygoing personality and his friendliness to children. They learned of his superstitious collection of hairpins in his back pocket; of his practice of strengthening his arms, one at a time, by extending Black Betsy out as far as he could and holding it there; and of his exercising his eye muscles by staring at a lit candle with one eye until his vision began to blur, then shifting to the other eye. Meanwhile, his legend grew with his prowess. Star pitcher Walter Johnson called him "the greatest natural ballplayer I've ever seen." Ty Cobb, American League batting champion, acknowledged Jackson's superior abilities. Babe Ruth copied his feet-together batting stance and his power stride into the pitch.

In 1915 Charles Comiskey, owner of the Chicago White Sox, bought Jackson for $65,000; he thus became the star of the pennant-winning club. When the United States entered World War I, Jackson was not eligible for the draft, because he was the sole support of his wife and his mother. When he went to work in the shipyards for his war effort, he was labeled a coward and a slacker.

The United States was different after the war, tainted by a growing cynicism. In baseball, gamblers and fixers openly operated in big league cities with impunity, while club owners swept all rumours of corrupted games under the rug, lest the public lose faith in the national pastime.

The White Sox, though runaway pennant winners in 1919, were a team of disgruntled underpaid players who were embittered by Comiskey's penuriousness, his failure to pay promised bonuses, and his high-handed refusal to discuss their grievances. It was also a team riddled with hostile cliques and dissension. The outcome was that eight of its ballplayers conspired with gamblers—including former boxer Abe Attell—to throw the World Series to the Cincinnati Reds.

The Black Sox Scandal, as the fix came to be called, was a fiasco for the players. The gamblers reneged on promised payments, leaving the disorganized and demoralized eight caught in a morass of lies and betrayals. Jackson, who was promised $20,000 for throwing the series (more than three times his $6,000 annual salary), in the end received only $5,000. The degree of his complicity in the scandal, however, has always been puzzling. Although he never returned the bribe, he went on to hit an outstanding .375 for the series while playing errorless ball in the field.

Jackson tried to meet with Comiskey after the series to tell him about the fix, but Comiskey refused to see him. Back home, Jackson had Katie write explanatory letters but received no reply. Typically, all reports concerning the fix were buried until a year later when the bubble finally burst. At the convening of the grand jury, Jackson confessed, attempting to make sense of what had made no sense to him. It was there, outside the grand jury room, that a young boy is claimed to have delivered the plaintive words that became part of American language: "Say it ain't so, Joe."

The eight ballplayers stood trial and were acquitted, but Judge Kenesaw Mountain Landis, newly appointed commissioner of baseball, banned them from ever playing professional baseball again.

Throughout the 1920s and '30s, Jackson played "outlaw" ball around the country under an assumed name, and all efforts at reinstatement were denied him. Retiring to Greenville with Katie, he owned a dry-cleaning shop, a pool parlour, and then a liquor store. Ty Cobb claimed that he drove through Greenville as an old man and stopped at Jackson's liquor store to buy a quart of bourbon, but Jackson failed to greet him. Cobb asked him, "What's the matter, Joe? Don't you remember me?" Jackson replied, "Sure I do, Ty; I just didn't think you wanted me to."

Jackson died of a heart attack shortly before he was to appear on Ed Sullivan's variety show, *The Toast of the Town*, as part of another attempt at his reinstatement. In subsequent decades his name continued to resonate fondly among the fans. Jackson's bat, Black Betsy, was exhibited for a time in the Baseball Hall of Fame. Despite his lifetime batting average of .356 and the numerous fans who have called for his induction, there is, as yet, no plaque commemorating his admission to the hall.

DEREK JETER

(b. June 26, 1974, Pequannock, N.J., U.S.)

As a shortstop for the New York Yankees, Derek Jeter was selected to multiple AL All-Star teams and has become one of the most popular players of his time.

Jeter grew up in Michigan and started playing Little League baseball when he was about five years old. After an impressive high school baseball record, including a .557 batting average in his junior year, he was drafted as a first-round pick in 1992 by the Yankees. He started at the minor league Class A Tampa Yankees and did poorly, with 21 errors in 58 games. Over the next few years, Jeter improved and was named Most Outstanding Major League Prospect by the South Atlantic League in 1993 and Minor League Player of the Year by *Baseball America* in 1994.

Derek Jeter, 2010. Brad Mangin/Getty Images

In 1996 Jeter became the starting shortstop for the New York Yankees. In his first season he carried a batting average of .314 and had 78 runs batted in (RBIs). He was named AL Rookie of the Year, and the Yankees won the World Series against the Atlanta Braves. In 1998 the Yankees had another World Series victory, this time against the San Diego Padres. The Yankees again beat the Braves in the World Series in 1999, and Jeter acquired a reputation as one of the premier postseason hitters in baseball after posting a combined batting average of .375 in the Yankees' three playoff series. In 2000 Jeter was named Most Valuable Player of the All-Star Game and the World Series, as the Yankees defeated the New York Mets to become the first team to win three consecutive World Series since 1974.

From 2004 to 2006 Jeter won three consecutive AL Gold Glove awards as the best-fielding shortstop in the league. He also won the AL Hank Aaron Award (for best overall hitter) and the AL Silver Slugger Award (for best offense at a position) in 2006, a season in which he finished second in the balloting for AL MVP. In 2009 Jeter recorded his 2,674th career hit, breaking the record for the most hits by a shortstop in major league history. The Yankees ended the 2009 season with a victory over the Philadelphia Phillies in the World Series.

RANDY JOHNSON

(b. Sept. 10, 1963, Walnut Creek, Calif., U.S.)

With five career Cy Young Awards (1995, 1999–2002) as the best pitcher in either the American or National League, Randy Johnson is considered one of the greatest pitchers in the sport's history.

Randall David Johnson excelled in both basketball and baseball through high school. He earned a scholarship to the University of Southern California, where he played basketball for a few years and starred on the baseball team from 1983 to 1985. The National League Montreal Expos drafted him after his junior season, and he made his major league debut on Sept. 15, 1988.

The physically imposing 6-foot 10-inch (2.08-metre) Johnson quickly built a reputation as the pitcher major leaguers most feared facing. His exceptional height (he was for a time the tallest player in major league history) and low delivery angle only increased the difficulty of hitting his fastballs (which could sometimes reach 102 mph [164 km/hr]) and hard-breaking sliders (pitches that appear to be heading toward a left-handed batter before suddenly veering toward the plate). The novelty of his height at first overshadowed Johnson's work on the mound, but as his pitching improved, the accolades increased. He was named to the first of his 10 All-Star Games in 1990 as a member of the American League Seattle Mariners, who had acquired him from the Expos the previous season. Johnson led the AL in strikeouts for four consecutive years (1992–95), and in 1995 he won the AL Cy Young Award. Johnson and the Mariners management began to have contract disagreements on a regular basis, and he was traded to the Houston Astros at the1998 trading deadline.

A free agent at the end of the 1998 season, Johnson signed with the NL Arizona Diamondbacks, where he led the NL in earned run average (ERA), innings pitched, and strikeouts on his way to the 1999 NL Cy Young Award. Johnson won Cy Youngs in each of the following three seasons, but his most impressive feat took place at the 2001 World Series, where he tied a record with three wins in a single World Series and earned Most Valuable Player honours, along with fellow pitcher Curt Schilling, while guiding the Diamondbacks to their first championship.

In 2004 he became the oldest player to pitch a perfect game and just the 17th pitcher to accomplish the feat.

After pitching for two seasons with the New York Yankees, Johnson was traded in 2007 to Arizona for a second stint with the Diamondbacks. The following year he recorded his 4,673rd strikeout, passing Roger Clemens for second place on the all-time strikeouts list—behind only Nolan Ryan. Johnson signed with the San Francisco Giants after the 2008 season. On June 4, 2009, he recorded the 300th victory of his career, a landmark that had been reached by only 23 other big-league pitchers in more than 120 years of American professional baseball. Johnson retired in January 2010.

GREG MADDUX

(b. April 14, 1966, San Angelo, Texas, U.S.)

One of the game's most successful pitchers, Greg Maddux is known for his accuracy and his ability to read opponents. He was the first pitcher to win four consecutive Cy Young Awards (1992–95).

From a young age Gregory Alan Maddux and his older brother, Mike (who also became a major league pitcher), were drilled in the fundamentals of the game by their father. Greg earned all-state honours in both his junior and senior years as a pitcher for Valley High School in Las Vegas, and, upon his graduation in 1984, he was drafted by the Chicago Cubs of the National League and assigned to the minor league system.

Late in the 1986 season, Maddux, just 20 years old, was called up to the big leagues. His performance that season—two wins, four losses, and a 5.52 earned run average—and the next (6–14, 5.61 ERA) was anything but masterful. Known as an overly emotional player who often taunted umpires and opposing hitters, Maddux, by his own later admission, was not a thinking pitcher but a "brain-dead heaver." All that began to change, however, when he adjusted the mechanics of his delivery. In 1988 he won 15 of his first 18 decisions and finished 18–8 with a 3.18 ERA. In 1989, as the ace of the Chicago pitching staff when the Cubs won the East Division crown, he went 19–12 with a 2.95 ERA. The next two seasons, pitching for losing teams, he won 30 games and lost 26. In 1992, with a 20–11 record and a 2.18 ERA, Maddux won his first Cy Young Award. Although he did not have a blazing fastball or a devastating curve, he was able to dominate hitters by studying their tendencies and then baffling them with the amazing accuracy and varying speeds of his pitches.

A contract dispute with the Cubs left him a free agent, and after the 1992 season he signed a five-year, $28 million contract with the Atlanta Braves. In his first three seasons with the Braves, he won the Cy Young Award each year while compiling a 55–18 record. In 1995 Maddux won a league-best 19 games while losing only 2, as he led the Braves to a World Series title. His league-leading ERA of 1.63, along with a 1994 mark of 1.57, made him the first pitcher since the legendary Walter ("Big Train") Johnson in 1918–19 to post an ERA of less than 1.80 in consecutive seasons.

Prior to the 2004 season, Maddux again became a free agent and returned to the Cubs. On July 26, 2005, he recorded his 3,000th strikeout, becoming the 13th pitcher to achieve that feat. During the 2006 season he was traded to the Los Angeles Dodgers, and after that season he signed with the San Diego Padres. In 2007 Maddux won a record-setting 17th Gold Glove award, capturing an 18th the following season. Also in 2008, after he was traded back to the Dodgers mid-season, Maddux became the ninth pitcher to win 350 games. He retired after the end of the 2008 season with 355 career wins, making him the second winningest pitcher in baseball's "live-ball era" (the period that dates from the introduction of hitter-friendly rules in 1920).

PEDRO MARTÍNEZ

(b. Oct. 25, 1971, Manoguayabo, Dom.Rep.)

Arguably the game's most dominant pitcher in the late 1990s and early 2000s, Pedro Martínez became the first Latin American pitcher to strike out 300 batters in a season in 1997.

Martínez began his journey to the major leagues by signing with the National League Los Angeles Dodgers in 1988, making his major-league debut with the Dodgers in 1992. In 1993 he was traded to the Montreal Expos, and the right-handed pitcher used his blazing fastball and ability to pitch inside to compile a record of 55 wins and 33 losses over four years with the club. He won the National League Cy Young Award—the most prestigious annual award given to a pitcher—in 1997.

Martínez signed a six-year contract worth $75 million in 1997 with the Boston Red Sox, making him the highest-paid player in baseball at the time. For 1998–2004 (he was on the disabled list for much of 2001), Martínez had 117 wins and 37 losses, winning the American League Cy Young Award in 1999 and 2000. In 1999 Martínez led the league in victories (23), earned run average (2.07), and strikeouts (313)—known as the Triple Crown of pitching. He became a fan favourite in Boston and was a member of their 2004 World Series championship team. Martínez became a free agent after the 2004 season and signed a $53-million, four-year contract with the New York Mets. In his first season with

Pedro Martinez, 2004. Jeff Gross/Getty Images

the Mets, he compiled a 15–8 record, with a 2.82 earned run average, but injuries caused him to spend significant portions of subsequent seasons on the disabled list and limited his effectiveness. Still, on Sept. 3, 2007, Martínez became the 15th pitcher (and first Latin American) in major league history to record 3,000 strikeouts. His play continued to decline, and, upon the termination of his contract with the Mets in 2008, there was among major league teams little interest in acquiring Martínez. The Philadelphia Phillies signed Martínez to a one-year contract at the All-Star break of the 2009 season.

Martínez lived in the Dominican Republic during baseball's off-season and was actively involved in community and charity work there. This community service combined with his on-field success made him, along with Hall of Famer Juan Marichal and Sammy Sosa, one of the most popular sports figures in the Dominican Republic.

MARK MCGWIRE

(b. Oct. 1, 1963, Pomona, Calif., U.S.)

Considered one of the most powerful hitters in the history of the game, Mark McGwire set a major league record for most home runs in a season (70) in 1998, breaking Roger Maris's mark of 61.

As a senior in high school, McGwire attracted more attention with his pitching than with his swing. The Montreal Expos drafted him as a pitcher in 1981, but instead he attended the University of Southern California, where he moved to first base, a position he was to maintain in the majors. Selected by the Oakland Athletics in the 1984 draft, McGwire joined the major league club in 1987 and quickly displayed the strength that would become his trademark. His 49 home runs that year set a rookie record and helped earn him American League Rookie of the Year honours. In 1989 his .343 postseason batting average guided Oakland to the World Series championship. Injuries, however, soon plagued McGwire, and from 1993 to 1995 he missed 290 games. In 1996, after briefly contemplating retirement, he became only the 13th player to hit 50 home runs in a single season. The following year he was traded to the National League's St. Louis Cardinals, for whom he posted 58 homers and with whom he elected to continue playing, ruling out free agency.

Attempts to top Maris's 37-year-old single-season home run record dominated the 1998 season. McGwire and the Chicago Cubs' Sammy Sosa thrilled fans with their home run derby, and midway through the year McGwire hit one of the longest homers of his career (545 feet [166 metres]). On September 1 he broke Hack Wilson's 68-year-old National League record (56 home runs), and six days later he tied Maris's mark. On September 8 McGwire hit his shortest home run (341 feet) of the year to break the record. The following year he became the second player (Sosa was the first) to hit 60 home runs in two seasons. McGwire held the home run record for only a brief period; the record was broken by Barry Bonds on Oct. 5, 2001. (Bonds hit 73 home runs that year.) McGwire announced his retirement from baseball after the 2001 season.

McGwire's legacy was tainted shortly after his retirement as a result of speculation that he had taken performance-enhancing drugs during his playing days. He thrived during the so-called "steroids era," when the assumed use of steroids by baseball players cast a pall over many of the batting records set in the 1990s. Additionally, McGwire admitted to taking a then-legal steroid precursor during his home run chase of 1998. In 2005 McGwire and five other active and retired major league players testified at a U.S. congressional hearing on steroids. McGwire's repeated refusal to answer direct questions about his alleged steroid use damaged his reputation with many baseball fans and brought new scrutiny to his achievements. Despite his 12 All-Star Game appearances and 583 career home runs, he was not elected to the Baseball Hall of Fame in his initial years of eligibility.

In October 2009 McGwire returned to baseball when he was hired as the Cardinals' hitting coach. Three months later he admitted to having used steroids intermittently from 1989 through the '90s, including during his record-setting 1998 season.

ALBERT PUJOLS

(b. Jan. 16, 1980, Santo Domingo, Dom. Rep.)

The Dominican-born American professional baseball player Albert Pujols is known as one of the most prolific hitters of the early 21st century.

José Alberto Pujols Alcántara was introduced to baseball early in life by his father, who was a popular pitcher in the Dominican Republic. The Pujols family immigrated to the United States when Albert was 16, and they eventually settled in Independence, Mo. Pujols impressed major league scouts with his play at both the high-school and collegiate level, and he was selected by the St. Louis Cardinals in the 13th round of the 1999 draft. He held out for a better signing bonus, however, and did not enter the minor leagues until the 2000 season. That was his only season in the minors, as an impressive performance in spring training earned him a spot on the Cardinals' 2001 opening-day roster.

Presumed to be a reserve as he entered his first season, Pujols instead played his way into the starting lineup. He appeared in 161 games, posted a .329 batting average with 37 home runs and 130 runs batted in, and was the unanimous choice for 2001 National League Rookie of the Year. Pujols continued to put up impressive offensive numbers in the following seasons and was twice (2002 and 2003) the NL Most Valuable Player runner-up to Barry Bonds. Pujols collected a number of other awards, including the 2004 NL Championship Series MVP and Silver Slugger awards in 2001, 2003, and 2004. In 2005 he hit .330 with 41 home runs and 117 RBIs and was named NL MVP.

In 2006 Pujols bettered the batting statistics of his previous season, hitting .331 with 49 home runs and 137 RBIs, and finished as MVP runner-up for the third time in his short career. That year he also experienced his greatest postseason success, as he helped lead St. Louis to a commanding four-games-to-one win over the heavily favoured Detroit Tigers in the World Series, giving the Cardinals their first title since 1982. In 2008 Pujols was named NL MVP after finishing the season with a .357 batting average and 116 RBIs. The following year he hit .327 with 47 home runs and 135 RBIs and won his third NL MVP award.

MANNY RAMIREZ

(b. May 30, 1972, Santo Domingo, Dom.Rep.)

Manny Ramirez is considered one of the greatest right-handed hitters in the history of the game.

Manuel Aristides Ramirez left the Dominican Republic in 1985 for the New York City borough of the Bronx, where he graduated from George Washington High School in 1991. He was drafted by the Cleveland Indians in June 1991, and in his first professional season, while playing for Cleveland's Burlington, N.C., minor-league affiliate, he was voted Appalachian League Player of the Year. Ramirez joined the Indians in 1993 and established himself as one of the most productive batters in Major League Baseball. Although sidelined by a hamstring injury for part of the 2000 season, he amassed 38 home runs and 122 runs batted in for the Indians in 118 games while compiling a .351 batting average. During the following winter, he signed an eight-year, $160 million contract with the Boston Red Sox.

Ramirez, who had been named an American League All-Star in each season since 1998, continued to produce in Boston. Additionally, his off-beat personality and unusual behaviour (such as occasionally playing in the outfield with a water bottle tucked into his back pocket) both on and off the field—which was usually excused by local media as simply "Manny being Manny"—served to lighten the mood around Boston's Fenway Park, where the team's failure to win a World Series since 1918 often created a defeatist and moribund atmosphere. In 2004 Ramirez sparked a postseason run for the Red Sox that resulted in the team's first World Series title in 86 years, and he was voted Most Valuable Player of the World Series. During that Series, Ramirez had seven hits in 17 at bats, including

Manny Ramirez, Sept. 24, 2010. Lisa Blumenfeld/Getty Images

a home run and four RBIs, for a .412 average during a four-game sweep of the St. Louis Cardinals. In 2007 Ramirez batted .296 during the regular season with 20 home runs and 88 RBIs, but it was his performance in the play-offs that was truly notable. He broke the career postseason home run record during the AL Championship Series, where his .409 batting average keyed a Boston rally from a three-games-to-one deficit over his old Cleveland Indians team, and the Red Sox went on to win another World Series, sweeping the Colorado Rockies in four games.

Ramirez's aloof attitude, history of questionable injury claims, and oft-expressed dissatisfaction with Red Sox management served to sour both the team and its fans on the slugger over his eight years in Boston. Soon after hitting the 500th home run of his career in 2008, he was traded to the Los Angeles Dodgers. Ramirez joined the Dodgers at the mid-season trading deadline and quickly endeared himself to Los Angeles fans. He was credited with bringing a looser attitude to his new team, which went from a 54–54 record when he arrived to a final 84–78 record, the National League West Division title, and a berth in the NL Championship Series. In 53 games with the Dodgers—approximately a third of the regular-season schedule—Ramirez hit .396 with 17 home runs and 53 RBIs and thereby supplied the team with some much-needed right-handed power. After heated negotiations between Ramirez's agent and the Los Angeles front office, he re-signed with the Dodgers in March 2009. Ramirez continued his hot hitting the following season: through the first 27 games of 2009, he was batting .348 with 6 home runs and 20 RBIs. But on May 7 he was suspended for 50 games because he had tested positive for use of performance-enhancing drugs; he claimed it was a false positive caused by his prescription medication. His play fell off after his return to the Dodgers, and he finished the season with a .290 batting average. He was waived by the Dodgers in August 2010 and was claimed by the Chicago White Sox. He went just 1-for-17 in five games with the Rays before abruptly retiring in April after he had reportedly tested positive for performance-enhancing drugs a second time.

ALEX RODRIGUEZ

(b. July 27, 1975, New York City, N.Y., U.S.)

Alex Rodriguez is a noted power hitter.

Alexander Emmanuel Rodriguez and his family moved to his father's native Dominican Republic when Alex was four, but they later relocated to Miami, Fla. There he became an excellent ballplayer at Westminster Christian High School, and in 1993 the Seattle Mariners selected Rodriguez (who would become familiar to baseball fans by his nickname, "A-Rod") as the first overall pick in the Major League Baseball draft. He made his debut with the Mariners at age 18, playing shortstop.

Rodriguez's first successful season came in 1996, when he accumulated a league-best .358 batting average with 36 home runs and 123 runs batted in. Over the next six seasons with the team, he continued to produce outstanding offensive statistics, most notably in 1998, when he became the third player in league history to hit 40 home runs and steal 40 bases in the same season. Before the 2001 season, when Rodriguez was a free agent, the Texas Rangers signed him to a 10-year $252 million contract, the richest contract ever given to an athlete at the time.

With the Rangers, Rodriguez continued to have great offensive seasons. He won Most Valuable Player honours in 2003 with a .298 batting average, 47 home runs, and 118 runs batted in. After that season, he was traded to the New York Yankees. In 2005 he posted a .321 batting

New York Yankee Alex Rodriguez hits his 600th career home run, Aug. 4, 2010. Michael Heiman/Getty Images

average, with 48 home runs and 130 runs batted in, to win his second MVP title. At Yankee Stadium on Aug. 4, 2007, at age 32, Rodriguez hit his 500th career home run, becoming the youngest player to accomplish that feat. The 2007 season was Rodriguez's best yet—he had a .314 batting average, with 56 home runs and 154 runs batted in—and he was named MVP for the third time.

In 2009 Rodriguez admitted that he used various performance-enhancing drugs from 2001 to 2003, a revelation that threatened to taint his seemingly extraordinary career accomplishments. His preseason admission was followed by a relatively sub-par regular season that saw Rodriguez fail to hit over 30 home runs and amass over 100 RBIs for the first time since 1997. His streak of nine consecutive All-Star Game selections also ended. However, he overcame his longtime reputation of faltering in the postseason by batting .365 with six home runs and 18 RBIs during the play-offs, and the Yankees went on to win the 2009 World Series. In 2010 Rodriguez became the seventh player in major league history to hit 600 career home runs.

EPILOGUE

O f all of the major North American professional sports, baseball has probably changed the least since its origin. The basics of the game—a ball, a wooden bat, the pitcher's mound, and the distance between the bases—are remarkably similar to their 19th-century analogues, which has allowed players, the baseball media, and fans to compare different eras with reasonable accuracy. As a result, many of Major League Baseball's long-standing records have transcended the game and become familiar with even the most casual of observers; numbers such as "56," "4,192," and "714" have not had their significance diminished in the years since those records were established, even if some have since been surpassed.

The historical consistency of the game has also led to greater controversy over the recent emergence of performance-enhancing drugs (PED) in baseball than in other sports, owing to the drugs' impact on baseball's hallowed record book. Baseball's recent effort to crack down on PED use has seemingly mitigated the problem for now, but the "steroid era" will forever tarnish the sport's history. Nevertheless, the game will persist, and its bright future will still surely resemble its past.

Appendix: World Series Results

WORLD SERIES*			
YEAR	WINNING TEAM	LOSING TEAM	RESULTS
1903	Boston Americans (AL)	Pittsburgh Pirates (NL)	5–3
1904	not held		
1905	New York Giants (NL)	Philadelphia Athletics (AL)	4–1
1906	Chicago White Sox (AL)	Chicago Cubs (NL)	4–2
1907**	Chicago Cubs (NL)	Detroit Tigers (AL)	4–0
1908	Chicago Cubs (NL)	Detroit Tigers (AL)	4–1
1909	Pittsburgh Pirates (NL)	Detroit Tigers (AL)	4–3
1910	Philadelphia Athletics (AL)	Chicago Cubs (NL)	4–1
1911	Philadelphia Athletics (AL)	New York Giants (NL)	4–2
1912**	Boston Red Sox (AL)	New York Giants (NL)	4–3
1913	Philadelphia Athletics (AL)	New York Giants (NL)	4–1
1914	Boston Braves (NL)	Philadelphia Athletics (AL)	4–0
1915	Boston Red Sox (AL)	Philadelphia Phillies (NL)	4–1

YEAR	WINNING TEAM	LOSING TEAM	RESULTS
1916	Boston Red Sox (AL)	Brooklyn Robins (NL)	4–1
1917	Chicago White Sox (AL)	New York Giants (NL)	4–2
1918	Boston Red Sox (AL)	Chicago Cubs (NL)	4–2
1919	Cincinnati Reds (NL)	Chicago White Sox (AL)	5–3
1920	Cleveland Indians (AL)	Brooklyn Robins (NL)	5–2
1921	New York Giants (NL)	New York Yankees (AL)	5–3
1922**	New York Giants (NL)	New York Yankees (AL)	4–0
1923	New York Yankees (AL)	New York Giants (NL)	4–2
1924	Washington Senators (AL)	New York Giants (NL)	4–3
1925	Pittsburgh Pirates (NL)	Washington Senators (AL)	4–3
1926	St. Louis Cardinals (NL)	New York Yankees (AL)	4–3
1927	New York Yankees (AL)	Pittsburgh Pirates (NL)	4–0
1928	New York Yankees (AL)	St. Louis Cardinals (NL)	4–0
1929	Philadelphia Athletics (AL)	Chicago Cubs (NL)	4–1
1930	Philadelphia Athletics (AL)	St. Louis Cardinals (NL)	4–2
1931	St. Louis Cardinals (NL)	Philadelphia Athletics (AL)	4–3
1932	New York Yankees (AL)	Chicago Cubs (NL)	4–0

YEAR	WINNING TEAM	LOSING TEAM	RESULTS
1933	New York Giants (NL)	Washington Senators (AL)	4–1
1934	St. Louis Cardinals (NL)	Detroit Tigers (AL)	4–3
1935	Detroit Tigers (AL)	Chicago Cubs (NL)	4–2
1936	New York Yankees (AL)	New York Giants (NL)	4–2
1937	New York Yankees (AL)	New York Giants (NL)	4–1
1938	New York Yankees (AL)	Chicago Cubs (NL)	4–0
1939	New York Yankees (AL)	Cincinnati Reds (NL)	4–0
1940	Cincinnati Reds (NL)	Detroit Tigers (AL)	4–3
1941	New York Yankees (AL)	Brooklyn Dodgers (NL)	4–1
1942	St. Louis Cardinals (NL)	New York Yankees (AL)	4–1
1943	New York Yankees (AL)	St. Louis Cardinals (NL)	4–1
1944	St. Louis Cardinals (NL)	St. Louis Browns (AL)	4–2
1945	Detroit Tigers (AL)	Chicago Cubs (NL)	4–3
1946	St. Louis Cardinals (NL)	Boston Red Sox (AL)	4–3
1947	New York Yankees (AL)	Brooklyn Dodgers (NL)	4–3
1948	Cleveland Indians (AL)	Boston Braves (NL)	4–2
1949	New York Yankees (AL)	Brooklyn Dodgers (NL)	4–1

YEAR	WINNING TEAM	LOSING TEAM	RESULTS
1950	New York Yankees (AL)	Philadelphia Phillies (NL)	4–0
1951	New York Yankees (AL)	New York Giants (NL)	4–2
1952	New York Yankees (AL)	Brooklyn Dodgers (NL)	4–3
1953	New York Yankees (AL)	Brooklyn Dodgers (NL)	4–2
1954	New York Giants (NL)	Cleveland Indians (AL)	4–0
1955	Brooklyn Dodgers (NL)	New York Yankees (AL)	4–3
1956	New York Yankees (AL)	Brooklyn Dodgers (NL)	4–3
1957	Milwaukee Braves (NL)	New York Yankees (AL)	4–3
1958	New York Yankees (AL)	Milwaukee Braves (NL)	4–3
1959	Los Angeles Dodgers (NL)	Chicago White Sox (AL)	4–2
1960	Pittsburgh Pirates (NL)	New York Yankees (AL)	4–3
1961	New York Yankees (AL)	Cincinnati Reds (NL)	4–1
1962	New York Yankees (AL)	San Francisco Giants (NL)	4–3
1963	Los Angeles Dodgers (NL)	New York Yankees (AL)	4–0
1964	St. Louis Cardinals (NL)	New York Yankees (AL)	4–3
1965	Los Angeles Dodgers (NL)	Minnesota Twins (AL)	4–3

YEAR	WINNING TEAM	LOSING TEAM	RESULTS
1966	Baltimore Orioles (AL)	Los Angeles Dodgers (NL)	4–0
1967	St. Louis Cardinals (NL)	Boston Red Sox (AL)	4–3
1968	Detroit Tigers (AL)	St. Louis Cardinals (NL)	4–3
1969	New York Mets (NL)	Baltimore Orioles (AL)	4–1
1970	Baltimore Orioles (AL)	Cincinnati Reds (NL)	4–1
1971	Pittsburgh Pirates (NL)	Baltimore Orioles (AL)	4–3
1972	Oakland Athletics (AL)	Cincinnati Reds (NL)	4–3
1973	Oakland Athletics (AL)	New York Mets (NL)	4–3
1974	Oakland Athletics (AL)	Los Angeles Dodgers (NL)	4–1
1975	Cincinnati Reds (NL)	Boston Red Sox (AL)	4–3
1976	Cincinnati Reds (NL)	New York Yankees (AL)	4–0
1977	New York Yankees (AL)	Los Angeles Dodgers (NL)	4–2
1978	New York Yankees (AL)	Los Angeles Dodgers (NL)	4–2
1979	Pittsburgh Pirates (NL)	Baltimore Orioles (AL)	4–3
1980	Philadelphia Phillies (NL)	Kansas City Royals (AL)	4–2
1981	Los Angeles Dodgers (NL)	New York Yankees (AL)	4–2

YEAR	WINNING TEAM	LOSING TEAM	RESULTS
1982	St. Louis Cardinals (NL)	Milwaukee Brewers (AL)	4–3
1983	Baltimore Orioles (AL)	Philadelphia Phillies (NL)	4–1
1984	Detroit Tigers (AL)	San Diego Padres (NL)	4–1
1985	Kansas City Royals (AL)	St. Louis Cardinals (NL)	4–3
1986	New York Mets (NL)	Boston Red Sox (AL)	4–3
1987	Minnesota Twins (AL)	St. Louis Cardinals (NL)	4–3
1988	Los Angeles Dodgers (NL)	Oakland Athletics (AL)	4–1
1989	Oakland Athletics (AL)	San Francisco Giants (NL)	4–0
1990	Cincinnati Reds (NL)	Oakland Athletics (AL)	4–0
1991	Minnesota Twins (AL)	Atlanta Braves (NL)	4–3
1992	Toronto Blue Jays (AL)	Atlanta Braves (NL)	4–2
1993	Toronto Blue Jays (AL)	Philadelphia Phillies (NL)	4–2
1994	not held		
1995	Atlanta Braves (NL)	Cleveland Indians (AL)	4–2
1996	New York Yankees (AL)	Atlanta Braves (NL)	4–2
1997	Florida Marlins (NL)	Cleveland Indians (AL)	4–3
1998	New York Yankees (AL)	San Diego Padres (NL)	4–0

YEAR	WINNING TEAM	LOSING TEAM	RESULTS
1999	New York Yankees (AL)	Atlanta Braves (NL)	4–0
2000	New York Yankees (AL)	New York Mets (NL)	4–1
2001	Arizona Diamondbacks (NL)	New York Yankees (AL)	4–3
2002	Anaheim Angels (AL)	San Francisco Giants (NL)	4–3
2003	Florida Marlins (NL)	New York Yankees (AL)	4–2
2004	Boston Red Sox (AL)	St. Louis Cardinals (NL)	4–0
2005	Chicago White Sox (AL)	Houston Astros (NL)	4–0
2006	St. Louis Cardinals (NL)	Detroit Tigers (AL)	4–1
2007	Boston Red Sox (AL)	Colorado Rockies (NL)	4–0
2008	Philadelphia Phillies (NL)	Tampa Bay Rays (AL)	4–1
2009	New York Yankees (AL)	Philadelphia Phillies (NL)	4–2
2010	San Francisco Giants (NL)	Texas Rangers (AL)	4–1

*AL—American League; NL—National League.
**One tied game.

GLOSSARY

abate To reduce in degree or intensity; moderate.

amyotrophic lateral sclerosis (ALS) A rare fatal progressive degenerative disease that affects pyramidal motor neurons, usually begins in middle age, and is characterized especially by increasing and spreading muscular weakness—called also Lou Gehrig's disease.

anabolic steroid Any of a group of usually synthetic hormones that increase constructive metabolism and are sometimes taken by athletes in training to increase temporarily the size of their muscles.

anticollusion Relating to the restriction of secret agreement or cooperation especially for an illegal or deceitful purpose.

antitrust Consisting of laws to protect trade and commerce from unlawful restraints and monopolies or unfair business practices.

arbitration The hearing and determination of a case between parties in controversy by a person or persons chosen by the parties or appointed under statutory authority instead of by a judicial tribunal provided by law.

balk An illegal motion by the pitcher in baseball toward the plate or toward a base when there are men on base, which results in the baserunners automatically advancing a base.

barnstorm To tour through rural districts staging performances.

berth Job, position, or place.

blithely Lacking due thought or consideration.

caustic Marked by incisive sarcasm.

corpulent Having a large bulky body.

cynicism The quality of being contemptuously distrustful of human nature and motives.

earned run average The average number of earned runs per game scored off a pitcher determined by dividing the total of earned runs scored against him by the total number of innings pitched and multiplying by nine.

echelon One of a series of levels or grades in an organization or field of activity.

franchise A team and its operating organization having membership in a professional sports league.

gentlemen's agreement An agreement secured only by the honour of the participants.

ghetto A quarter of a city in which members of a minority group live especially because of social, legal, or economic pressure.

humidor A case or enclosure in which the air is kept properly humidified.

idiosyncratic Distinguished by peculiarity of constitution or temperament or an individualizing characteristic or quality.

imbroglio An intricate or complicated situation.

incorrigible Something or someone incapable of being corrected or reformed.

integration Incorporation as equals into society or an organization of individuals of different groups (as races).

intemperate Lacking moderation; excessive.

invective An abusive expression or speech.

jerry-built Carelessly or hastily put together.

journeyman An experienced usually competent or reliable workman in any field, usually as distinguished from one that is brilliant or colourful.

magnate A person of rank, power, influence, or distinction often in a specified area of activity.

moribund Being in a state of inactivity or obsolescence.

motif A usually recurring salient thematic element; a dominant idea or central theme.

pedestrian Commonplace, unimaginative.

pennant A flag emblematic of championship.

penuriousness The quality or state of being extremely frugal.

precarious Dependent on uncertain premises; dubious.

precipitous Very steep, perpendicular, or overhanging in rise or fall.

presage To give an omen or warning of; foreshadow.

prodigious Exciting amazement or wonder.

promulgate To put (a law) into action or force.

putout The retiring of a base runner or batter by a defensive player in baseball. Also, the official credit given a baseball player for making a putout.

quintessence The most typical example or representative.

reticent Restrained in expression, presentation, or appearance.

sacrifice bunt A bunt in baseball laid down with less than two out that enables a base runner to advance a base while the batter is put out at first base and that is not recorded as an official time at bat (also called a sacrifice hit).

segregation Forced social separation or isolation by race, class, ethnic group, or other characteristic.

spendthrift A person who spends improvidently or wastefully.

strike zone The area (as between the knees and shoulders of a batter in his natural stance) over home plate through which a pitched baseball must pass to be called a strike.

supernal Superlatively good.

swarthy Possessing or being a dark colour or complexion.

turnverein An association of gymnasts and athletes; an athletic club.

Yom Kippur The Day of Atonement, this is the most solemn and important of the Jewish holy days. Marked by prayer and fasting, it is observed on the 10th day of the Jewish calendar month Tishri (which usually occurs in September or October).

BIBLIOGRAPHY

Historical works include Lawrence Ritter and Donald Honig, *The Image of Their Greatness: An Illustrated History of Baseball from 1900 to the Present*, updated ed. (1984); and Lawrence S. Ritter (comp.), *The Glory of Their Times: The Story of the Early Days of Baseball Told by the Men Who Played It*, new ed. (1984). For a history of black players and the Negro leagues, see Robert Peterson, *Only the Ball Was White* (1970, reprinted 1984), and Peterson's article for *Encyclopædia Britannica* on the Negro leagues. David Quentin Voigt, *Baseball, an Illustrated History* (1987), includes such topics as black baseball and intercollegiate sports.

The *Official Baseball Guide*, containing records and a narrative review of the previous season, and the *Official Baseball Register*, giving the career record of each major league player of the previous season, are published annually by *The Sporting News*. The standard reference work covering the records of professional players since 1871 is Joseph L. Reichler (ed.), *The Baseball Encyclopedia*, 7th rev. ed. (1988). Organization and play of the game itself is the basis of Joe Brinkman and Charlie Euchner, *The Umpire's Handbook*, rev. ed. (1987). Bill James and John Dewan, *Bill James Presents the Great American Baseball Stat Book*, ed. by Geoff Beckman et al. (1987), is a massive collection of the game's statistics.

Information on baseball played outside the United States may be found in Robert Whiting, *You Gotta*

Have Wa (1990), and *The Chrysanthemum and the Bat: Baseball Samurai Style* (1976); Peter Bjarkman, *Baseball with a Latin Beat* (1994); Marcos Bretón and José Villegas, *Away Games* (1999); Alan M. Klein, *Sugarball: The American Game, the Dominican Dream* (1991); Samuel A. Regalado, *Viva Baseball* (1998); Rob Ruck, *The Tropic of Baseball: Baseball in the Dominican Republic* (1991); and Michael M. Oleksak and Mary Adams Oleksak, *Béisbol: Latin Americans and the Grand Old Game* (1991).

INDEX